Shopping

Shopping

A Century of Art and Consumer Culture
Edited by Christoph Grunenberg and Max Hollein

With essays by Chantal Béret, Rachel Bowlby, Anne Friedberg, Thomas Girst, Boris Groys, Christoph Grunenberg, K. Michael Hays, Martin Hentschel, Max Hollein, Thomas Kellein, Eva Kraus, Michael Lüthy, Ingrid Pfeiffer, Rolf Quaghebeur, Julian Stallabrass, Katharina Sykora and Mark C. Taylor

Hatje Cantz Publishers

Supported by:

LIVERPOOL
the world in one city

Project part-financed by the European Union
European Regional Development Fund

Media Partner:

*The*Guardian

Contents

Foreword

Since Walter Benjamin described the *flâneur* of the Parisian arcades of the nineteenth century, the browsing, selection, purchase and consumption of commodities has been recognised as a defining activity of modern urban life. Today, shopping once again occupies a central place in the public imagination. Not only has shopping become a prime leisure activity but the infatuation of contemporary artists with the sophisticated strategies of display, distribution and consumption has reached a critical point. *Shopping: A Century of Art and Consumer Culture* is the first exhibition to examine in-depth the act of shopping as a dominant cultural phenomenon of the twentieth and twenty-first centuries and explore the creative dialogue between art and commercial presentation. This collaboration between Tate Liverpool and the Schirn Kunsthalle Frankfurt brings together around 70 artists and more than 200 works, looks at the many mutations that the theme of shopping in art has undergone over the last century.

The historical starting point of *Shopping* is Eugène Atget's photographs of Paris storefronts from exactly a century ago, a time when the department stores – Emile Zola called them 'cathedrals of consumption' – fundamentally changed the shopping experience in the great metropolitan centres. Further important chapters in the early interaction of art and consumption are the serial arrangement of products in Bauhaus photography and the exploration of the 'body as commodity' in Surrealism. A critical phase in the exhibition is the multi-faceted tendencies of the 1960s with important examples from Pop Art and Fluxus. We are especially proud to have been able to document and, in some cases, even reconstruct a number of important historical ensembles of works or installations, such as Claes Oldenburg's *Store*, 1961; Gerhard Richter and Konrad Lueg's *Living with Pop – A Demonstration for Capitalist Realism*, 1963; *The American Supermarket*, 1964; and the *Fluxshop* of 1964–65. We have also been fortunate to maintain the curatorial principle of bringing together representative groups and significant installations rather than single works, including substantial installations by Christo, Joseph Beuys, Jeff Koons, Sylvie Fleury, Damien Hirst and Andreas Gursky.

Any project of the scale and ambition as *Shopping* is not possible without the support of many. First of all, we would like to thank those who have contributed financially to its realisation. We are most grateful to The Henry Moore Foundation for its continued generous support of Tate

Liverpool programmes. We also thank The Liverpool Culture Company Limited whose contribution in support of the Liverpool bid for European Capital of Culture in 2008 is most welcome in this latest collaboration between institutions in two European cities. *Shopping* is the first exhibition at Tate Liverpool to be supported by The Guardian Newspapers and we look forward to a fruitful collaboration. The largest, and one of the most spectacular installations in *Shopping*, Guillaume Bijl's *New Supermarket* was only possible through the generous support of Tesco Stores PLC who supplied fixturisation products and expertise to create the unique experience of a contemporary supermarket in a museum. We would especially like to thank Antony Bunce and Ray Williams who were most helpful in making this ambitious project happen. Debenhams in Manchester, with the help of Comme Ca PR, made their shop windows available for the presentation of a variety of works and installation in the most appropriate setting for an exhibition on shopping. We would like to thank Nick Harvey, Manager at Debenhams Manchester and Alyson Doocey and Claire Turner of Comme Ca PR.

The response to *Shopping* in Liverpool has been enthusiastic and we are pleased to present the exhibition in a city with such a distinct history in retail. Liverpool is not only the home of important department stores such as Lewis's, but also the bridgehead for important developments arriving from America: the first Woolworth store in Great Britain opened here in 1909 and, in more recent history, the first T.K. Maxx. It is particular pleasing to present an exhibition on the theme of shopping at a time when major developments in regional and urban regeneration are centred around important retail projects. We are grateful for the support of the Liverpool City Council, in particular David Henshaw, Chief Executive and Charlie Parker, Executive Director, Regeneration. We also would like to thank Ed Oliver and the Liverpool Stores Committee for their collaboration on the promotion of *Shopping*.

All of this would not have been possible without the artists and our greatest thanks have to go to them. *Shopping* includes a number of new works and ambitious installations as well as site-specific projects outside the Gallery. Particular thanks go to Guillaume Bijl, Common Culture, Andreas Gursky, Jenny Holzer, Surasi Kusolwong, Michael Landy, Sze Tsung Leong, Paul McCarthy and Ben Vautier. One of the highlights of *Shopping* is the reconstruction of the important *American Supermarket* exhibition, which was first presented in 1964 at the

Bianchini Gallery in New York. We are most grateful to Ben Birillo, who originally organised the exhibition and who most generously shared his recollections and advice. We are also much indebted to Sara Seagull and Larry Miller of the Robert Watts Studio Archive who assisted generously in the reconstruction of *The American Supermarket*.

We are extremely grateful to the private collectors and museums and galleries who allowed us to borrow their works. Without their co-operation *Shopping* would have not been possible.

The publication that accompanies and contextualises *Shopping* was a particularly challenging project. We would like to thank the authors for their insightful essays and the translators for their sensitive translations. A special thank has to go Hatje Cantz Publishers and, in particular, the excellent work of Karin Osbahr and Markus Hartmann. We also thank Christian Wurster for his elegant design. At Tate Liverpool, Cecilia Andersson and Natalie Rudd contributed their ideas and tireless research to making this such a richly illustrated and comprehensive book. We would also like to thank Jemima Pyne, Communications and Publishing Manager who co-ordinated the authors, translators and publisher.

We are also very pleased about the collaboration with the Schirn Kunst-halle Frankfurt and would like to especially thank Ingrid Pfeiffer whose devotion to the many aspects of this exhibition contributed decisively to its realisation. Ingrid Pfeiffer led the complex logistics for *Shopping*, working closely with the Registrars Karin Gruening and Elke Walter. Many at Tate have contributed to the success of *Shopping*. We like to thank the Director of Tate, Nicholas Serota, and Sandy Nairne, Director: Programmes who supported this project from the beginning and were instrumental in securing important loans. Jim France, Director of Collection and Research Services also actively supported the exhibition and we are grateful to him and the Conservators Mary Bustin, Elizabeth McDonald and Jo Gracey for their work in Frankfurt and Liverpool. Sophie Harrowes, Director of Communications and Nadine Thompson, Head of Press Office were also most generous with their media and marketing expertise.

At Tate Liverpool we have to mention, above all, the curatorial team that participated in curating the exhibition and editing the catalogue: Natalie Rudd and Cecilia Andersson's contribution to both was exemplary. In the last few months Jemima Montagu joined the Team and was instrumental in realising the reconstruction of *The American Supermarket* and actively shaped the presentation in Liverpool. Claire Young assisted with the recreation of the signage for the *American Supermarket* and Rosey Blackmore at Tate Publishing realised the reprinting of the Lichtenstein and Warhol paper bags originally produced for the *American Supermarket*.

Lindsey Fryer, Vicky Charnock, Elisa Oliver and Catherine Sadler of the Education Department provided many angles of interpretation, ranging from the investigation of patterns of consumption in Liverpool to academic conferences. Helen Stalker, Registrar at Tate Liverpool, expertly oversaw the complex logistics that come with such a large exhibition. The challenging installation with many large-scale works and ambitious reconstructions was as always efficiently managed by Ken Simons and Barry Bentley and their team. We are also grateful to Catherine O'Reilly and Tracey Ruddell of our Communications Team at Tate Liverpool for the careful handling of the promotion and press for *Shopping*. Jayne Hobin and her team effectively led the challenging development work, necessary for such an ambitious project. Finally, we would like to thank Helen Watters, Assistant to the Director at Tate Liverpool who was involved in and supported most aspects of the exhibition. Thanks to all of them and to the many others at Tate Liverpool who have contributed to *Shopping*.

Christoph Grunenberg
Director
Tate Liverpool

Max Hollein
Director
Schirn Kunsthalle Frankfurt

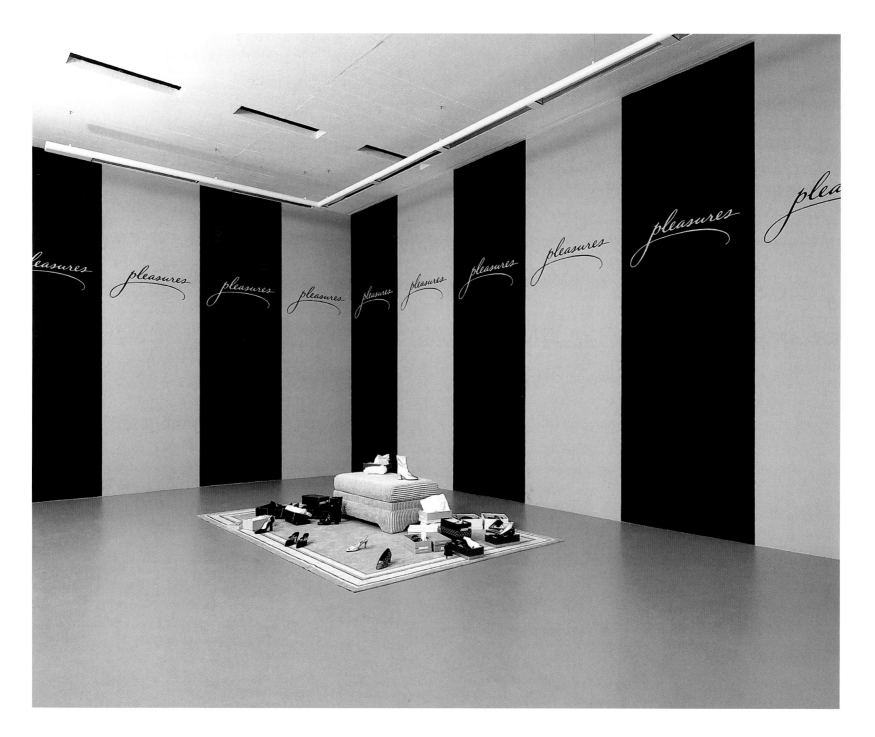

Sylvie Fleury **Untitled** 1992 and **Pleasures** 1996

Shopping

Max Hollein

The beautiful new world of consumer goods is booming. Not merely in the analyses of major commercial undertakings and lifestyle conglomerates, but also according to the views of cultural theoreticians and art historians. Shopping, wandering idly, strolling, selecting and consuming are identified both as the primary leisure occupation of our affluent Western society as well as being recognised as the determining activity at the root of modern urban life in all its facets. Purchasing is much more than the mere satisfying of everyday needs: it is the important ritual of public and communal life, through which identity is created and changed. It is possible that this also results from a capitulation before the superior power of our consumer society, but many have dared to take the plunge into the very pleasant hot water and do not find themselves opposed to this phenomenon, but in a position of fascinating participation and involved observation – and that right in the eye of the shopping hurricane.

Only ten years ago the cultural theoretician Boris Groys stated with regard to the contempt for consumption and its motives: 'Nothing in the modern consumer society is consumed with such relish as criticism of consumption. Merely to consume appears to be morally reprehensible – one should primarily produce, make, be creative.'[1] This ethical denial of the intellectual as opposed to the market- and, thus, system-dominating consumer society underwent a clear change. These days the theme, both in theory and analysis, exerts an unusual, thoroughly attractive fascination. We no longer allow ourselves to be corrupted by the orgiastic delight in shopping, in plunging into this living world of ideas of happiness. Wandering idly through the pedestrian zones and purchasing according to the principle of desire is the embodiment of

our freedom, open luxury and superabundance the sharpest weapons against any criticism of the capitalistic system. The act of purchasing, the modern hunting and gathering, becomes the spiritual and creative confession of our lifestyle society. Even Sunday – as the former Lord's day – increasingly becomes in this cultural circle the consumption-free day of idleness, a circumstance that it is necessary to combat and where one looks with envy at the paradisiacal possibilities of 'shop around the clock' in the US.

Karl Marx and Friedrich Engels naturally knew about the culturally political power of consumer goods: 'The bourgeoisie attracts through the rapid improvement of all instruments of production, through the infinitely facilitated communications of all, even the most barbarous nations in civilisation. The cheap prices of its goods are the heavy artillery, with which it shoots the Chinese walls into the ground, with which it compels the most stubborn xenophobia to capitulate.'[2] The worldwide standardisation of consumer goods, through a unified cultural, marketing and working area, ensures on the one hand an enclosed shopping zone of transcontinental dimensions, while on the other hand one must not underestimate the purchasing act as patriotic tool. In a unified world of consumer goods, in times of crisis politicians as well as marketing experts gladly bet on a non-existent patriotic preference for the place of origin and call for the purchase of national products – thus, driven by the national self-preservation instinct, shopping can become a political statement.

At the latest the theory of the post-modernists perceived our society as consumerist in the broadest sense, in which we, as consumers, are less attracted by products and services than by projected contents and characteristics. In such a hyper-system, an article, a product – freed from its inherent, profane functional value – can play a completely new, manipulable and manipulating role with regard to its content and our expectations and requirements. We observe a charging of the contents and aestheticising of even the most profane, basic products, which results in the fact that even the purchase of the most everyday articles becomes a wistful act of personal self-definition. The boundaries become blurred, the context expands, the status of the product as well as its radiating power comes to the fore. As Walter Benjamin observed, 'The objective environment of the human being assumes ever more relentlessly the characteristic of the article.'[3]

But consumers often have to recognise that it is only in its original context, the department store, that an article is animated with the beauty that makes it so seductive and aureate – in dull, everyday life functional value and barter value diverge too greatly. This discrepancy, however, is no longer held against the new world of consumer goods: the consumer does not alter his purchasing behaviour, but his everyday environment – everything must remind one of the atmosphere of the purchasing palaces. The everyday surroundings are adapted to the appearance of the shopping temple. In this act of appropriation the consumer becomes the artist of popular culture.

The surface attractions of the presentation of consumer goods have their effect. However, the theatrical staging, the glamour of the world of goods not only attracts the purchaser, but is also noticed by the artist. The first moment a store decided logistical storage and sales-orientated presentation of goods were no longer a compelling unity, a new aesthetic of presentation was rung in. The emergence of large shopping precincts and pavements hand in hand with the evolution of the wide display window provided for a new awareness of life and a quantum leap

into the aesthetics of consumer goods. The incipient evolution of the modern shopping enterprise, from the stores and sales arcades of the late nineteenth century via the department store to the mega mall, was not merely a distinguishing and characteristic development of the twentieth century, but also had a lasting effect upon the art of that period.

In that respect this exhibition follows the fundamentally creative dialogue between art and the consumer aesthetics of the businesses and purchasing houses, and underlines the considerable interaction between art and the presentation of goods. The methods and special effects of modern shopping – the endless, the excessive, the superabundance, the created fireworks of colours and shapes, the emphasising of the surface and the easy decodability find an echo in their systematic method, fascination, beauty and perfidy not only in our media society but also in the art of the period. During the whole of the twentieth century artists were fascinated by the magnitude of the temple of consumption and enticed by the subtlety of the commercial methods of display and presentation. Walter Benjamin's *flâneur* of the Parisian arcades experiences the strolling, selecting, purchasing and consuming as an activity determining modern life. The sophisticated and developing strategies for the sale and presentation of consumer goods create a utopian world of desires, longings and promises. From this the question frequently arises: Which is the consumer and which the product? Or have both these worlds in fact long been united?

Logically the new lifestyle businesses define themselves spatially and functionally not as places of the profane purchasing act but as cultural forums of our society. In their presentation and spectacle, in their focusing on observation and experiencing, they become not unlike the modern exhibition house – and vice versa. For Jean Baudrillard the ubiquitousness of the system and the aesthetics of shopping represent the end of the complex diversity of human life: 'We have reached the point where "consumption" has grasped the whole of life … work, leisure, nature and culture all previously dispersed, separate, and more or less irreducible entities that produced anxiety and complexity in our real life, and on our "anarchic and archaic" cities, have finally become mixed, massaged, climate-controlled, and domesticated into the single activity of perpetual shopping.'[4] Shops thus become on the one hand all-embracing living spaces and on the other hand local filters, meeting places for similarly-minded people. They provide the customer with branded goods, which act as signal beacons for fellow humans, a sign of recognition and understanding even outside the temple of consumption. Shops have long ago either stripped or completely assimilated the forum as the primary area for public meeting. As neuralgic places of public life they are both: a many-faceted manifestation and representation of the self-conception of our leisure society, as well as an environment of seduction and validation of the individual. Shopping serves the narcissistic fulfilment of desire in the same way as it enables participation in an easily consumable, collective feeling of happiness.

[1] Boris Groys, 'Der Wille zur totalen Produktion', in *Frankfurter Allgemeine Zeitung, Bilder und Zeiten*, no.114, 16 May 1992.

[2] Karl Marx and Friedrich Engels, *Manifest der kommunistischen Partei*, Berlin 1989, p.17. I am indebted to Rudolf Herz of Munich for drawing my attention to this quotation.

[3] Walter Benjamin, 'Über einige Motive bei Baudelaire', in *Illuminationen*, Frankfurt am Main 1977, p.239

[4] Jean Baudrillard, 'Consumer Society', in *Jean Baudrillard, Selected Writings*, ed. Mark Poster, Stanford, California 1988, p.29ff.

Wonderland: Spectacles of Display from the Bon Marché to Prada

Christoph Grunenberg

Dying of Consumption

Shopping is the crucial, penultimate step in the circulation of commodities. What interests us in particular about this stage in the life of commodities is the pre-terminal process of inspecting, admiring, selecting and purchasing of goods. In the moment of purchase, the commodity undergoes a magical transformation (or 'transubstantiation', as Karl Marx also called it), turning a product into money.[1] Without this act, the product remains a worthless entity into which companies have invested capital – research and development, production, distribution, marketing and advertising – and which costs them money with every minute that it lies unsold on the shelf of the department store or supermarket.[2]

In particular the aspect of presentation, seduction through and acquisition of commodities – the scintillating stages leading up to the crucial moment of purchase – was a long neglected phase in the analysis of the continuous cycle of exchange. Karl Marx largely overlooked this particular aspect in his *Capital*, stating that 'our present interest is in the sphere of exchange'.[3] Marx concentrated his attention on the economic aspects of production and trade, mostly ignoring the rituals and locales of shopping and the intricate techniques of seduction.

Successive generations of economists have followed his example and ignored the consumer and the contradictory mechanism of consumption. In his chapter on 'Commodity Fetishism', Marx acknowledged that the commodity form has 'nothing whatever to do with the physical properties'.[4] He also recognised the shift from the concentration on the pure use or exchange value of a product towards the emerging commodity spectacle, which invested objects with new and mutable meanings as 'not simply as a form of exchange but as a powerful and essentially unstable form of representation'.[5] Marx famously described the commodity functioning as a 'social hieroglyph', as the 'definite social relation between human beings' assumes 'the semblance of a relation between things'. Nevertheless, he closely tied the perception of a commodity with its reflection of the 'social character of ... [men's] own labour', that is 'material expressions of the human labour expended in their production'.[6]

It was the rapidly developing network of institutions of distribution, promotion and exchange that was to further refine an intricate system of complex meanings and delicate social gradations. From the second half of the nineteenth century, distribution and consumption were recognised as an increasingly central aspect of the capitalist economy, as the commodity became more and more dissociated from the idea of labour. Over the last two decades, critical attention has shifted from production to consumption and the consumer, suggesting that consumption is a much more complex and multi-layered process than just manufacturing, advertising and selling a product.[7] Meaning is created not only by *what* we buy, but also *where* and *how* and what happens to the product once it is in our possession.

The Rise of Modern Consumer Culture

The rise of modern consumer culture can be traced back to the mid-nineteenth century and the radical development of new material goods,

Welwyn Garden City Stores 1960s

Welwyn Garden City Stores 1960s

new methods of promotion and dissemination and new 'democratic' forms of consumption, developments that initially were most pronounced in the consumer revolution that took place in France.[8] Technological advances, industrial mass-production, rapidly improving and expanding systems of mass transportation, new methods of communication, increases in disposable incomes and proliferating channels of distribution all contributed to the accelerated expansion of the retail sector. Modern consumer culture in the nineteenth century was defined by the emergence of department stores with a fixed-price system and the introduction of credit; the availability of a wide choice of standardised goods; the access of a wider range of social groups to these more affordable commodities; mass consumption with its need for the constant expansion of an ever more elaborately staged spectacle of seduction; the increasing importance of consumer goods as cultural signifiers and modes of social distinction; and, finally, the emergence of shopping as an acceptable leisure activity. The rise of the department store in the middle of the century was the most prominent and spectacular manifestation of this new culture of uninhibited consumption and exchange. Retail developed into a major branch of the economy and a significant employer. In only twenty-five years, the Bon Marché department store in Paris saw a rapid expansion from just 12 employees and a turnover of 450,000 fr. in 1852 to 1,788 employees and a turnover of 73 million fr. in 1877. By 1887 the Bon Marché took up a whole city block covering 52,800 square metres.[9]

In the nineteenth and early twentieth centuries, modern men and women's relationship to commodities changed radically as a process took place that increasingly separated the producer from the ultimate consumer. The establishment and expansion of colonial empires provided cheap raw materials and introduced objects never seen before

along with a dream-world of exotic images, tastes and smells. Commodities were now often first encountered in shops or department stores or – with the rapid expansion of mail order houses, particularly in the US – delivered directly to the consumer's doorstep. Consumer culture saw an incredible proliferation of 'things' and desperately increasing pressures on producers to distribute them to consumers. It was now possible to own several machine-made dresses and more than just the one household pot traditionally used for a variety of purposes. Although the actual product played an important role in this process, there was also an increasing emphasis on the enhancement of the 'mysterious' character of the commodity.[10] As time, effort and capital expended on the production of the commodity decreased, the resources invested into transportation, presentation, marketing and selling increased proportionally.

The New Emphasis on Distribution

In 1929, the American journal *Commerce Monthly* explained the increased importance of distribution as a result of ever more efficient methods of mass production:

So greatly has potential output been increased by the application of machinery to manufacture that the limits of operation are now set rather by the number of customers who can be found to buy than by any difficulty in securing men and machines to make the goods. This situation has gradually transformed a seller's market into a buyer's market. The impact of the industrial revolution has passed from the field of production to that of distribution, and the problems of marketing the output of mass production have come to overshadow those of production itself.[11]

The rise of new methods of retailing – from the opulent department-stores of the nineteenth century to the epidemic spread of so-called chain stores in the early decades of the twentieth century – were the direct outcome of this process. It no longer sufficed to present a stock range of standard products that satisfied consumers' basic and limited needs. In fact, shopping was no longer about satisfying basic needs such as shelter, food and clothing, but about creating new needs, selling products that the consumer was not even aware that he or she needed. The American journalist and cultural critic Samuel Strauss explained the new situation producers and distributors found themselves in by the 1920s: 'Formerly the task was to supply the things that men wanted; the new necessity is to make men want the things which machinery must turn out if this civilization is not to perish... the problem before us today is not how to produce the goods, but to produce the customers.'[12]

Presentation is Everything

Over the last century, the rapid development in the major industries of advertising, marketing, public relations and consumer research reflects the unstoppable rise of the spectacle of consumption. Image, design, styling, branding and packaging became the central focus while the actual process of production became an almost negligible factor. The logical consequence has been a growing separation between retail and production and an exponential growth of the service industries, which do not require factories and workers and therefore do not have to deal with material products. As the surface appearance of the commodity takes precedence, the context in which products are offered to the consumer logically has to support the image projected. Objects are no longer defined by their function but by what Georg Simmel, in a review

of the Berlin Trade Fair in 1896, called the 'shop-window quality of things':

> The production of goods under the regime of free competition and the normal predominance of supply over demand leads to goods having to show a tempting exterior as well as utility. Where competition no longer operates in matters of usefulness and intrinsic properties, the interest of the buyer has to be aroused by the external stimulus of the object, even the manner of its presentation.[13]

Commercial methods of presentation evolved as the locales of shopping expanded in scale and importance. Sales and marketing managers, publicity and advertising representatives, shop window designers and decorators are the professions that emerged as department stores developed into major establishments with hundreds or thousands of employees.[14] Whether a major discount supermarket or an exclusive boutique, the presentation of the product is an essential element of the package offered. The carefully staged coincidence of image and brand identity – a well-designed product of a familiar and highly regarded brand presented in the right setting – should be hard to resist. Presentation is everything in capitalism and what was described in *Commerce Monthly* a few months before the Wall Street Crash in 1929, summarised the successful transformation over the previous fifty to sixty years of Western economies into 'consumer cultures'.

The Spectacle of Consumption

The rising tide of mass-produced commodities that swept through the nineteenth century called for new forms of representation in the service

L.-C. Boileau **Bon Marché** Paris, 1876. Cross-section of staircase

of publicity, promotion and distribution. Many different forms of advertising were developed – from printed newspaper announcements, posters, billboards, and shop window displays to gigantic world fairs and expositions. By the early twentieth century, these forms had created their own iconography, resulting in a unifying and sophisticated spectacle that 'enforced likeness and consolidated a dominant machinery of specifically capitalist representation'.[15]

The history of modern consumer culture is therefore in essence also a history of the continuous evolution and ever increasing sophistication of commercial display and presentation methods. From the Bon Marché in 1850s Paris to Rem Koolhaas' recently opened Prada store in New York, retail has always been an extravagant spectacle that can compete with the most lavish opera production or latest cinematic special effects. Style is not the question here – whether neo-baroque excess or Calvin Klein minimalism, surrealist commodity fetishism or typological Bauhaus seriality – what counts is the successful attraction of attention and awakening of unknown desires.

In the multiplying retail outlets of the great cosmopolitan centres, everything was done to attract consumers, to draw their gaze towards the brightly lit and sumptuously decorated show windows, to entice them to enter the store and wander through the aisles with the hope that some exquisitely displayed product or the latest novelty would turn the *flâneur* or *flâneuse* into a spending customer. The most defining feature of the temples of consumption in the late nineteenth-century was their fantastic splendour, their celebration of an illusion of accessible luxury through material and decorative excess. In the great expositions and large department stores of the period, 'this new and decisive conjunction between imaginative desires and material ones,

between dreams and commerce, between events of collective consciousness and of economic fact' became increasingly pronounced.[16] It was the beginning of a culture of make-believe, of continuous sensational entertainment – an extraordinary exhibition on display twenty-four hours around the clock, a spectacle performed for consumers to forget themselves and spend, spend, spend. It was a spectacle, however, that required and received the willing complicity of the contemporary consumers who not only desired it but enjoyed being entertained.

The luxurious architecture was itself a major means of attracting attention towards the new retail establishments. Department stores soon took up whole city blocks and the architectural decoration often surpassed even the grandest public building. Emile Zola famously described the unparalleled opulence of commercial architecture in *The Ladies' Paradise*: 'The high plate-glass door, facing the Place Gaillon, reached the mezzanine floor and was surrounded by elaborate decorations covered with gilding. Two allegorical figures, two laughing women with bare breasts thrust forward, were unrolling a scroll bearing the inscription: *The Ladies' Paradise*.'[17] For his extension of the Wertheim department store in Berlin (1904–05), Alfred Messel chose the late Gothic style, reconfiguring a building type which in medieval times had functioned as an open market hall. The imposing structure facing the Leipziger Platz lacked the typically wide expanse of shop window and instead featured high, open arcades and slender, perpendicular windows stretching over several floors. The use of the Gothic architectural style for the Wertheim extension transformed a mundane shop into an awe-inspiring cathedral of consumption: 'When, of an evening, you stand at a distance and the massed windows are flickering with diffused and, at the same time, subdued lights – you believe you must

Alfred Messel **Department Store Wertheim** Leipziger Straße, Berlin 1904–05

stay until the first organ note sings out to you from this lofty hall.', wrote one critic admiringly of Messel's Wertheim store.[18]

The radical change in the distribution of consumer goods was complemented by the emergence of a new class of urban consumer who was highly mobile, had access to a growing disposable income and had increasing leisure time. Customers were not only to come from the immediate neighbourhoods but had to be enticed from all over the city, facilitated by the creation of the *grands boulevards* and efficient systems of mass transportation. Commodities were also constantly on the move, increasing the distance between factories, the locales of shopping and the homes where consumption took place. Department stores became prominent destinations for tourists; already in 1872 the Bon Marché was promoted as a sightseeing stop and the store offered tours through its various departments as well as behind the scenes.[19] Consumers and retailers thus entered a dynamic relationship in which patronage was exchanged not necessarily just for goods but also for services, entertainment, advice, leisure and social interchange.

Shopping as Entertainment

The attraction of potential customers through free entertainment is almost as old as the department store itself. In New York, Alexander T. Stewart's second department store, which opened in 1862 on Broadway and 10th Street, featured an organ which was played throughout the day. From the 1870s, the Bon Marché in Paris organised extravagant concerts often attended by thousands: 'In less than hour the store, glutted with merchandise, abandoned to a world of gnomes or genies, is rapidly transformed, as in a fairyland, into a bewitching palace, daz-

zling with its lights, filled with flowers and exotic bushes whose effect is splendid.'[20] The Dufayel department store in Paris featured a theatre for 3,000 guests and a Cinematograph Hall for 1,500, attracting 'many people to the store ... an ingenious and profitable method of advertising'.[21] In 1902, the opening celebrations for the new Marshall Field and Co. store in Chicago featured extravagant decorations with 'cut flowers on every counter, shelf, showcase, and desk' as well as banners and six string orchestras distributed over various floors. 'The opening was one of the grandest events that has ever been known in Chicago,' one eye witness marvelled, 'in a word, simply Wonderland'.[22] At the turn of the twentieth century, the large department stores had become amusement palaces that disguised their true commercial purposes behind an elaborately staged spectacle. Significantly, Marshall Field refused to sell any goods on the opening day of its new store, concentrating all attention on the lavish show that firmly logged the store not only in the city's but also the country's imagination.[23]

Americans especially excelled at the creative fusion of retail and entertainment, and soon gained an international reputation for staging the most lavish and extravagant spectacles of consumption. One of the leading German department store entrepreneurs, Oskar Tietz, visited France, England and the US to inform himself of the latest retail developments. He enticed the chief decorator away from a Chicago department store and hired a New York sales and advertising manager for his Berlin store.[24] In the US, pioneers from other branches of popular entertainment crossed over to become leading retail entrepreneurs – film producer Adolph Zukor – opened one of the best-known low price department stores in New York under the name 'Penny Arcade'.[25] In particular, theatre impresarios and stage designers made an easy transition to shop and window display. Lee Simonson, a leading stage

Kyllmann & Heiden **Kaisergalerie** Berlin, 1869–73, Photograph 1885

designer of the 1920s, not only applied his knowledge in the retail sector but also explored the parallels between the display of merchandise and of art objects in museums.[26] The designer Norman Bel Geddes, who worked for a time as a theatrical stage designer specialising in lighting, pronounced the store 'a stage on which the merchandise is presented as the actors'.[27] The most prominent example, however, was L. Frank Baum, the author of *The Wonderful Wizard of Oz* (1900), who established his own store, worked as a pioneering shop window designer and founded the influential trade magazine *The Show Window*. By the 1920s, merchandising and shop window display had become a highly specialised profession that required fantasy, a flair for invention and an instinct for spectacle. However, extravagant shop window displays were themselves overtaken by ever more outrageous publicity stunts and pseudo-events, concerts, parades and festivals that transported customers and passers-by into a carefree and comforting dream-world.

Window and Counter-Shopping

Shopping had become a significant leisure activity and the department store the premier destination for lengthy excursions that involved much more than taking care of urgent shopping errands. It is worth quoting in full Gustav Stresemann's detailed account of the shopping experience in Berlin at the turn of the century:

> Meanwhile the department stores have taken it upon themselves to do more and more for the comfort of their customers. In Berlin, Wertheim has already set up a kind of counter inside his establishment where for payment one can drink beer, coffee, chocolate, fancy cake etc. Nowadays if one hears a family say: 'We're going to Wertheim'

that does not mean first and foremost that we need something particularly necessary for our housekeeping but one is talking about an excursion, which one is going to make to a beautiful place in the neighbourhood. For this one chooses an afternoon when one has most free time and, if possible, one arranges to meet acquaintances ... If one has come across acquaintances or brought them along, one sits chatting for some time, each shows the others her purchases, thereby gaining mutual encouragement for fresh expenditure. Time passes in looking at the different departments or at the clothes of the women, who are purchasing, in conversation and so on and when one suddenly looks at one's watch and sees that it is high time to return home, then simultaneously one frequently becomes aware of the fact that, instead of the single bow tie, which one initially intended to buy, one is loaded down with a whole bundle of the most varied kinds of things. Perhaps for a while one feels remorse and resolves that one will never again be so thoughtless but as soon as one has entered the department store to make a small purchase the play starts anew.[28]

Department stores encouraged the leisurely 'window- and counter-shopping' which had become respectable social activities. Unlike the *flâneur* of the Parisian arcades, the modern shopper was no longer a suspicious character but was encouraged to stroll, linger and make use of the establishments' lavish facilities without having to make a purchase. Until the early nineteenth century, entering a shop still 'entailed an obligation to make a purchase'. The opening in 1852 of the Bon Marché in Paris by Aristide Boucicault introduced fixed and clearly marked prices that applied to the whole range of goods and did away with lengthy negotiation over the value of a product. The fixed price policy opened the *grand magasins* to customers from a wider social

Félix Vallatton **Le Bon Marché** 1898

Distant Customers

The relationship between customer and retailer gradually became both more formalised and more distant, characterised by a certain degree of passivity on the part of the buyer, who was made to feel increasingly comfortable in the anonymity of the large department stores. In these intensely public places where large masses of people converged, the individual has to retreat, becoming reserved and even apathetic, in order to preserve his or her privacy: 'Active verbal interchange between customer and retailer was replaced by the passive, mute response of the customer to things – a striking example of how "the civilizing process" tames aggressions and feelings towards people while encouraging desires toward things.'[30] However, the type of 'medium-grade objects' offered at reasonable prices in department stores were mass-produced, standardised, without defining characteristics and usually displayed in large numbers. The spectacle of consumption was a necessary development to engage the increasingly distanced customer, to challenge him or her to see in the commodities more than just functional articles which one might need or not.[31]

The elaborate staging and dramatic display of commodities had become a fundamental necessity on which survival of not only the retailer but also the producer depended. The grand architecture of the department store, the large, fantastic window displays, the polished glass cases displaying goods in sophisticated arrangements, the attentive shop assistants, the free entertainment and multiple services offered were all important elements in the production of a spectacle of consumption. Attention shifted away from the commodity to multiple associations, cleverly evoked through subliminal advertising, exotic displays or lavish packaging. The frame had become far more elaborate than the work of art itself.

The Phantasmagoria of Consumption

The department store at the turn of the century was the pinnacle of the modern economic *Gesamtkunstwerk*, a monument to the seduction of the senses through colour, material, texture, movement, sound and form. Many contemporary descriptions and literary accounts describe the experience as overwhelming and perplexing, in particular for those who encountered modern city life for the first time, as the protagonists in Emile Zola's *The Ladies Paradise*:

The shop which suddenly had appeared before her, this building which seemed so enormous, brought a lump to her throat and held her rooted to the spot, excited, fascinated, oblivious to everything else ... With its series of perspectives, with the display on the ground floor and the plate-glass windows of the mezzanine floor, behind which could be seen all the intimate life of the various departments, the spectacle seemed to Denise endless... Denise stood transfixed before the display at the main door. There, outside in the street, on the pavement itself, was a mountain of cheap goods, placed at the entrance as a bait, bargains which stopped the women as they passed by ... It was a giant fairground display, as if the shop were bursting and throwing its surplus stock into the street.[32]

The primary principle was that of variation: 'Change, change and yet more change. The very goods themselves, which are on offer, are certainly the thing, which achieves the greatest possible effect of change.'[33] Both inside the store and spilling onto the street, the modern urban passer-by faced a superabundance of objects in endless variations of shapes, forms and colours. Octave Mouret, Zola's fictional department store owner in *The Ladies' Paradise*, stands for the revolutionary school of window dressing that dominated the last two decades of the nineteenth century. He pioneered 'the school of the brutal and gigantic in the art of display', which supplanted 'the classic school of symmetry and harmony achieved by shading'. Watching a salesman attempt 'to put some blue silks next to grey and yellow ones, then stepping back to see how the colour blended', Mouret intervened:

'But why are you trying to make it easy on the eye?' he said. 'Don't be afraid to blind them … Here! Some red! Some green! Some yellow!' He had taken the pieces of material, throwing them together, crumpling them, making dazzling combinations with them … He wanted avalanches, as if they had fallen at random from gaping shelves, and he wanted them blazing with the most flamboyant colours, making each other seem even brighter. He used to say that customers should have sore eyes by the time they left the shop.[34]

The increasing disorientation caused by the mystifying juxtaposition of disparate and unrelated objects and superimposition of imagery characterises the shift from the early consumer culture of the 1851 Crystal Palace in London to the excesses of the 1900 Grand Exposition in Paris. The penchant for exotic environments in the world expositions of the second half of the nineteenth century was continued in the department stores with their Oriental salons and Egyptian halls. Rosalind Williams described the style of decoration in Parisian *grand magasins* as 'chaotic-exotic', capturing the collision of disconnected objects and boundless variety in the extravagant staging of escapist fantasies. The Trocadéro and department store shared the stylistic themes of 'syncretism, anachronism, illogicality, flamboyance, childishness', creating a phantasmagoric dream-world of consumerism in which sales were achieved through appealing to the imagination and by transporting the customers to distant places and pasts.[35]

However, a sense of bad taste emerged in both the products and their arrangement. There was too much, too loud and too cheap. Reviewing the Berlin Trade Exhibition in 1896, Simmel disapproved the fact that every 'fine and sensitive feeling … is violated and seems deranged by the mass effect of the merchandise offered'. At the same time, he also had to acknowledge that these exaggerated displays satisfied exalted, contemporary sensibilities: 'the richness and variety of fleeting impressions [being] well suited to the need for excitement for overstimulated and tired nerves'.[36]

Shop 'til you Drop: The Exhaustion of Consumption

The spectacle of consumption at the turn of the century had emerged from the unregulated and pre-institutionalised spectacle of the nineteenth-century street, 'where an astonishing variety of goods and entertainment offered by itinerant peddlers and showmen was consumed in a carnival atmosphere', the street functioning both as 'showcase and show'. Department stores and other commercial outlets interiorised these traditions, 'especially in their miscellaneousness, the strident

View of Leipziger Straße Berlin, 1909

pitch of their promoters, and their emphasis on consumption as show.'[37] Everything seemed to be directed towards creating a permanent state of distraction, a constant series of small shocks and surprises that pulled the consumer from one attraction to the next. Simmel, again on the Berlin Trade Fair, detected mesmerising entertainment as one of the main techniques of capitalist promotion:

> In the face of the richness and diversity of what is offered, the only unifying and colourful factor is that of amusement. The way in which the most heterogeneous industrial products crowded together in close proximity paralyses the senses – a veritable hypnosis where only one message gets through to one's consciousness: the idea that one is here to amuse oneself.[38]

The relentless onslaught of visual impressions, it was feared, would push the modern individual into a state of nervous exhaustion on the brink of madness.

Department stores and shops were only one element in a newly emerging, lively culture of entertainment, which included trade fairs and expositions, amusement parks, music halls, theatres, nickelodeons and penny arcades, cinemas, bars and restaurants. Electricity, in particular, radically transformed the experience of city centres into a fairyland, 'a make-believe place where obedient genies leap to their master's command, where miracles of speed and motion are wrought by the slightest gesture, where a landscape of glowing pleasure domes and twinkling lights stretches into infinity'.[39] Shop windows were lit by new, powerful lights that not only illuminated the displayed goods but also basked the prospective shoppers and street in the warmth of the bright lights. At night, the shop window became even more effective than during the

daytime. As the source of illumination was moved inside the window, any reflection of the pedestrian *flâneur* was avoided, enhancing the illusion of there being no barrier between the consumer and the desired goods. Day and night had become indistinguishable, adding another ambiguity to the already confusing spectacle of the emerging modern metropolis.

In the modern city, with its bustling masses of industrious employees, eager consumers and pleasure-seeking members of a new leisure class, multiple impressions and stimuli competed for attention and were necessary not only for spatial orientation but for pure survival, as Benjamin described: 'Moving through this traffic involves the individual in a series of shocks and collisions ... Whereas Poe's passersby cast glances in all directions which still appeared to be aimless, today's pedestrians are obliged to do so in order to keep abreast of traffic signals.'[40] Perception in the modern city thus had a distinctly cinematic quality, occurring in transience as the rushed individual took in the dynamic spectacle unfolding on the street. The shifting gaze of the mobile consumer could not escape the attractions of the commodity spectacle which parasitically took over every surface: shouting from shop fronts and windows, from posters and billboards, in newspapers and illustrated magazines, inscribed on buildings and even projected into the sky at night, moving on the sides of buses and trams and on signs carried by sandwich-board men until, in the first decade of the twentieth century, the viewers' frantic movements were temporarily arrested and the image itself became animated on the silver screen.

A crisis of consumption gripped the leading entrepreneurs and emporiums at the turn of the twentieth century, fearing that the overwhelmed

Bernhard Sehring **Department Store Tietz** Leipziger Straße, Berlin, 1898

Roof Garden of the Kaufhaus des Westens Berlin, 1920s

consumer would soon no longer be able to consume. In a vicious cycle of competitive outperforming and endless exaggeration, exhilaration gave way to indifference which, in turn, had to be broken by even more daring publicity stunts, material excesses and unlikely juxtapositions of exotic artefacts and commodities. Titillated and stimulated into a state of delirious apathy, retailers, aesthetic reformers and cultural critics alike realised that the old strategies of escalating excess in product design, decoration, promotion and advertising had lost their effectiveness. Not unlike today, the sense of restless dissatisfaction was also interpreted as a symptom of a deeper, spiritual crisis penetrating society, as Simmel analysed: 'The lack of something definite at the centre of the soul impels us to search for momentary satisfaction in ever-new stimulations, sensations, and external activities.'[41] While it was impossible to arrest or even redirect the global progress of capitalism, it might at least be possible to rescue shopping from the association with conspicuous displays of vulgarity and bad taste with which it became increasingly associated.

Shopping Relief

The larger department stores offered respite from the seductive onslaught of commodities in winter gardens, tea rooms, libraries, reading rooms and parlours reserved exclusively for ladies.[42] The Wertheim flagship store on the Leipziger Platz in Berlin revitalised the fatigued consumer in its spectacular palm house. The Kaufhaus des Westens (KaDeWe) in Berlin featured a spectacular roof terrace on which customers rested on deck chairs, pretending to sail on a majestic ocean liner through the swell and surge of metropolitan Berlin. As much as they provided comfort, these facilities were also a form of publicity

which had 'such a curious psychological effect, particularly upon the female world'.[43] But these luxurious oases of silence and peace offered only temporary relief before the hardened shopper was thrown again, revitalised, into the battle of consumption. By the early twentieth century, the architecture, decoration and display in some department stores had become so fantastic and ostentatious that a backlash was inevitable. The responsibility to curb these excesses of uninhibited capitalism fell to the artistic and architectural avant-gardes.

Some of the most significant reforms in the final years of the nineteenth and early years of the twentieth centuries took place in Germany. The German Werkbund (founded in 1907) took a leading role in these reforms, coupling its ambitions for the improvement of the design of industrial products with social concerns and the support of consumer interests. Every aspect of daily life was to be penetrated by aesthetic considerations and promoted through a new artistic culture. The artists, designers and architects as well as the businessmen, industrialists and politicians associated with the Werkbund took an active interest in retail architecture and questions of decorative arrangement of commodities. The design of shop fronts, windows and interiors was seen as a special challenge as there 'goods and purchasers meet each other'.[44] In 1910 a higher technical college devoted to decoration was founded in Berlin and the epochal Werkbund exhibition of 1914 in Cologne featured a whole street presenting exemplary shop display.[45]

Reforms of Shopping I: The Department Store

The Wertheim department store was an early example of the particularly German concern with curtailing the excesses of industrial capi-

Emil Schaudt **Kaufhaus des Westens** Berlin, 1907

talism epitomised by the more profusely decorated foreign stores.[46] Wertheim was praised for its lack of declamatory signage and advertising: 'Dumb in the midst of loud noise, proud and self-confident like the gigantic trees in front of it, majestically, almost ceremonially its structure rises up on the corner. A department store? But no advertising sign, no flag, nothing colourful proclaims its purpose by day, nor any light effects in the evening.'[47] Instead, the architecture communicated through its 'considerable, reticent beauty' the ambitious quality of products on sale and the kind of bourgeois customer which they attracted.[48] Wertheim's windows on the Leipziger Street, however, functioned as prime advertisement, dominated by the urge to open the whole interior to the 'covetous gaze of Woman,'[49] the 'essence of the display window hereby intensified into the gigantic.'[50] The idea of 'the total shop window' culminated in Bernhard Sehring's Kaufhaus Tietz (Berlin, 1899-1900), Victor Horta's L'Innovation (Brussels, 1901) and Frantz Jourdain and Henri Sauvage's La Samaritaine (Paris, 1905) which all featured the near dissolution of the façade with the absence of any structural elements.[51]

The impression of Wertheim's interior, however, particularly in the central atrium, contrasted with the relative discretion of the exterior: 'humans in uninterrupted streams at almost any time of day; never-ending, vast rows of sales' stands; a sea of massed goods, spread out; ... colours, glitter, light and noise: a monstrous confusion, seemingly without design and order.'[52] While Wertheim featured the usual spaces for refreshment and relaxation, it was clear that, as Göhre ascertained, 'peace and quiet and the department store are totally opposed to each other, completely mutually exclusive things'.[53]

In contrast, the KaDeWe (opened in 1907) featured a closed and clearly structured façade that demonstrated restraint and solidity. The depart-

ment store was complimented for its 'uniform artistic design worked out to the last detail, using only genuine materials (wood, metal and stone), avoiding all ostentation'.[54] While there were still large sale spaces on the ground floor and grand interior courtyards for relaxation, the store also featured many smaller, architecturally distinct departments. Each of the sixty-five departments, as one contemporary critic observed, presented itself 'to a certain degree as an intimate specialist shop and, therefore, during the course of a long series of purchases one does not suffer from nervous exhaustion as quickly as one does in colossal stores'.[55] The more intimate atmosphere yet spatially more generous layout of the KaDeWe not only relieved customers from the pressures of crowds but also increased the distance from the goods, thus allowing a more civilised shopping experience for the upmarket customer.

Reforms of Shopping II: The Artistic Shop Window

In 1905, the politician Friedrich Naumann argued that the modern department store required, 'no unnecessary interior decoration ... since the goods themselves wished to provide its decoration and must remain distinct if the public is to see what's what. For practical reasons all dark corners and narrow angles must be avoided and thus there are no distracting false small decorations, which is very agreeable.'[56] The presentation of commodities moved away from a disjointed agglomeration, as described by Zola, towards a more rational and typological arrangement, reflecting the need to channel the gaze as well as direct the emotional investment of the over-distracted metropolitan inhabitant. Karl Ernst Osthaus, who was instrumental in the reform of modern shop-window decoration, blamed the persistence of 'panoptical portrayals' on the 'hypertrophic atmosphere of display window com-

Franz Habich **Haberdashery Department in the Kaufhaus des Westens** Berlin, 1907

petitions', with their sensational arrangements of elaborate tableaux organised around particular merchandise. The city streets already offered enough distraction and the 'mystery of the union of the purchaser with the goods demands concentration'.[57]

Karl Ernst Osthaus deduced the argument for artistic display from the alienation of labour and production as he saw it manifested in the type of display favoured in northern European countries (contrasting it with some Oriental cultures where no shop windows were necessary or the view opened directly onto a workshop): 'Thus for most people the most important source of interest in work has run dry, its most indispensable basis removed from the sense of style. What effect does this have on the display? It must seek to heighten the interest through artistic means. Must exhibit great splendour, must entice, stimulate desire.'[58] The Werkbund attempted to counteract a crisis of consumption, out of which grew a crisis of representation as the commodity was stripped of all marks of its production. Osthaus presented an admittedly mythicising conception of pre-industrial work, and set against the alienation and fragmentation caused by industrialisation the Werkbund's programme of artistic integrity which was to transform the commodity into a cultural product with a convincing wholeness and material authenticity.[59] The shop owner was now to take on a decidedly educational role, responsible for the development of taste among the broader population.[60] The reforms in shop and window display design centred on the essential values and characteristics of the merchandise itself, attempting to give a sense of authenticity to the commodity, as well as the store in which it was offered: 'The new window intends to be objective. Each article, instead of telling stories, will be itself. The display will be a display, something put together, which does not appear to be linked by any "literary" connection. The garment is an article, not the cover-

ing of an expectant, eavesdropping waxen beauty.'[61] The narrative was to be avoided at all cost, whether in illustrative tableaux resembling elaborate stage sets or in the displays of 'Bismarck towers made from chocolate or soap, those temples made out of stearin candles and with Raphaelesque angels in old tomes decorated with sentimental trash'.[62] For more opulent commodities the background was to be as neutral as possible and avoid any props or foreign adornments. For less glamorous products the presentational reserve could be somewhat relaxed.[63] The style of the display was to grow out of the inherent nature of the commodity and was to be logically coherent, avoiding incongruous embellishments or juxtapositions such as 'if the lady in front of the mirror was surrounded by twenty corsets on stands or a similar number of pieces of washing, which covered the floor'.[64]

The Werkbund was divided over the subject of the standardisation of industrial products (the *Typisierung* of commodities) versus the application of artistic principles to production and presentation by the so-called 'individualists', a fundamental debate that affected attitudes on shop window decoration and design.[65] The artistic camp categorised commodities according to a formalist emphasis on colour, form and line and on whether their painterly or plastic nature required juxtaposition or subordination.[66] August Endell's acclaimed shop design for the Salamander shop in Berlin, for example, concentrated on the company's logo, displaying a small selection of the product (shoes) in front of tastefully patterned backgrounds. Despite his plea for objectivity, Osthaus praised the 'mystic magic' of the windows, with 'sparkling areas of deep-coloured mirrors it positioned the lighting fixtures towards the street, the light trickling down from above over the goods. Trademarks, changed into magic symbols, glisten with burning features'.[67] Packaging also became a major area of artistic influence which allowed

August Endell **Salamander Shoe Store** Tauentzienstraße, Berlin, c. 1910

August Endell **Interior of Salamander Shoe Store** Potsdamer Straße, Berlin, c. 1910–11

the decorator to present stacks and rows of identical or identically packaged products in intricate, often symmetrical patterns, playing with the simple shapes and clear design of rectangular boxes.

Accumulation of related products was allowed as long as a causal relationship existed between the displayed objects, as for example with a shop window that presented 'all parts of Weck's cooking equipment grouped together; it provides a sort of object lesson in the application and use of the equipment and, as a result, heightens the interest.'[68] However, arranging items according to function posed a new dilemma, since it directed the emphasis away from the mechanised production process towards the consumer, who would ultimately use the product.[69] The strictly rational and geometrical arrangement of commodities seemed to follow the principles of non-objective art that were emerging at the same time. The machine aesthetic was translated into the commercial sphere through three-dimensional compositions of actual factory- and mass-produced commodities. But despite overcoming displays mimicking organic, natural forms in nature – waterfalls of silk or soaps in floral arrangements – abstraction itself failed to reveal the true relationship between production and the product.[70] The decorative stacking and serial arrangement of attractively packaged products ultimately told little about the genealogy of the commodities and the actual conditions of production in factories, and thus contributed little to decreasing the alienation of the consumer from the consumed objects.

I Can See Clearly Now: The Reformed Shopper

In the capitalist economy, perception had not only become disjointed by the uncontrolled proliferation of commodities and relentless spectacle of promotion but also through the atomisation of surfaces through intricate decoration – an almost destructive act by which the modern individual would 'see beyond' the ordinary visible: 'take it to pieces, dismember it, take bits out, observe that part for a moment, this part more closely and a third part down to the smallest detail, each according to its practical interest'.[71] A newly ordered and regulated vision as promoted by the Werkbund was to have an almost restorative and soothing function. The turn towards artistic presentation was also supported by solid economic interests, as Simmel observed: 'It is at the point where material interests have reached their highest level and the pressure of competition is at an extreme that an aesthetic ideal is employed.'[72] Tasteful shop windows and the restrained display of merchandise actually introduced a real sales advantage: the consumer was no longer torn between numerous offers but able to concentrate attention on individual objects.

Mass consumption required a new, specially programmed and sophisticated consumer who, like the modern worker, was subjected to scientific investigation and determination following the efficiency doctrines of Taylorism and Fordism. Like production, consumption was to be optimised for maximum profit return and every aspect of selling from shop architecture, effective displays and circulation patterns to the consumer's own behaviour was scrutinised and analysed. Women, for example, were diagnosed as better shoppers: 'Scientists affirm that women are less often colorblind than men. It is asserted that a woman has a much wider range of vision than a man has. With her eyes fixed straight ahead she observes persons and things farther to the right and to the left than men do.'[73] Perception had become an instrument of desire, reducing, as Marx had predicted, vision to a 'sense of having'.[74] As much as men were reconfigured into perfect machines of

Julius Klinger **Shop Window Display for A. Rosenhain**
Berlin, 1909

Weck's Preservation, Halbach Company
Shop Window Display Competition, Hagen, 1910

production, women were assigned the complementary role of consuming automatons. Male and female activities thus converged in a productive union, which would maintain the continuous flow of capital.

Reforms of Shopping III: Rational Shopping

While the reforms of shop and window display initially had demonstrable economic results, the lack of spectacle in the rationalised shop window was soon criticised for 'a certain uniformity, not to say boredom'.[75] The pronounced puritan tendency inherent in modernism made for an uncomfortable relationship with the voracious and unquenched demands of consumer capitalism. Can shopping ever be totally free of subconscious desires, class aspirations or just simple pleasures afforded by little luxuries and novelties? The challenge to modernist artists and designers of the 1920s and 1930s was to transform shopping into a democratic, rational and controlled activity, employing a formal vocabulary that categorically denied any superfluous decoration, sensual surfaces or precious materials. In the extended austerity of the 1920s, conspicuous consumption remained something to beware of, while a collaboration with industry – with its corresponding sales and performance pressures – was high on the modernist agenda.

The reform attempts of the Werkbund continued into the 1920s and 1930s and the display of commodities in expositions and trade fairs figured prominently in the work of Bauhaus. The Schocken department store chain worked closely with the Bauhaus, commissioning display tables and the company's entire typographical output.[76] Erich Mendelsohn's series of Schocken stores combined dynamic form, functionality and transparency in buildings that, through their innovative

use of light, transformed the architecture itself into spectacular propaganda or, as Adolf Behne put it, 'Reklamearchitektur'. Like the exterior, the wide open sale spaces with a minimum of decoration were more reminiscent of a factory floor than the aristocratic spaces of the pre-war department stores. Now the openly displayed merchandise on simple tables and display cabinets was deemed advertising enough without any further decorative additions or themed arrangements. The company's business principles, written in large capital letters over each sales counter, featured as a constant reminder to the consumer of the store's honesty and commitment to quality. The department store architecture and strategies of display were seen as a continuous whole, developing out of the utilitarian integrity of the products. Mendelsohn went even further declaring that 'the beauty of the whole results technically from the new means [of production]'.[77]

Functionalism propagated displays that concentrated on the products themselves, reflecting their function and genesis out of the modern industrial process. The design was to be free from artistic considerations which, ultimately, had nothing to do with the function or production of a utilitarian object.[78] The most consistent shop windows and displays of goods at trade fairs and consumer shows featured the serial arrangement of objects based on an uncompromising functionalism. Large numbers of identical or related goods were arranged in simple geometric patterns and rarely featured any display props or decorative backgrounds. The pronounced social agenda of some of these exhibitions was demonstrated by the focus on consumer interests and needs. The arrangement of simple everyday objects was 'not determined by production and its laws, but by [the object's] application'.[79] The doctrine of functionalism with its rationalised treatment of modern living and the scientific analysis of domestic work processes was most consistently

Erich Mendelsohn **Department Store Schocken** Stuttgart, 1928–29

Erich Mendelsohn **Department Store Schocken** 1928–29

realised. In the 1932 *Wohnbedarf* (*Household Furnishings*) exhibition, traditional crockery sets were split up so that 'for example with the drinking utensils, nowhere appears a service, but all teapots, all coffeepots, all teacups etc., are arranged in one row after another. With this one wanted to force the visitors to clearly realise the function and meaning of every single receptacle.'[80]

The gospel of rationalisation took the glamour out of shopping and transformed consumption into an almost mechanical activity entirely based on sensible considerations of need, function and price. In 1928, an article entitled 'Planned Shopping' in a German trade union journal took exception to the time wasted by housewives on unnecessary shopping trips and advocated planned shopping with productive weekly deliveries that would completely abolish the need for time-intensive and exhausting excursions to the shops.[81] Time for shopping was to be reduced so that working-class women could devote more time to political work and education.

However, how were more expensive and precious products to be advertised? How was the reductive modernist presentation to be reconciled with demands of storeowners to appeal not only to reason but also to deeper and more powerful desires? The answer lay in the splendid isolation of commodities, a strategy enthusiastically endorsed by Fernand Léger: 'In shop windows a single useful commercial object isolated in front of a coloured background has a higher publicity value than 200 objects piled on top of each other.'[82] The displays followed modernist principles of simplicity yet employed the generous use of space as an indicator of taste, elegance and luxury. Redefining the modernist democratic agenda, Frederick Kiesler used the formal principles of abstraction, simplicity and asymmetry to great dramatic effect in his windows

for Saks Fifth Avenue 'to stimulate desire. That is why show windows, institutional propaganda, and advertising were created and why their importance is continually increasing.'[83] Kiesler managed to reintroduce spectacle into contemporary display, fusing modernist aesthetics with entertainment, stage design and commercial interests. This, however, also implied that the commodity could no longer be reduced to a purely functional object, and once again conjured alluring visions of affluence, luxury and excessive consumption.

Twentieth-Century Display Styles

The dominant display trends emerging in the first decades of the twentieth century could be categorised into two basic trends. On the one hand, there is the staging of spectacular displays that frequently degenerated into feasts of material exuberance with their typically disruptive invasion of architectural, bodily and mental space. This bias has often been associated with anti-modernist tendencies based on the ostentatious indulgence in frivolous, sensual and luxurious pleasures, waste of material resources and human perceptual energies. On the other hand, there were the well-meaning reform attempts instigated by concerned representatives of both the avant-garde and enlightened business community. Their attempts to contain the deluge of commodities and capitalism's tendency towards ruthless promotion, seduction and exploitation led to the application of first artistic, and then strict utilitarian principles, to commercial display.

By the 1920s, these two extremes of presentation were well established, and over the past century shop displays have oscillated between these two polar opposites. The presentation of art in galleries and museums

Hans Finsler **Hermes-Service** 1931

Frederick Kiesler **Saks Fifth Avenue** New York, 1927–28

has simultaneously fed off and inspired commercial displays. The spectacle periodically resurfaces, as with the Surrealists' installations that revisited the Paris of Atget's shops and flea markets and that cleverly explored the indeterminate status of the mannequin between life and death. Today's minimalist shops have their origin in the so-called 'white cube' galleries, mimicking art's pretence at an autonomous space free from the debasing influence of commerce, and employing the same strategies of aesthetic enhancement and elevation through elegant isolation.

From Passive Consumer to Anti-Globalism Activist

There is a long tradition in left-wing and Marxist, academic theory to present consumers as repressed, controlled and regulated subjects without individual will, manipulated by clever, irresistible strategies of psychological seduction: 'There is in fact a maliciousness in the flattery of the goods. … Those served by capitalism are in the long run its unconscious employees', writes Wolfgang Fritz Haug, for example, in 1971.[84] Consumers have never been hapless and near-comatose victims of the evil system of capitalist exploitation, led into temptation by subliminal messages that sell us everything from toasters to cars by appealing to our hidden, sexual urges. Neither has the nightmare vision of an all-consuming *Society of the Spectacle* in which we are subjected to the 'omnipresent affirmation of a choice *already* made in production and corollary consumption' become reality.[85] Shoppers have always made decisions based on necessity, functionality and taste as well as being consciously influenced by advertising and marketing. We are seduced by hot brands and expensive fashion labels and, in most cases, we know why, and take great pleasure in the meaning bestowed

onto us by wearing Gap, Ralph Lauren, Boss and Rolex, or whatever the latest must-have logo may be. The great failures of marketing history – think of the introduction of New Coke or the countless new breakfast cereals and lifestyle magazines that fail each year – clearly demonstrate that, whatever the advertising budget, success cannot be manufactured. The proliferation of television programmes that present commercials from around the world for pure entertainment indicates that nowadays, it is more important to intrigue though originality and humour than to clumsily appeal to sexual desires, lifestyle aspirations and class status.

As a matter of fact, with emerging localised variations and rapidly shifting taste patterns, strategies of consumption have become so complex that predicting, not to mention manipulating consumer taste has become a pseudo-scientific growth industry. Chasing the ever more powerful youth market, large companies employ style scouts and 'street crews' that feed back up-to-date information from the front-line of consumption about what is currently perceived as cool, hip and trendy.[86] It no longer suffices to associate oneself with a particular brand, as its image may have been hijacked and radically transformed by non-target groups or (horror!) might already be three days out of fashion. A well-known example is Tommy Hilfiger, which managed to function successfully in parallel markets: as an upscale fashion brand projecting an all-American, aristocratic New England, 'my-ancestors-came-over-on-the-Mayflower' image, and at the same time was a preferred clothing label customised by black rap culture (which in turn was appropriated by white middle-class kids).

For the radical counter culture of the 1960s and 1970s, anti-consumerism was an essential element of their political philosophy – to the extreme

'White Weeks' in the Department Store Tietz
Leipziger Straße, Berlin, c. 1926

of endorsing stealing in order to subvert the existing capitalist order.[87] Nowadays, 'ironic consumption', as Naomi Klein describes it, allows critical consumers to enjoy forbidden fruits with a knowing wink:

> They were now finding ways to express their disdain for mass culture not by opting out of it but by abandoning themselves to it entirely – but with a sly ironic twist. They were watching *Melrose Place*, eating surf'n'turf in revolving restaurants, singing Frank Sinatra in karaoke bars and sipping girly drinks in tikki bars, acts that were rendered hip and daring because, well, *they* were the ones doing them. Not only were they making a subversive statement about a culture they could not physically escape, they were rejecting the doctrinaire puritanism of seventies feminism, the earnestness of the sixties quest for authenticity and the 'literal' readings of so many cultural critics.[88]

Even the radical opponents of globalisation and full-time anarchists battling exploitative multinational conglomerates have had to come to terms with the fact that the almighty allure of shopping can affect even the most devoted anti-capitalist, as poignantly depicted in a recent *New Yorker* cartoon. The pleasures of consumption and powerful appeal of brands have even penetrated alternative communities that believe themselves resistant to the powerful spin machines of advertising and marketing. Instead of Prada stilettos it might just be Birkenstock sandals. Shopping today transcends political, ideological and ethnic boundaries and has become a kind of universal, fundamentally human activity. The joys of consumption, it seems, will continue to be at the centre of modern life for a long time.

[1] Karl Marx, *Capital*, vol.1, *Der Produktionsprozess des Kapitals*, London: Dent and New York: Dutton 1974, p.85.

[2] The practice of charging producers for the privilege of advantageous placement on supermarket shelves (preferably at eye height, at the ends of shelves facing the highly frequented central aisles) puts a very concrete value on this cost. In the US this kick-back system is euphemistically called 'slotting allowance'. James B. Twitchell, *Lead us into Temptation: The Triumph of American Materialism*, New York: Columbia University Press 1999, p.124.

[3] Marx, *Capital*, vol.1, p.81.

[4] Ibid. p.45.

[5] Twitchell, *Lead us into Temptation*, p.69.

[6] Marx, *Capital*, vol.1, pp.45, 47.

[7] In 1988, Grant McCracken was still able to state that the history of consumption 'has no history, no community of scholars, not tradition of scholarship' and is 'preparadigmatic'. *Culture and Consumption: New Approaches to the Symbolic Character of Consumer Goods and Activities*, Bloomington and Indianapolis: Indiana University Press 1988, p.28.

[8] See Rosalind H. Williams, *Dream Worlds: Mass Consumption in Late Nineteenth-Century France*, Berkeley, Los Angeles and Oxford: University of California Press 1982, pp.7–12. Some writers have located the origins of modern shopping as 'a discrete consumer activity' as early as the second half of the eighteenth century. See Elizabeth Kowaleski-Wallace, *Consuming Subjects: Women, Shopping, and Business in the Eighteenth Century*, New York: Columbia University Press 1997. Chandra Mukerji, in *From Graven Images: Patterns of Modern Materialism*, New York: Columbia University Press 1983, detects evidence of modern consumption ('commercial capitalism') in the fifteenth and sixteenth centuries, concentrating on goods and

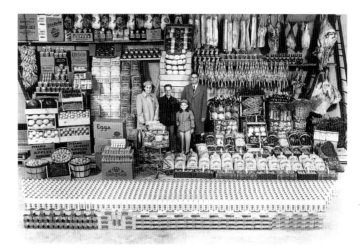

Alex Henderson's illustration to **Why Eat Better** in **Better Living** November 1951

their meanings rather than 'industrial capitalism' and its effects. While the origins of the 'consumer revolution' might reach back into the eighteenth century and earlier, modern forms of consumption (or 'shopping') most distinctly emerged in the nineteenth century. For a useful discussion of these competing theories see McCracken, *Culture and Consumption*, pp.3–30.

9 Michael B. Miller, *The Bon Marché: Bourgeois Culture and the Department* Store, Princeton, New Jersey: Princeton University Press 1981, pp.40–3.

10 Marx, *Capital*, vol.1, pp.43ff.

11 A. M. Michener, 'The New Emphasis in Distribution', *Commerce Monthly*, no.10, Apr. 1929, pp.3–11; repr. in Daniel Bloomfield (ed.), *Selected Articles on Trends in Retail Distribution*, New York: H. W. Wilson Company 1930, p.71.

12 Quoted in Ric Burns and James Sanders with Lisa Ades (eds.), *New York: An Illustrated History*, New York: Alfred A. Knopf 1999, p.338.

13 Georg Simmel, 'The Berlin Trade Exhibition', (1896) in David Frisby and Mike Featherstone (eds.), *Simmel on Culture: Selected Writings*, London: Sage 1997, p.257.

14 H. Gordon Selfridge's *The Romance of Commerce* (London: The Bodley Head 1918) contains an expansive chart illustrating the organisation of a twentieth-century department store. Amongst the many staff that are concerned directly with presentation and promotion are in particular the Publicity Department (with sub-departments for Newspaper Advertising; Catalogues & Curculars; Letters; Posters, Hoardings, etc., House Sign Cards) and the Display & Trims Department (with sub-departments for Windows; Outlying Windows; Interior Displays; Merchandise Displays; Flowers & Palms; Electricity; Flags and Scenic Work).

15 Thomas Richards, *The Commodity Culture of Victorian England: Advertising and Spectacle, 1851–1914*, London and New York: Verso 1991, p.251.

16 Williams, *Dream Worlds*, p.65.

17 Emile Zola, *The Ladies Paradise* (1883), trans. Brian Nelson, Oxford: Oxford University Press 1995, p.4.

18 Paul Göhre, *Das Warenhaus*, Die Gesellschaft: Sammlung sozialpsychologischer Monographien, ed. Martin Buber, vol.12, Frankfurt am Main: Literarische Anstalt Rütten & Loening 1907, p.8.

19 Miller, *The Bon Marché*, p.169.

20 *L'Orphéon*, 5 Jan. 1886, quoted in Miller, *The Bon Marché*, p.172.

21 Quoted in Williams, *Dream World of Consumption*, p.94.

22 Quoted in William Leach, *Land of Desire: Merchants, Power, and the Rise of a New American Culture*, New York: Vintage 1993, p.31.

23 'I have read everything that I could see in print about your opening,' department store pioneer John Wanamaker of Philadelphia wrote to Marshall Field's manager, H. Gordon Selfridge, 'and confess that I feel more interest in what you are doing than in any other business except our own. I hope to make a visit to see with my own eyes.' Quoted ibid. p.31.

24 Helmut Frei, *Tempel der Kauflust: Eine Geschichte der Warenhauskultur*, Leipzig: Edition Leipzig 1997, pp.80, 82.

25 Ibid. p.169.

26 Lee Simonson, 'Skyscrapers for Art Museums', *American Mercury*, vol.11, no. 44. August 1927, pp.399–405.

27 Leach, *Land of Desire*, pp.306–7.

28 Gustav Stresemann, 'Die Warenhäuser – ihre Entstehung, Entwicklung und volkswirtschaftliche Bedeutung', *Zeitschrift für die gesamte Staatswissenschaft*, no.56, 1900, pp.713–14

29 Williams, *Dream Worlds*, p.67. However, this new system was slow to take hold in some countries and in 1906 H. Gordon Selfridge was still shown the door by a shop

"I totally agree with you about capitalism, neo-colonialism, and globalization, but you really come down too hard on shopping."

Koren, Cartoon in **The New Yorker** 23 July, 2001

walker in a London department store after responding in the negative to a question about whether he wished to make a purchase. Bill Lancaster, *The Department Store: A Social History*, London and New York: Leicester University Press 1995, p.75.

30 Williams, *Dream Worlds*, p.67.

31 'By stimulating the buyer to invest objects with personal meaning, above and beyond their utility, there arose a code of belief which made mass retail commerce profitable. The new code of belief in trade was a sign of a larger change in the sense of the public realm: the investment of personal feeling and passive observation were being joined; to be out in public was at once a personal and passive experience.' Richard Sennett, *The Fall of Public Man*, New York: Alfred A. Knopf 1977, pp.144, 145.

32 Zola, *The Ladies' Paradise*, pp.4–5.

33 Göhre, *Das Warenhaus*, p.30.

34 Zola, *The Ladies' Paradise*, p.48.

35 Williams, *Dream Worlds*, p.69.

36 Simmel, 'The Berlin Trade Exhibition', p.255.

37 William R. Taylor, *In Pursuit of Gotham: Culture and Commerce in New York*, New York and Oxford: Oxford University Press 1992, p.70.

38 Simmel, 'The Berlin Trade Exhibition', p.255.

39 Williams, *Dream World*, p.85.

40 Walter Benjamin, 'Some Motifs in Baudelaire', in *Charles Baudelaire: A Lyric Poet in the Era of High Capitalism*, trans. Harry Zohn, London and New York: Verso, 1997, p. 132.

41 Georg Simmel, *The Philosophy of Money* (1900), ed. David Frisby, London and New York: Routledge 1990, p. 484. See also Don Slater, *Consumer Culture & Modernity*, Cambridge: Polity Press 1997, pp.104–105.

42 By the late nineteenth century, a variety of services were standard features in large department stores. When Selfridges opened in London in 1909, the American-owned department store offered a Bureau of Information as well as 'a library and Silence Room, a First Aid Ward, a Bureau de Change, Patriotic Rooms ... Railway Steamship and Theatre Booking Offices, Parcel and Cloak Check desk – with gratuities neither expected nor allowed ... a Post and Telegraph Office, a Savings Bank, a Luncheon Hall, a tea garden open to the sky'. Quoted in Lancaster, *The Department Store*, p. 75.

43 Alfred Wiener, 'Das Warenhaus', *Jahrbuch des Deutschen Werkbundes*, vol.2, 1913, p.45.

44 August Endell, 'Ladeneinrichtungen', *Jahrbuch des Deutschen Werkbundes*, vol.2, 1913, pp.55–58; quoted in Endell, *Vom Sehen: Texte 1896-1925 über Architektur, Formkunst und 'Die Schönheit der großen Stadt'*, ed. Helge David, Basel, Berlin and Boston: Birkhäuser 1995, p.106.

45 On the relative failure of the shopping street at the Werkbund exhibition, see Silke Strempel, 'Karl Ernst Osthaus: Förderer der künstlerischen Schaufenstergestaltung', in Michael Fehr, Sabine Röder and Gerhard Storck (eds.), *Das Schöne und der Alltag: Die Anfänge des modernen Designs 1900-1914*. Cologne: Wienand Verlag pp.396–8.

46 Alfred Messel's Wertheim department store was erected in three phases: 1896–7, 1899–1900 and 1904–6. Kathleen James, 'From Messel to Mendelsohn: German Department Store Architecture in Defence of Urban and Economic Change', in Geoffrey Crossick and Serge Jaumain (eds.), *Cathedrals of Consumption: The European Department Store, 1850-1939*, Aldershot, Brookfield (Vermont), Singapore and Sydney: Ashgate 1999, p.260.

47 Göhre, *Das Warenhaus*, p.7.

48 Ibid. p.9.

49 Karl Scheffler, 'Korrespondenzen: Berlin', *Dekorative Kunst*, vol.1, no.4, 1898, p.187. Quoted in Jenny Anger, 'Forgotten Ties: The Suppression of the Decorative in German Art and Theory, 1900-1915', in Christopher Reed (ed.), *Not at Home: The Suppression*

of Domesticity in Modern Art and Architecture, London: Thames & Hudson 1996, p.135.

50 Göhre, *Das Warenhaus*, p.12.

51 Helga Behn, *Die Architektur des deutschen Warenhauses von ihren Anfängen bis 1933*, diss., University of Cologne, 1984, p.88.

52 Göhre, *Das Warenhaus*, p.15.

53 Ibid. p.27.

54 Leo Colze, *Berliner Warenhäuser* (1908), Berlin: Fannei Walz 1989, p.21.

55 M. Napsilber, 'Das Kaufhaus des Westens', *Der Roland von Berlin*, vol.5, 28 Mar. 1907, p.446. Quoted in Frei, *Tempel der Kauflust*, p.114.

56 Friedrich Naumann, 'Das Neue Geschäftshaus', (1905) in *Werke*, vol.6, *Ästhetische Schriften*, ed. H. Ladendorf, Cologne-Opladen: Westdeutscher Verlag 1964, p.74.

57 Karl Ernst Osthaus, 'Das Schaufenster', *Jahrbuch des Deutschen Werkbundes*, vol.2, 1913, pp.60, 62.

58 Ibid. p.59.

59 Frederic J. Schwartz, *The Werkbund: Design Theory and Mass Culture before the First World War*, New Haven and London: Yale University Press 1996, pp.47, 51.

60 By the end of the first decade of the twentieth century, department stores were acknowledged to contribute to the aesthetic refinement of all classes, taking on an educational function not unlike those of museums: 'When today palace upon palace lines up along the major traffic arteries of the state capital, when display windows, suffused with light, containing the most outstanding products of all the industries of civilised people not only entice one to buy, but also speak plainly to our aesthetic sense, when today even the little man is in a position, for a price, to acquire luxury articles, this is solely thanks to the modern departmental store system.' Colze,

Berliner Warenhäuser, p.11.

61 Osthaus, 'Das Schaufenster', p.61.

62 Ibid. p.61.

63 Ibid. pp.64–65.

64 Ibid. p.61.

65 For an account of this debate, see Joan Campbell, *The German Werkbund: The Politics of Reform in the Applied Arts*, Princeton, New Jersey: Princeton University Press, 1978, pp.57–68.

66 Osthaus, 'Das Schaufenster', pp.67–68.

67 Ibid. p.63.

68 Ibid. p.67.

69 Schwartz, *The Werkbund*, p.101.

70 Christoph Asendorf, *Batteries of Life: On the History of Things and Their Perception in Modernity*, trans. Don Reneau, Berkeley, Los Angeles and London: University of California Press 1993, p.101.

71 August Endell, 'Die Schönheit der Großen Stadt' (1908) in *Vom Sehen*, p. 182.

72 Simmel, 'Berlin Trade Fair', p.257.

73 Paul H. Nystrom, *Economics of Retailing* (1930), repr. New York 1978, vol.1, p.28, n.3.

74 Karl Marx, *Economic and Philosophic Manuscripts of 1844*, New York 1968, p.140.

75 Paul Westheim, 'Schaufenster und Schaufensterdekorateure', *Kunstgewerbeblatt*, vol.22, no.7, 1911, p.132. Quoted in Schwartz, *The Werkbund*, p.105.

76 Frei, *Tempel der Kauflust*, p.132.

77 Quoted in James, 'From Messel to Mendelsohn', p.268.

78 'We ought not to conceal the fact that the artist has nothing more to look for in advertising than in medicine, in criminal science, in locomotive construction or in

street cleaning.' Adolf Behne, 'Kultur, Kunst und Reklame', *Das Neue Frankfurt*,
no.3, 1926–27, repr. in Heinz Hirdina (ed.), *Neues Bauen, Neues Gestalten: Das Neue
Frankfurt/die neue stadt: Eine Zeitschrift zwischen 1926 und 1933*, Dresden: Verlag
der Kunst 1984, p.231.

[79] Wilhelm Lotz, 'Werkbundausstellung "Wohnbedarf" Stuttgart 1932', *Die Form*, vol.7,
no.7, 15 Jul. 1932, p.223.

[80] Ibid. p.224.

[81] Mary Nolan, *Visions of Modernity: American Business and the Modernization of
Germany*, New York and Oxford: Oxford University Press 1994, p.224.

[82] Fernand Léger, 'Color in the World and the New Pictorial and Decorative Realism of
the Object', unpub. transcript of lecture given at Museum of Modern Art, New York,
n.d. (early 1940s); Alfred H. Barr, Jr., Papers, Archives of American Art, Roll 3264,
Frame 138.

[83] Frederick Kiesler, *Contemporary Art Applied to the Store and its Display*, New York:
Brentano's 1930, p.79.

[84] Wolfgang Fritz Haug, *Kritik der Warenästhetik*, Frankfurt: Suhrkamp 1971, p.65. Cf.
Twitchell, *Lead us into Temptation* – one of the most eloquent defenders against the
cultural pessimism that inevitably describes individuals as brain-dead manipulated
robots. He has convincingly described consumption as active, creative and cultural.

[85] Guy Debord, *The Society of the Spectacle* (1967), Exeter: Rebel Press 1987,
sect.1, para.6.

[86] Naomi Klein, *No Logo*, London: Flamingo 2000, p.75.

[87] Abbie Hoffman's *Steal This Book*, New York: Pirate Editions 1971.

[88] Ibid. pp. 77–78.

Duty-Free Shopping

Mark C. Taylor

The camera zooms in on a serious President Bush as he appears to be addressing the nation on the latest developments in the war against terrorism. Then he speaks:

'America is asking what is expected of us.'
[Images of people going about everyday activities flash across the screen.]

'Go about your business.'
[Images of business people rushing through office buildings.]

' Fly!'
[Images of airports, pilots, passengers, planes.]

'Enjoy life!'
[Images of stores and people shopping.]

'American has overcome challenges before and we will again.'
(American Travel Association, 2002)

For the United States the difference between the first and second halves of the twentieth century can be understood in terms of the changing relation between shopping and war. During World Wars I and II, posters depicting a stern Uncle Sam challenged citizens to support the war effort by using their savings to purchase war bonds. Some fought in distant lands and others worked at home in factories producing materials needed to defeat the enemy. While World War II was good for the economy and helped pull the country out of depression, the diversion

of resources and conversion of factories to serve the ends of war resulted in a scarcity of consumer products. By the end of the war, pent up demand created the conditions for an economic revival in the late 1940s and early 1950s. During subsequent decades, this consumer revolution led to an economy fueled more by consumption than production. When the twentieth century abruptly ended on 11 September 2001, the significance of this transformation became fully apparent. The initial trauma of the collapse of the Twin Towers was unprecedented in the history of the United States, but the impact of the attack on the global economy was no less surprising for most analysts. Faced by a different kind of conflict at home and abroad, President Bush called for national support for a new war by issuing a new economic challenge: 'Go shopping!' At first, this appeal seems ludicrous, for it appears to mock the necessity of individual sacrifice for the good of the whole country. *Ask not what your country can do for you but what you can buy for your country*. The more, the better. During this time of trial, to forego spending, it seems, is to concede defeat to those who would drag us back to the Middle Ages. In post-industrial society shopping is not only an economic necessity, but is actually a patriotic duty. Yet are matters so simple? When shopping becomes a duty, is it any longer really shopping? Or must shopping always be duty-free? And is shopping an adequate response in this moment of complexity?

In 1843 – nine years before Bon Marché opened its doors – Søren Kierkegaard published his first major work, *Either-Or*. In the preface, the pseudonymous editor, Victor Eremita, explains that the two volumes were written by different authors: A, whose identity remains obscure and seems to be multiple, and B, Judge William. A and B represent what Kierkegaard elsewhere describes as two stages on life's way or, perhaps more accurately, styles of life – the aesthetic and the ethical.

Andy Warhol **Dollar Signs** 1981

Ethical life, Judge William explains, is devoted to duty, i.e. the fulfilment of one's moral obligations as defined by the codes and mores of society. For the ethical person, life is a serious and often weighty affair. Long-term obligations must always control short-term desires, and, therefore, the future consistently governs the present. The aesthete, by contrast, lives for the moment. Inasmuch as duty inhibits the satisfaction of fleeting desires, the aesthete regards it as both repressive and an impediment to self-fulfilment. Though seeming to be driven by natural impulses, aesthetic life is actually impossible without coy cultivation.

A's understanding of aesthetic life begins to emerge in his intriguing essay entitled 'The Rotation Method'. One of the greatest threats to pleasure, he warns, is boredom. 'Boredom', according to A, 'depends on the nothingness that pervades reality; it causes a dizziness like that produced by looking down into a yawning chasm, and this dizziness is infinite.' When overwhelmed by this sense of nothingness, the person suffering from boredom 'cries out for change'.[1] A's response to this desperate need for change is 'the rotation method', which can take one of two forms. In the 'inartistic' version, one follows the strategy of the farmer who repeatedly changes the field where he plants his crops. 'One tires of porcelain dishes and eats on silver; one tires of silver and turns to gold ... This method defeats itself; it is plain endless.' In contrast to this 'extensive' method, the 'artistic' approach A prefers is 'intensive': 'My method does not consist in change of field, but resembles the true rotation method in changing the crop and the mode of cultivation. Here we have at once the principle of limitation, the only saving principle in the world. The more you limit yourself, the more fertile you become in invention.'[2] To accomplish the self-limitation necessary for aesthetic pleasure, it is necessary to forget the past and let go of the future by

giving up hope. The aesthete lives in and for the moment. 'Enjoying an experience to its full intensity to the last minute will make it impossible either to remember or forget.'[3]

Conversely, remembering and forgetting make it impossible to enjoy an experience to its full intensity. Always in conversation with Judge William whose sense of duty, as we have seen, leads to a preoccupation with the future at the expense of the present, A counsels the aesthete to forget not only the past, but, more importantly, the future. He concludes, 'it is impossible to live artistically before one has made up one's mind to abandon all hope'.[4] To abandon hope, however, is to lose all sense of purpose. For Judge William, life without purpose is unbearable, but for A, the only life worth living is purposeless. The aesthete, therefore, faces the paradoxical task of purposively pursuing purposelessness.

The reason Kierkegaard describes A's life as aesthetic now becomes clear. Though commentators have long recognised that Judge William is a paradigm of Kantian ethics, the way A's life embodies Kantian aesthetics has gone unnoticed. A's purposive purposelessness is the existential enactment of Kant's notion of beauty. In the *Third Critique*, Kant defines beauty as 'intrinsic finality' or 'purposiveness without purpose' ('Zweckmässigkeit ohne Zweck'). In contrast to extrinsic teleology in which means and ends are externally related in a utilitarian manner, in inner teleology, means and ends are reciprocally related in such a way that each is a condition of the other and both taken together constitute their own end or purpose. The beautiful work of art formed by the reciprocal relation of its parts has no utilitarian value but is its own end or purpose. When this aesthetic is translated into a form of life, purposiveness without purpose becomes activity for its own sake. By engaging in an activity for no purpose other than the activity itself, one becomes totally immersed in the fleeting present without regard for past or future. For A, such purposeless activity is the antidote to boredom.

While the birth of the department store in Europe and the United States was still a decade away and the transition from industrial to consumer capitalism was taking over a century to complete, Kierkegaard's analysis of aesthetic existence anticipated one of the most important contemporary forms of life. When shopping is duty-free, it is an effective expression of A's rotation method. There are, of course, two basic kinds of shopping: shopping to fulfil needs, and shopping for shopping's sake. In the first instance, shopping is purposeful – people shop to live; in the second instance shopping is purposeless – people live to shop. If shopping is to hold boredom at bay, it must enact what Nietzsche eventually labels 'the eternal return'. 'The essential thing', for A, 'is never to stick fast ... Everything doubtless will return, though in a different form; that which has once been present in the rotation will remain in it but the mode of cultivation will be varied.'[5] A continuous flow of new products keeps the shopper in play.

But is there not a hidden purpose to ostensibly purposeless activity? In a consumer economy, isn't shopping for shopping's sake useful? Doesn't shopping serve the interests of capital by keeping the wheels of production turning? To answer these questions, it is necessary to trace the unexpected extension of Kantian and Kierkegaardian aesthetics into the realm of economics.

During the winter of 1857–58, Marx developed a series of reflections in seven notebooks, which were unknown until they were published in 1953 under the title *Grundrisse*. Anticipating insights he would later elabo-

rate with more rigor in *Capital*, Marx's thought-in-process presents some of his most seminal ideas. The most important part of his analysis for our purposes is his emerging understanding of money and capital. As always, Marx appropriates and subtly displaces Hegelian ideas to develop his argument. In effect, Marx interprets money and, by extension, capital in terms of Hegel's understanding of the absolute. By using Hegel in this way, Marx indirectly returns to Kant. Hegel's entire system is an elaboration of Kant's account of the beautiful work of art in terms of inner teleology. In Hegelian speculation, intrinsic purpose becomes the structure of self-referentiality, which grounds all thought and being. For Marx, the absolute, which makes the world go round, is money, whose developed form is capital. 'The continual movement in circuits of the two antithetical metamorphoses of commodities, or the never ceasing alteration of sale and purchase is reflected in the restless currency of money, or in the function that money performs as a *perpetuum mobile* of circulation.'[6] Marx's foundational distinction between use value and exchange value is strictly parallel to Kant's distinction between extrinsic and intrinsic teleology. 'Only with *capital*', Marx argues, 'is exchange value posited as exchange value in such a way that it preserves itself in circulation.'

> The first quality of capital is, then, this: that exchange value deriving from circulation and presupposing circulation preserves itself within it and by means of it; does not lose itself by entering into it; that circulation is not the movement of its disappearance, but rather the movement of its real self-positing as exchange value, its self-realization as exchange value.[7]

Like the beautiful work of art, capital has no end other than itself: the purpose of capital, in other words, is capital. Simultaneously the presup-

Andy Warhol **Bonwit Teller Window Screen** 1957 (reconstruction 1997)

position and result of circulation, 'capital is a constantly self-renewing circular course of exchanges'.[8] In ways that are not immediately obvious, art and capital meet in shopping. When shopping is duty-free it is an art. Shopping is exchange for the sake of exchange, which eternally returns to preserve itself. If people only shop for what they need, the economy eventually grinds to a halt. The post-industrial economy is sustained by consumer spending, which must be excessive.

It took almost a century for these speculative ideas to weave themselves into the fabric of everyday life. With characteristic insight and prescience, Warhol declared, 'All department stores will become museums and all museums will become department stores.'[9] Throughout the history of modernism, art and commerce are not only closely related but are actually extensions of each other. By the beginning of the twenty-first century, Warhol's prediction has come true: department stores *are* museums and museums *are* department stores. Stores and museums are not so much selling commodities as styles of life, as well as commodified art.

The trajectory from speculative philosophy to the speculative economy of consumer and finance capitalism is unexpectedly reflected in the glass of display windows. Glass, of course, plays an important role in art and architecture throughout the twentieth century. For many, the clarity and transparency of glass express the values and virtues of modern art and life. The significance of glass, however, is not merely symbolic; its value is also economic. Indeed, Bill Lancaster goes so far as to insist that the Crystal Palace (1851), with which modern glass architecture arguably began, 'started a consumer revolution'.[10] This surprising claim becomes plausible when the impact of glass architecture on shopping is considered.

By the middle of the eighteenth century, large plate glass was being used in construction. As Ann Friedberg points out, 'it did not take shopkeepers long to realize the window might be a prime proscenium for commodity display'.[11] Shop windows had far-reaching effects on economic activity as well as social interaction. In open markets and windowless stores, the process of exchange had been face-to-face. Moreover, prices were not fixed but were subject to negotiation. In this situation, the economic relation was inescapably personal. Since in many cases, the shop where commodities were sold was also where they were produced, the site of consumption and the site of production was the same.

All of this changes with the introduction of windows. There are, of course, two basic kinds of store windows. On the one hand, windows open closed walls to expose interior to exterior and vice versa; on the other hand, windows that display goods are self-contained and closed off from the interior of the shop, thereby preserving it from exposure. Needless to say, these two kinds of windows can be combined to create scenes that leave backstage commercial machinations open to inspection.

Display windows transform the exchange relation in several important ways. When goods are displayed in windows, it is possible to shop without entering into a personal relationship with the merchant. As windows proliferate, shoppers gradually become anonymous faces in the crowd. When the activity of shopping is reduced to gazing through store windows, vision becomes the dominant sense. The glaze of glass eliminates smell, sound and tactility to create the *aestheticisation of the commodity*. Thing disappears into image, which is crafted to solicit the desire of the consumer. Glass is actually a technology of desire. By staging a constant interplay of proximity and distance, glass keeps desire in play by refusing to deliver what the consumer wants. 'Look but don't touch' is the motto describing the foreplay of the designing merchant.

By the early decades of the nineteenth century, glass had extended from store windows to building architecture. The transformation of separate shops, enclosed by the iron-and-glass architecture of the arcades, into department stores created what Walter Benjamin, following Louis Philippe, labeled 'temples of commodity capital'.[12] The opening of Bon Marché, designed by L.C. Boileu and Gustav Eiffel in 1852, marked a new chapter in the economic history of the West. Other markets and department stores quickly followed: Les Grandes Halles (1853–58), Printemps (1865) and Galleries Lafayette (1895). In the United States, Macy's opened in 1857. Department stores extended and accelerated developments set in motion by the invention of plate glass and display windows. One of the most important innovations introduced was the creation of a fixed-price system. Benjamin already recognised the significance of this price revolution. Commenting on Bon Marché's explosive growth, he quotes Georges d'Avenel's 'Le Mécanisme de la vie moderne: Les Grands Magasins'.

> The originality consisted in selling guaranteed merchandise at discount prices. Items, first of all, were marked with fixed prices, another bold innovation which did away with bargaining and with 'process sales' – that is to say, with gauging the price of an article by the physiognomy of the buyer; then the 'return' was instituted, allowing the customer to cancel his purchase at will; and finally, employees were paid almost entirely by commission on sales. These were the constitutive elements of the new organization.[13]

This new organisation was nothing other than the system of mass consumption necessitated by modern mass production. As new modes of production and consumption required new promotion and marketing strategies, the display window became the focus of experimental designs. Though windows filled with commodities began to appear in the United States as early as the 1840s, it was not until after the turn of the century that window display became an art. From 1897–1902, L. Frank Baum, who published *The Wizard of Oz* in 1900, edited a highly influential monthly journal entitled *The Show Window*, whose primary purpose was to advance the 'arts of decoration and display'. Using the latest mechanical devices and electrical technology, Baum sought to create spectacular displays, which, in his terms, would 'arouse in the observer the cupidity and longing to possess the goods'.[14] As window dressers developed their art, they often entered into collaborative relations with museums and employed artists to create enticing displays.

There is, of course, a long history of cooperation among modern art, industry and commerce. During both its European and American phases, the Bauhaus was dedicated to fostering collaboration between art and industry. Russian Constructivism as well as the Werkbund and De Stijl sought to bridge the worlds of art and business. In the United States, John Dewey promoted an 'arts-in-industry' movement, which contributed to the establishment of Pratt Institute and the New York School of Fine and Applied Arts, later the Parsons School, where commercial art was taught after 1900.[15] Such alliances were not limited to applied and commercial arts. Many of the great modern museums were, after all, created by successful capitalists. The Brooklyn Museum, Newark Museum, Metropolitan Museum of Art, Museum of Modern Art and Guggenheim were all established and endowed by wealthy business people. Without denying their interest in art, it is undeniable

Simon Doonan **Shop Window for Barneys 575 Fifth Avenue** New York, April 2002

that in many cases, supporting museums was good business. In the early decades of the last century, the directors of the Brooklyn and Newark Museums sponsored extensive expositions of industrial goods. But it was the prestigious Metropolitan Museum of Modern Art that exercised the greatest influence in industrial design. In 1914, the Met hired Richard Bach to fill the newly created position of associate in industrial arts. 'Bach recognized', William Leach points out, 'perhaps better than the others did how strategic "design" was to the success of mass production. The surfaces and shapes of many kinds of objects, not their underlying structure or function, so Bach understood, offered the greatest potential for business profits. Indeed, "design alone" might yield "the entire profit".'[16] Under Bach's leadership, the Met established a design service and created workshops and laboratories for the development of commercial products. In 1927, the Met co-sponsored the first Macy's Exposition devoted to a consideration of the impact of modern art on industrial design.

The collaboration between art and commerce extended from institutional arrangements to individual artists and commissions. Leach goes so far as to argue that 'it was in the department stores, not in the museums, that modern art and American art found their first true patrons'. Infatuated by the 1913 Armory Show, the Gimbel brothers displayed modern masters like Cézanne, Picasso and Braque in store galleries.[17] In addition to exhibiting art created in the studio, stores also employed artists to develop new work for their windows. While in most cases window designers remained anonymous, it was not uncommon for established artists to do store windows. In her insightful and beautifully illustrated study *Windows: The Art of Retail Design*, Mary Portas maintains that 'it was Salvador Dalí who really made shop windows respectable'.[18] As window designs became more sophisticated, the

line separating high and low, fine art and commercial art, artist and artisan, and art and business became more obscure.

The two most important twentieth-century window designers in the United States were Gene Moore, who is best known for his work at Tiffany's, and Simon Doonan, who transformed Barneys in the 1980s and 1990s. From his early years at Delman's in the late 1930s, Moore actively supported artists. Reflecting on his long career in his autobiography, Moore notes that he commissioned more than 800 works from artists.

> From my first windows at Delman's through sixteen years at Bonwit Teller and now thirty-five at Tiffany's I've always given artists credit. I was the first display director to do so regularly, and the knowledge that their name would appear on a credit card – a slip of paper – in the window next to their art has drawn artists to me. I'm constantly commissioning artists to make me specific objects for use in the windows I've planned, but also ask artists to bring me their 'serious' art. At Bonwit's, particularly during the late 1950s, I turned the windows into a modern art gallery, with works by as many as ten artists displayed in the windows alongside mannequins dressed in merchandise.[19]

The careers of some of the most important artists of the last half of the twentieth century were launched in Moore's windows. The first exhibitions of the paintings of Warhol and Johns were in Moore's windows at Bonwit Teller, where he also exhibited the work of Rauschenberg and Rosenquist. Tiffany's, however, is where Moore really made a name for himself. Well into the 1950s, Tiffany's had remained a paragon of 'good taste' and conservative design. When Walter Hoving took control

Simon Doonan **Shop Window for Barneys 575 Fifth Avenue** New York, March 2002

of Tiffany's in 1955, the approach to advertising and marketing changed dramatically. His son, Thomas Hoving, as Director of the Met, would transform the museum world in the 1970s with commercial marketing practices developed at Tiffany's. One of Walter Hoving's first moves was to hire Gene Moore to develop window designs that would transform Tiffany's and in the process change retail practices throughout the commercial world.

Faced with a daunting challenge, Moore turned to artists with whom he had worked in the past. Warhol, Johns, Rauschenberg and Rosenquist followed Moore to Tiffany's. With their help and contributions from many lesser-known designers and artists, Moore made store windows integral to the Tiffany's brand. Though Warhol made no distinction between his commercial and fine art, Johns and Rauschenberg always did window displays under the shared pseudonym of Matson Jones. Moore's collaboration with artists fulfiled Warhol's prediction about the future of department stores and museums. While Warhol transformed the store window into a museum, Thomas Hoving converted the museum into a store window. After taking over the Met, Hoving invited his father's famous window designer to create a permanent display for the Museum's Greek and Roman gold and silver collections.

The only window designer who comes close to Moore's commercial importance and artistic influence is Simon Doonan. Doonan, who left the Metropolitan Museum of Art's Costume Institute to join Barneys in 1986, prefaces his autobiography, *Confessions of a Window Dresser*, with an epigram from Oscar Wilde's *The Picture of Dorian Gray*: 'We can forgive a man for making a useful thing as long as he does not admire it. The only excuse for making a useless thing is that one admires it intensely. All art is quite useless.'[20] Protests to the contrary notwith-

standing, Doonan finds the uselessness of art quite useful. Riding the wave of the 1980s art boom, Doonan created unrivalled display windows, which, in many cases, were more creative and provocative than the art in downtown galleries and uptown museums. In addition to his experience at the Met, Doonan brought with him a history of West-Coast design, which drew on the dark side of LA life, as well as a fascination with the excesses of punk.

Barneys was founded by Barney Pressman in the 1930s as a men and boy's discount clothing store in New York's Hell's Kitchen. With each succeeding generation of Pressmans, Barneys became more upmarket. Barney's son, Fred, introduced American men to designer clothing: Givenchy, Chardin, and, most importantly , Giorgio Armani. Joshua Levine, who chronicles the store's history in *The Rise and Fall of the House of Barneys*, claims that Fred Pressman 'discovered Giorgio Armani'. Though the relationship eventually dissolved in contentious litigation, Barneys and Armani never would have become what they did without each other. Levine concludes: 'Barneys was the store that Giorgio built. He owed Barneys a lot, but Barneys owed him even more.'[21]

When in turn Gene Pressman took over from his father, his ambition was nothing less than to transform Barneys into a new Bauhaus. Doonan recalls the challenge:

Gene's Bauhaus vision was not an end in itself. The upscale pedestrian traffic that pulsed across New York's 57th Street and down Fifth Avenue was his ultimate goal. He envisioned hordes of eager beavers packing the sidewalk on Seventh Avenue, just as they did uptown at the stores with which he was now competing: Bergdorf Goodman (disparagingly referred to by everyone at Barneys as Berger King),

The Art of the Motorcycle Exhibition at the Guggenheim Museum, Las Vegas, 2001

Henri Bendel, and Saks. He charged me with making the windows so beyond the valley of gorgeousity that they would make the 17th street downtown store a major destination for the rich uptown fashion addicts, and the entire world.[22]

During the era of postmodern appropriation, Barneys windows became indistinguishable from the art displayed in nearby galleries. Eagerly promoting business as art and art as business, Doonan admits:

I became an enthusiastic proponent of this entente cordiale between art and commerce and regularly invited artists either to create their own installations or to loan individual pieces for window-display purposes. Sandy Skogland, Josh Gosfield, Annette Lemieux, Duane Michaels, Candyass, David Seidner, Konstantin Kakanias, and Michael Byron all designed entire installations from scratch. Countless others loaned art or participated in group installations, into which clothing was thrown.[23]

Even more important than the cooperation between business and art was the buzz generated by Doonan's ability to make Barneys part of the downtown art scene and the celebrity culture surrounding it. His calculated strategy was enormously successful:

It was not just the physical plant that made Barneys groovy. The downtown location of the original store gave Barneys an art world alliance not shared by any of the snotty uptown competition; Ross Bleckner and Jean-Michel Basquiat were not shopping at Lord & Taylor. Given the proximity to arty SoHo, it was inevitable that downtown Barneys would become the eighties art boom headquarters for artists who were starting to make money and wanted to look spiffy.·[24]

One of the most remarkable things about the Barneys phenomenon is that it occurred in the wake of what appeared to be an economic catastrophe. Doonan started working at Barneys one year before the 1987 stock market crash. Many analysts thought the collapse foreshadowed a long economic downturn, but the market quickly rebounded and continued as if nothing had happened. Throughout the 1980s, the rise of the art market paralleled the rise of the stock market. After October 1987, art seemed to many investors a safer bet than stocks. Paintings, which sold for record prices, were locked away in personal and corporate vaults at home and abroad.

As the art market boomed, artists were caught up in a culture of celebrity greater than anything Warhol could have anticipated. Artists became media stars whose personae created the market value of their work. The aura spread from person to artwork; bad art by big names brought excessive prices. As the stakes of the game escalated, even collectors became celebrities courted by the media and featured in glossy magazines. With the market expanding faster than the capacity for production, artists scrambled to meet consumer demand. When originals could not be produced fast enough, many artists followed the lead of architects like Frank Gehry and Michael Graves and began to create a variety of products that could be marketed in high-end stores and retail outlets.

There was, however, a darker side to the frenzy in the 1980s art world. Throughout the decade, the AIDS epidemic ravaged the art community. Red ribbons and AIDS benefits seemed to mark a pause in Gordon Gekko's culture where greed was good. As always, however, ostensibly good actions had ulterior motives. AIDS benefits were remarkably effective advertising and marketing strategies. Once again, Barneys led the way. In 1986, Doonan staged an extravaganza:

The Art of the Motorcycle Exhibition at the Solomon R. Guggenheim Museum, New York, 1998

The Levi Jean Jacket Auction, benefiting Saint Vincent's AIDS care program. Iman, Fran Lebowitz, Deborah Harry, Cornelia Guest, and 80 more celebrities and models teetered down the Andrée Putman – designed staircase in a silent runway auction of jean jackets customized by the major artists and designers of the moment – including Basquiat, Armani, Cutrone, YSL, Warhol, Alaïa, Rauschenberg, Valentino, and Haring. The highlight for me was Madonna modeling the jacked created by her AIDS-afflicted artist friend Martin Burgoyne and, on a lighter note, an exuberant John Galliano being thrown out by security guards after he yanked off B-52 Kate Pierson's giant red bubble wig while she was modeling Karl Lagerfeld's jacket. J'adore![25]

Such outlandish decadence only seemed to increase the aura of Barneys and the enterprise continued to grow. Expansion, like the fashionable art fuelling it, had become an end in itself. In 1993, Barney Pressman's discount clothing store, which had started in Hell's Kitchen, moved uptown to Madison Avenue and 57th Street, the most expensive real estate in the world. A year later, Barneys, which by now had also become a leader in women's fashion, invaded the West coast by opening a luxurious store in Beverly Hills. Expressing supreme confidence in this moment of triumph, Doonan summed up the Barneys revolution with words as excessive as his window designs.

The unapologetically hip luxe of the Barneys image has redefined high-end retailing without precedent … The cognoscenti grooviness of the original Barneys store has become an axiom for hip consumerism; if a character in a movie needs to look upscale and trendy, they dress him from Barneys, and then shove a Barneys bag into his hand.[26]

Less than two years later, the house of Barneys collapsed. On 11 January 1996, Barneys filed for bankruptcy. Like companies financed by junk bonds, Barneys proved to be a speculative house of cards without a secure foundation.

Doonan concludes his revealing memoir with a homage to the person he dubs 'the patron saint of window dressing' – Andy Warhol. Whether or not he deliberated followed Warhol's script, Doonan surely subscribed to his gospel: 'Being good at business is the most fascinating kind of art.'[27] Throughout the late 1980s and early 1990s, Barneys and artists formed an alliance that was mutually profitable. In 1997, ten years after Warhol's death, the Andy Warhol Museum organised an exhibition, *The Warhol Look*, which travelled to Madison Avenue (i.e. the Whitney Museum). An entire section of the show was devoted to Warhol's work as a window dresser. With the pride of a devoted disciple, Doonan ends his confession with an image from the Warhol exhibition accompanied by the following caption:

The Warhol Look show also featured a reconstructed Barneys window by myself in 1989, showing Andy as the compulsive collector surrounded by Russell-Wright china, Hunan-wok menus, physique mags, and cookie jars. Honesty forces me to admit that I did get a massive frisson from being included in a major museum show with the likes of Gene Moore. Andy Warhol's prediction about the museums becoming department stores and vice versa seemed as if it had finally become a vague possibility. My window was opposite a window done by Rosenquist in the 1950s, Barneys 17th Street, 1989.[28]

In 1989 – the year of the collapse of the Berlin Wall – Thomas Krens was named Director of the Guggenheim Museum. In the early years of

Giorgio Armani Exhibition at the Solomon R. Guggenheim Museum, New York, 2000

Giorgio Armani Exhibition at the Solomon R. Guggenheim Museum, New York, 2000

his tenure, Krens' signature image found him posed in front of a Warhol self-portrait. It did not take long for an art world baffled, if not outraged, by the appointment of an outsider from a sleepy New England college to one of the most prestigious and powerful museum positions to suspect that Krens's carefully conceived game plan was little more than a footnote to Warhol's dictum 'Business art is the step that comes after Art'.[29] What Barneys was to business and art in the late 1980s and early 1990s, the Guggenheim was to art and business throughout the decade of the 1990s.

Krens undeniably combines passionate vision, intellectual insight and business savvy in a way no one ever has in either the museum or corporate world. When he assumed control at the Guggenheim, the institution was facing a financial crisis that made it necessary to float a large bond issue and to deaccession several paintings from the collection. For an art world already suspicious of Krens's business background and seemingly slim museum experience, these moves amounted to heresy. In the furor provoked by the museum's financial manoeuvering, commentators and critics missed the larger significance of one of Krens' early exhibitions – *The Great Utopia: The Russian and Soviet Avant-Garde, 1915–1932* – for his vision of the relationship of art, politics and economics. While planning began before the collapse of the Soviet Union while Krens was still at Williams College, the show did not open until 1992. In retrospect, it is clear that both Krens' strategy in bringing the exhibition to fruition and the content of the show anticipated the course the Guggenheim would follow in the 1990s. Krens was one of the first to realize the far-reaching economic and political importance of knowledge and culture in an information society. In the contemporary world, art has more to do with politics and economics than with aesthetics. The only reason *The Great Utopia* survived the demise

of the Soviet Union was that from the outset, Krens conducted negotiations with the Ministry of Foreign Affairs rather than with the Ministry of Culture. After the Cold War, culture became more politicised than ever. Having learned his lessons in art and business well, Krens put on display the lessons the Soviet avant-garde had to teach about the politics of art. Not limited to painting and sculpture, this exhibition also included important sections devoted to architecture, graphic design (i.e. advertising), textile design and porcelain. From Moscow to Fifth Avenue the economic system changes, but the mission remains the same: collapse the distinction between high and low in order to bring art to the masses and, in the process, make a profit.

A full consideration of the role of the Guggenheim in art and society during the 1990s must wait for another occasion. In this context, it is necessary to limit the discussion to the way in which Krens's strategy brings to closure the relation between shopping and art that we have been tracing. As he pondered the Guggenheim's financial crisis in the late 1980s, Krens quickly realised that neither private donations nor public support could any longer provide the resources museums needed. The only solution, he concluded, was to forge mutually profitable alliances with corporations and business interests. The unlikely laboratory for Krens's experiment was an abandoned factory in a down-and-out New England mill town. In the late 1980s, Krens advanced a proposal that seemed preposterous at the time: convert the decaying Sprague Electric complex in North Adams, Massachusetts, into the largest museum of contemporary art in the world. What eventually made this unlikely undertaking successful was Krens's canny decision to pitch it as a plan for economic redevelopment rather than a cultural project. With persistence and flair rivalling P.T. Barnum, Krens persuaded the state to buy into the plan. A decade-and-a-half and four

Claudio Silvestrin **Emporio Armani** Milan, 2001

governors later, Mass MOCA is a successful museum delivering much of what Krens had promised.

The strategy devised in planning Mass MOCA laid the foundation for Krens' most successful project to date – Guggenheim Bilbao. By the middle of the 1990s, the United States was in the midst of what would become the longest economic boom in its history. The explosive growth of the dot-coms drove speculative markets to unprecedented heights. Krens was the right man in the right place at the right time. Having absorbed the marketing lessons of the 1980s and with a sophisticated understanding of finance capitalism, he extended his Mass MOCA model to create a blueprint for bringing together art, travel and entertainment to create profitable economic networks. Bilbao, like Mass MOCA, was conceived and promoted as an economic development project. What made Bilbao a success, however, was not merely financial planning by investment bankers but, more importantly architecture. Krens recognised the economic potential of celebrity architecture, which was one of the products of 1980s postmodernism. In Frank Gehry, Krens found the architect who secured the Guggenheim brand. Success tends to breed success; as the impact of the Guggenheim Bilbao on the international travel industry and local economy became clear, other museums and cities rushed to appropriate the strategy. All the while, Krens's vision was growing more global. As he developed partnerships and alliances with cultural institutions and corporations around the world, critics accused Krens of franchising the museum; but the museum continued to prosper.

While corporate sponsorship of the arts is not, of course, new, Krens took it to unprecedented heights. Beyond the widely accepted practice of soliciting corporate contributions to support operations and exhibitions, he mounted highly successful shows consisting of products made by sponsoring companies: *The Art of the Motor Cycle* (sponsored in 1998 by BMW) and *George Armani* (sponsored in 2000 by Armani, which also made a substantial contribution to the museum prior to the show). Fred Pressman might have discovered Armani, but Krens put him on the cultural map in a way no designer ever had been before. Attempting to explain the rationale for the exhibition in the preface to the catalogue, Krens writes:

> While design and objects of material culture have traditionally been considered secondary to the 'high' arts, since the beginning of twentieth century artists and designers have blurred those distinctions in their melding of aesthetics and function, of art and everyday life. The Guggenheim has consistently investigated the central role that design has played in modern culture since 1991, when it expanded its vision to include architecture, design, and new media … Guggenheim exhibitions … [have] presented a range of artistic languages, including art, architecture, fashion, and design, demonstrating the fusion that often occurred between them.[30]

Krens simultaneously extended and reversed trends in the museum world. Throughout the 1990s, financially stressed museums steadily expanded their marketing and sales operations to increase income or create new revenue streams. Museum stores popped up everywhere and every exhibition ended in a salesroom filled with reproductions and products, which were indistinguishable from the paraphernalia Hollywood creates for major film releases. While refining these tactics, Krens also developed other strategies. In addition to commodifying works of art, the Guggenheim also aestheticised commodities. When Krens put BMW motorcycles and Armani suits on display, he reversed established retail practices. Moore, Doonan and their stable of artists turned the store window into a museum, but the Guggenheim transformed the museum into a store window. Critics began to wonder if anything was not for sale. Krens's comment on the Armani exhibition suggests that he saw the show as an extension of the avant-garde's effort to bring art to the masses. Though it remains unclear whether he regarded this gesture as ironic or even parodic, there can be no doubt about the importance of bridging high and low for Krens's agenda. Recent world events, however, have conspired to jeopardise this effort and to pose new challenges for the overall strategy. Three weeks after the collapse of the Twin Towers, the Guggenheim opened two new museums in Las Vegas – Guggenheim Hermitage and Guggenheim Las Vegas – both designed by Krens' chosen successor to Gehry, Rem Koolhaas. These new ventures are backed by the Venetian Resort and Casino. The two Vegas museums bring high art to what might well be described as the world capital of popular – if not low – culture. What began in Moscow as *The Great Utopia* ends in Las Vegas as faux Venice. Malevich, Rodchenko and Tatlin would not be amused. Whether Guggenheim Las Vegas and Hermitage Guggenheim can survive the economic disruption caused by 11 September remains to be seen.

It is already obvious that another Krens–Koolhaas project, designed around shopping, has been at least a partial casualty of new economic realities. On 18 December 2001, the fashion section of the *New York Times* carried an article by Guy Trebay and Ginia Bellafante entitled, 'Prada: Luxury Brand With World-Class Anxiety', which began:

> Teetering on high heels at the top of a stair overlooking Mercer Street last Friday evening, the willowy Estée Lauder model Carolyn Murphy surveyed a crowd of fashion's elite and whispered, 'This is so bizarre.'

The occasion was a long-anticipated party celebrating the opening of Prada's 24,000 square-foot store in SoHo. Ms. Murphy could have been referring to the unseasonal December weather. But she could easily have been editorializing about the crowd, a throng drawn from a rarefied sphere where the worlds of business, fashion, film, art and architecture intersect.

The article failed to note that the Broadway and Prince location of the new Prada store is the site of the SoHo Guggenheim. Reversing Barneys move from downtown to uptown, shortly after becoming Director, Krens moved uptown downtown by creating his first branch of the expanded Guggenheim in SoHo. The logic seemed compelling at the time: increase interest and thus attendance and sales by bridging the worlds of upper and lower Manhattan – and all they represent. But just as down-town Barneys had trouble uptown, so the uptown Guggenheim struggled downtown. Attendance languished and Krens was forced to develop an alternative strategy by forging an alliance with Prada.

As the success of Bilbao rested on Gehry's architecture, so, Krens wagered, the Guggenheim–Prada project would turn on Koolhaas's architecture. Koolhaas was commissioned to design a Prada store for the basement and half of the first floor of the SoHo Guggenheim. The other half of the first floor was supposed to be a state-of-the-art museum store, which would market an expanded product line through guggenheim.com. In this venture, Krens was betting a significant part of the museum's future on the continued growth of shopping for luxury goods. By the time the Prada store opened, however, the plan had unravelled. Declining museum attendance combined with an already bad economy forced the Guggenheim to abandon its SoHo outpost and

Museum Shop Guggenheim Museum Las Vegas, 2001

to suspend the operation of guggenheim.com. While some analysts attempted to see the new Prada store rising in the midst of the dust of disaster as a hopeful sign of economic recovery and cultural renewal, a more measured assessment leads to a more sober conclusion.

In the aftermath of 11 September, it is no longer clear that the business strategies and marketing practices of the 1990s are sufficient to revive a worsening economy already seriously wounded by the dot-com melt-down. Nor is it obvious that this is a short-term problem. Prada is almost as distressed as the Guggenheim. Having expanded to 150 stores, adding twenty-six in 1998 alone, Prada is struggling to service a $1.6 billion debt load at a time when sales are declining. The new flagship emporium cost a cool $40 million. Though financial analysts remain skeptical about the economic prudence of such expenditures, Miuccia Prada and her husband, Patrizio Bertelli, claim to remain confident in their venture. Trebay and Bellafante conclude, 'It would appear that the Prada strategy is to invigorate the act of shopping by creating museums of consumerism.' But it now seems evident that museums can no more save fashionable clothing stores than shopping can save museums. Rather than a new beginning, the SoHo Prada will more likely mark the end of an era.

The decade of the 1990s was a hyperreal period for the United States. Political victory over the only other superpower combined with an unprecedented economic boom to create a sense of confidence bordering on arrogance. With finance capitalism running wild, playing the market became an end in itself. As important as making a profit was being in play. People who had never ventured into the market became virtually addicted to the game. Celebrity financial analysts displaced celebrity designers on new TV, radio and Internet programmes. The result was a financial–entertainment complex in which the market fed the media and the media fuelled the market. When NASDAQ's Times Square display became the best digital show in town, it was clear that the art of finance had become an end in itself. And yet, all the while people knew the game was not quite real. When pressed, few denied that the bubble eventually would burst. Most gamblers, however, did not want to pick up their chips while the ante continued to grow. When the Twin Towers collapsed and all the symbolic weight they bore went up in smoke, new realities shattered comfortable illusions. It is not just that we are facing a new economic and political condition, but, much more importantly, the very rules of the game have changed. In the uncertain world into which we are moving, shopping will not solve our problems even if the President declares it a duty.

No one understands this better than Rem Koolhaas. Though it might prove to be a financial disaster, his SoHo Prada store is a stunning architectural success. Never before has store design been more spectacularly successful. Art, architecture, fashion and commerce are brought together through the most sophisticated information and telematic technologies to create a new kind of environment. But this moment of success might also be the moment of failure. Koolhaas could hardly have anticipated how quickly the world would confirm an observation recorded in his book, *Projects for Prada*, published on the occasion of the opening of the new store: 'In a world where everything is shopping... and shopping is everything... what is luxury? Total luxury is NOT shopping.'[31]

In the wake of disaster, we might become free from the duty to shop. And life just might not be so boring, after all.

Rem Koolhaas **Prada Soho** New York, 2001

1 Søren Kierkegaard, *Either-Or*, vol.1, trans. David Swenson and Lillian Marvin Swenson, Princeton, New Jersey: Princeton University Press 1959, p.287.

2 Ibid. pp.287–8.

3 Ibid. p.288.

4 Ibid.

5 Ibid. p.292.

6 Karl Marx, *Capital*, New York: International Publishers 1972, vol.1, p.130.

7 Karl Marx, *Grundrisse*, trans. Martin Nicholaus, New York: Penguin Books 1993, pp. 259–60.

8 Ibid. p.261.

9 Quoted in Mary Portas, *Windows: The Art of Retail Display*, New York: Thames and Hudson 1999, p. 14.

10 Bill Lancaster, *The Department Store: A Social History*, London and New York: Leicester University Press 1995, p.16.

11 Ann Friedberg, *Window Shopping: Cinema and the Postmodern*, Berkeley: University of California Press 1993, p.65.

12 Walter Benjamin, *The Arcades Project*, trans. Howard Eiland and Kevin McLaughlin, Cambridge, Mass.: Harvard University Press 1999, p.37.

13 Ibid. pp.59–60.

14 Quoted in William Leach, *Land of Desire: Merchants, Power, and the Rise of a New American Culture*, New York: Random House 1993, p.60.

15 Leach, *Land of Desire*, p.156. In developing this account, I have followed Leach's fine history of the period.

16 Ibid. p.171.

17 Ibid. p.136.

18 Portas, *Windows*, p.8.

19 Gene Moore, *My Time at Tiffany's*, New York: St. Martin's Press 1990, p.67.

20 Simon Doonan, *Confessions of a Window Dresser*, New York: Penguin Group 1998, p.8.

NASDAQ Building Times Square New York, 2002

21 Joshua Levine, *The Rise and Fall of the House of Barneys*, New York: William Morrow
   and Co., 1999, pp.74, 205.

22 Doonan, *Confessions*, pp.68-71.

23 Ibid. p.111.

24 Ibid. p.108.

25 Ibid. p.112.

26 Ibid. p.116.

27 Andy Warhol, *The Philosophy of Andy Warhol*, New York: Harcourt Brace 1975, p.92.

28 Doonan, *Confessions*, p.229.

29 Warhol, *The Philosophy*, p.92.

30 Thomas Krens, *Giorgio Armani*, New York: Solomon R. Guggenheim Museum 2000,
   p.viii.

31 Rem Koolhaas, *Projects for Prada, Part 1*, Milan: Fondazione Prada Edizioni 2001.

Barbara Kruger **Untitled (I shop therefore I am)** 1987

The Artist as Consumer

Boris Groys

It is a long time since consumption became the new leading ideology of our society. Belief in production, which was characteristic of early industrial capitalism, no longer exists. Since the demise of the Soviet style of socialism, it has become clear that a society that devotes itself to the forced development of production at the expense of personal consumption thereby ruins its economy. The historic conflict between the ideals of work asceticism and consumption has not been resolved through ethical reflection but through economic rationality: contrary to the opinion of many sociologists and economic theorists, decadent consumption has proved itself to be economically more effective when compared with the protestant work ethic. That is to say that production does not make headway if there is a lack of demand. Thus, today it is not production but consumption that is considered to be the citizen's primary duty. In times of crisis and war, modern politicians no longer demand that one should be thrifty and tighten one's belt still further, but, on the contrary, that one should buy more, so that the economy can keep running. Consequently, labouring under social pressure, modern society finds itself under an almost inescapable compulsion to consume.

All theories that attribute constant consuming to individual desire are, therefore, underestimating the moral nature of the shopping urge. To behave in a responsible manner towards society nowadays means for an individual to buy as much as possible – regardless of whether he wishes to do so or not. The individual who buys too little is regarded by society as a selfish human being, egotistical, misanthropic and not interested in the well-being of the economy, upon which he ultimately depends. This view is particularly noticeable in the spontaneous, nega-tive reaction aroused by someone who does not dress fashionably or has not got the latest PC – he immediately makes himself an outcast, hostile to the economy and thus anti-social. Fashion, which directs consumption behaviour, therefore serves as a visible sign both of social conformity and of being loyal to the economy. The negative opinion of resistance to consumption which predominates today is not so novel: Marcel Mauss has noted that all archaic cultures despised those who hoarded their treasures instead of bringing them into circulation.[1] And Georges Bataille has correctly ascertained, within the framework of his general economic theory, that senseless and aimless extravagance is indispensable for economic development.[2]

One cannot help asking what position art occupies in this current situa-tion, characterised by the granting of a social licence to consumption. At first glance art is put in a difficult position, for the artist is regarded primarily as a producer who serves the art market, in its turn part of the general commodity market. Seen in this perspective the position of the artist does not seem particularly advantageous in two respects. On the one hand the individual artist cannot compete under mass con-sumption conditions with fashion, advertising or commercial design. At the same time, however, because of the general denigration of pro-duction, the artist appears to lose his traditional esteem as a model, creative or even genial producer. Traditionally, artistic creativity was regarded as the embodiment of true, authentic human production. This ideal has not only been socially devalued by the revaluation of con-sumption, but its basic theory has also been questioned. It is said that the structuralistic post-structuralistic discourse has brought about the death of the author, by which is meant that the artist is incapable of bringing genuine, original things of significance and form into the world: every artist is primarily a user, a consumer of the medium in which he works, and can produce nothing other than that which his chosen medium, be it language or picture, allows him to produce. The artist has thereby been robbed of his cultural mission, and subjected to the logic of general social consumption.

Such an estimation – incidentally rather widespread – overlooks, however, the fact that the social role of the artist has undergone a far-reaching change during recent decades. From being a model producer, the artist has become a model consumer. Above all, within the framework of installation art as well as in new media, the artist works equally with both self-produced as well as externally-produced objects. The act of art production has itself become an act of shopping. The artist draws on pictures and objects from the mass culture in which he lives, and changes them for the creation of his own areas – just as every consumer does. Only the artist does it in an exhibition room, and thereby in an ostentatious and exemplary manner. Certainly, since Duchamp and then Pop Art the artist has regarded himself not as a producer but much rather as an exclusive consumer of anonymously produced and continually circulating things. No artist will today claim that he is the source of his work or that he produces original things of significance or form. Nowadays art no longer stands at the fount of artistic work but at its end. The signature of an artist no longer means that he has produced a specific object, but that he has made use of this object – and done so in a particularly interesting manner. If he is successful, the artist recaptures his claim to authorship by using serial, anonymous, impersonal production of pictures and things in a way that is recognised by society. It is not by chance that the modern artist no longer wishes to be creative, but critical. A critical attitude, however, is more characteristic of the consumer that the producer. The producer does not criticise; instead he offers his production to the critical judgement of the consumer, who enjoys the privilege of testing and assessing the offering to hand. But the desire of promoted modern art to be critical rather than creative shows clearly enough the complete reversal of the artist's role from producer to consumer.

It is particularly interesting to note that the theoretical criticism of the concept of creativity initially followed a completely different political pattern from the one of making a consumer out of the artist. The criticism of the gilding of art production initially had the aim of dethroning the artist and placing him on a par with other modern producers. The famous demand made of art by the historic avant-garde that it should reveal its technical processes and surrender the concept of genius, initially had as its sole aim the attainment of parity between the artist and the industrial worker. In the twentieth century art production was formalised, subjected to techniques and depersonalised to such an extent by the avant-garde (from Malevich and Mondrian via Albers and Sol LeWitt to Buren, to mention only the painters) that most traces of the physical presence of the artist in the work of art were intentionally expunged, and it came more and more to resemble a product produced by industrial means. At the same time ready-made techniques were being developed as well as different variations of media art, which have made the eradication of the artist's physical presence almost complete.

However, the cleansing of art from any reference to physically performed work in its creation has not, in the final analysis, had the effect of placing the artist on a par with the industrial worker. Quite the opposite: the artist has radically distanced himself from every kind of production and instead has placed himself much closer to administration, planning and leadership roles – and, ultimately, close to consumption.

The artist's insight has become 'disembodied' and all-consuming; it does not 'work', but only criticises, assesses, decides, selects and combines. It is an insight that can always be 'embodied' again, as often as anyone has the desire to reconstruct the processes that the artist has revealed. This change shows up particularly clearly in the altered position of the artist in the temporal economic theory of insight. The colossal investment in work, time and effort, which were necessary for the creation of a typical work of art, were irritatingly disproportionate to the conditions of art consumption, for after the artist had had to labour at his work for a long period, the beholder was able to consume the work effortlessly and at a single glance. This gave rise to the traditional superiority of the consumer, of the beholder, of the collector over the artist-painter as a supplier of pictures, which he had to produce in wearisome, physical toil. As photographer, video artist or ready-made collector, the present-day artist places himself on the same level as the art collector with regard to expenditure of time and effort.

In a corresponding manner the museums and other art collections nowadays do not function as places in which the unrepeatability of the historical – the work of the past – is represented, but as archives, in which various strategies of insight are stored and may be retrieved at any time and reintroduced. One can hardly consume, in the traditional sense, a major display of the kind created by artists of today – previously one could purchase a painting or sculpture and bring it home. Displays in which new media are used are frequently not even consumable mentally, for the video material is simply too extensive to be viewed in its entirety during the time that a normal visit to an exhibition lasts. This clearly shows that such a display is an act of consumption and not of production. The visitor is certainly allowed to view the art, but he is not its real consumer. Instead he takes as his model a specific type of con-

sumption, which the artist demonstrates in his exhibition, in the same way that in former times the aristocratic lifestyle provided an example for the other classes. The present-day art consumer no longer consumes the artist's work; he invests his own energy in trying to consume like an artist.

This is not only a question of an individual takeover of single items from the domain of mass culture, in the sense of the ready-made praxis. The artist is increasingly not only taking over objects from the outside world, but also assuming various social roles. Having often appeared as preacher, prophet, teacher, revolutionary, seducer, display artist or entertainer, he is now also casting himself as social and institutional critic, ethnologist, sociologist, curator, art critic or even as terrorist. The further the development of art proceeds, the more roles the artist takes on, in an increasingly explicit manner. Artists now prepare food for exhibition visitors, fit them up with new hair-dos, wash their feet or sell them small souvenirs. These non-artistic roles are played out away from the exhibition hall: excursions, readings and political events are organised, artists get involved in town planning and intervene in everyday life. The assumption of foreign social roles equates with their consumption; work itself becomes an item to consume, exactly like alienated, industrial production.

The position of art described here is, by the way, not all that new: the works of art from the old, pre-modern periods, which we see collected and exhibited in our museums, are similarly not kept there because they derive from the creativity of famous producers – for in those ancient times the artists were regarded as tradesmen and servants and for the most part remain unknown – but because they were formerly used by the aristocracy in their palaces or during sacred ceremonies. It was, therefore, not the origin in the sense of a paternity on the part of the producer, but a specific – aristocratic or sacred – usage that originally ennobled these things and made them into works of art. Historically such usage has always been of central significance for the whole culture – and for the whole economy, for every economy eventually ends up at a dead end if it exclusively orientates itself on the profane needs of the people. The so-called 'natural' human needs are extremely limited – and very easy to satisfy. A developed economy can then only climb higher if it exceeds the natural needs of the people, if the consumer consistently replaces his natural needs with artificial, freely-discovered desires, if he begins to strive after the unnecessary, the superfluous, the luxurious.

In former times it was the aristocracy's social function to promote exemplary and innovative consumption and to continually discover new, artificial, exquisite needs, towards which production could orientate itself. The traditional artist-craftsman merely satisfied these desires through his production. And in this sense his efforts were secondary, although he functioned as producer of his works. Almost immediately after the abolition of the traditional role of the aristocracy as a result of the French Revolution, the middle classes understood that the expansion of the economy to the masses and the fulfilment of their natural needs, which Jean-Jacques Rousseau had preached in his time, was not sufficient for the development of the modern economy. Imitation of the lifestyle of the fallen aristocracy began directly after the French Revolution, in which, from the start, artists clearly played a leading role. Even the poets and artists of the romantic period developed a cult of extravagance, of luxury, of the refined and exclusive life, of unusual taste. Different variations of dandyism and decadence followed, all of which pursued the aim of continually developing new forms of the un-

natural, 'sick', fictitious lifestyle. The artist became the modern economy's special envoy for seeking out and developing new consumption desires, which included, incidentally, the desire for simplicity, directness and asceticism.

While in this way the artist assumed the position of the pure beholder, the exemplary consumer, he compensated for the deepest trauma of modern times, namely the loss of the aristocracy. Nowadays one visits a major exhibition or display in the same way that one previously visited an aristocratic palace. As an idler with the sovereign insight, the artist of today is that ceaseless consumer, whose innovative, 'unnatural', purely artificial consumption behaviour represents the objective of every well-functioning economy. Art thereby becomes the open horizon, the last frontier, the avant-garde of the modern economy. Present-day art shows that one can make everything into an object of desire if the artist redefines desire and gives it a new direction. In his article 'Der Begriff des Politischen' ('The Concept of the Political') of 1932, Carl Schmitt noted, with reference to the Early Romantics, 'The way from the metaphysical and moral to the economic passes via the aesthetic and the way via the still so sublime, aesthetic consumption and enjoyment is the safest and most comfortable way to economising spiritual life.'[3] In modern times the artistic avant-garde functions as an economic avant-garde or, it could be said, as the pseudo-aristocracy of a society organised on the basis of the economy.

In direct contrast, it is also frequently said that art can play no leading, innovative role in consumption, because art is itself dictated by the market. This equating of innovation in art with the changes in fashion governing commercial mass culture, is, however, as questionable as it is widespread. There is an important difference between art and commercial mass culture: art has at its disposal an archive, and mass culture does not. This difference becomes immediately clear if one asks how each sector would carry out a temporal diagnosis to distinguish between the new and the old. In order for such a differentiation to be complete, a historic archive is needed for the comparison of various periods in time, including the present. Only when such comparisons are made can the specifically new of the present be distinguished from the old. And since the individual person is probably incapable of a sufficiently comprehensive temporal overview, we are directed to the archives of our culture. If we turn to the art sector, it is the archive of valorised artistic tradition – as represented in museum collections, books on the history of art and practical artistic instruction – that not only makes such a diagnosis possible, but also demands that it is done.

Artistically obsolete for us, therefore, is not merely that which belongs to the past; past or present, it is something with which we are already familiar from our art archives. And we consider art to be new when it does not resemble the art preserved in our archives. It is for precisely this reason that the art archive constantly drives us on to do something new instead of repeating the past, for, in view of its lasting presence, such a repetition seems to be a superfluous imitation of what is already extant. If this archive did not exist and the old art, instead of being preserved, was regularly destroyed, there would be no reason to produce anything new. Furthermore, if a comparison could not be made between new and old, neither would an appropriate distinction be possible.

This is exactly the way in which present-day fashion, advertising and commercial design function. Since old stock is regularly removed from the boutiques and supermarkets, these sectors of the industry have a short memory. The introduction of the new functions primarily as a revival, though one cannot say instantly to what extent such a revival corresponds with the historical model. In order to be able to do that one must create a special fashion archive, which for a normal customer would be largely irrelevant. The market, therefore, cannot dictate innovation, as is often assumed. Rather the market operates in a zone of indistinguishability between new and old. The mass consumer consumes what pleases him – without a clear criterion of the distinction between old and new.

The most consistent form of consumption is, however, general annihilation – the definitive use of all things. Death is an ideal consumer because it consumes everything; only for death is it true that anything goes. Every consumer, if he takes to this field, will in the long run become similar to death, or consumed by death himself. Now the history of art, as is well-known, begins as the archiving of death – through the erection of burial places, pyramids and museums. Art consumes death – it consumes consumption – and at the same time archives this consumption. Present-day art does not function very differently. Yet it is highly characteristic that art, if it devotes itself to the subject of mass consumption, begins to collect and to archive precisely that which is the first thing to be annihilated and rejected by consumption and thrown into the rubbish. Andy Warhol was primarily interested in packaging, containers and posters – all those things first removed from a purchase and thrown away. Further examples are too numerous to be quoted individually. In any case we certainly know that our museums of contemporary art are filled with rubbish: food remnants, cigarette ends and broken glass. But while art is consuming consumption and archiving scenes of this consumption, it succeeds in escaping simple subjugation under the constant changes in fashion, and simultaneously creates new, critical variants of consumption. The artist of today, therefore, proves to be not only a simple consumer, but a consumer of consumption – and thereby the author of new forms of critical consumption behaviour.

[1] Marcel Mauss, 'Gabentausch'; in Idem., *Soziologie und Anthropologie*, Frankfurt am Main: Fischer 1989, vol.2, p.28f.

[2] Georges Bataille, 'Der verfemte Teil' (La part maudite) in Idem., *Aufhebung der Ökonomie*, Munich: Matthes & Seitz 1967, p.62f.

[3] Carl Schmitt, *Der Begriff des Politischen*, Berlin: Duncker & Humboldt 1963, p.83.

'… therefore I am'
The Shopper-Spectator
and Transubstantiation
through Purchase

Anne Friedberg

The Shopper's Gaze

To shop: as a verb, it implies choice in the relation between looking and having. *Shopping* is a mode of visual speculation that combines expertise, diversion, self-gratification and physical movement. The visual practice of shopping developed in the nineteenth century as the architecture of arcades and department stores, the arrangement of merchandise in display, and the *mise-en-scène* of the shop window facilitated and encouraged the *mobilised* gaze necessary for such leisurely inspection of goods.

> How can a window sell goods? By placing them before the public *in such a manner that the observer has a desire for them*, and enters the store to make the purchase. Once in, the customer may see other things *she* wants, and no matter how much she purchases under these conditions *the credit of the sale belongs to the window.*[1]

The above principle of visual display was articulated by L. Frank Baum in a remarkable treatise of 1900, *The Art of Decorating Dry Goods Windows,* written several months before he wrote the children's classic *The Wonderful World of Oz,* itself a fable about advertising and display. Baum made his living as a window dresser before he began to sell the fiction that transformed his career. Between 1897 and 1902, Baum edited *The Show Window,* a trade periodical that elaborated techniques for catching the eyes of passing window-shoppers and turning them into absorbed spectators and eager buyers.

'The credit of the sale belongs to the window': as Baum described it, the framed visual display of the shop window triggers a causal circuit where the framed image produces a direct stimulus to induce the desire to buy. There is a similarly innate relationship between the speculative visual practice of shopping and another visual practice that has its roots in nineteenth-century visual culture – cinematic spectatorship. Like the shop window, the cinema relies on a proscenium for visual display and its moving images play upon this same imaginary relation between *looking* and *having.*

In *Window Shopping: Cinema and the Postmodern* (1993), the development of the moving image is situated amid changes in nineteenth-century commercial culture – the rise of department store shopping and packaged tourism – which were reliant on a newly mobilized gaze.[2] Seen in this context, the moving image emerged as a combination of the nineteenth century contrivances that produced a mobilised visuality and the apparatuses that produced a virtual visuality (from the 'captured historical moments' reproduced in the panorama and diorama to photography's more exacting indexical record).

What moving pictures offered – from their very beginnings – were imaginary visual tours through alternative worlds: visual experience as an indirect form of possession. As films themselves became commodified – as admission was charged, and as audiences lined up and paid for the movies – the spectator invested in a particularly intangible product. Films became one of many newly-marketed 'commodity experiences' (including amusement parks, packaged tours, sporting events) that did not directly sell a product, but offered the same premium that consumerism promised – *transformation through purchase.* More than any other major industry, the moving image industry

Audrey Hepburn in **Breakfast at Tiffany's** 1961, directed by
Blake Edwards

The Show Window 1897–1902 magazine edited by
L. Frank Baum

turned the image – and the experience that it produces – into a product itself.

The mobilised gaze of the pedestrian stroller – the *flâneur* described by Baudelaire and Walter Benjamin – was a privilege of a certain gender and class; and yet in the context of a burgeoning consumer culture, the mobilised contemplative gaze of the *flâneuse* – as shopper – provided a new set of powers and behaviours for women in urban space. Endowed with purchasing power, the *flâneuse* became a key target of consumer address. While acquiring new freedoms of lifestyle and choice, women became subject to new desires created by advertising and consumer culture.

In this way, the speculative gaze of the shopper and the newly-fashioned gaze of the movie spectator shared a cultural logic. The shop window trained the eye and became a proscenium for the visual intoxication of the viewers who strolled by, the site of seduction of consumer desire. The same impulses that sent the *flâneur* through the arcade, the *flâneuse* into the department store, the tourist to the World Exhibitions or on the packaged tour, also sent the spectator into the panorama, diorama and – eventually – to the cinema. The cinema relied on a similar proscenium, a framed visuality that became a commodity itself. Like the department store and its show windows, the movies extended visual access to luxury goods. In *Contemporary Art Applied to the Storefront and its Display* (1930), Austrian architect Frederick Kiesler imagined a more direct incorporation of the moving image and the sales window. Describing the potential for film as a 'sales robots' on the inside of the store, Kiesler corroborated the power of the film to sell: 'SALES ROBOTS ... Films which show desired merchandise to customers and explain its qualities and merits. The sales

person may wait on someone else in the meanwhile. The screen acts as an auxiliary robot. Such "Screen sales" unquestionably have their place in the store of tomorrow.'[3]

The Spectator-Shopper

The cinema, as it developed in the first decades of the twentieth century, offered its spectators a virtual form of shopping. Movie-going was analogous to browsing without obligation to buy. The cinema spectator engaged in the contemplative visual examination of lifestyles and products, of characters and behaviours, imaginatively 'tried on' other identities. If the ethic of consumerism offered a population the boons of living well and accumulating goods, the movie screen was an ideal space for exhibiting these objectives. A working-class spectator had only to pay a small price to share in this spectacle of acquisition and possession. While feature films may not have been designed to sell a product directly, they offered many of the same bonuses that advertising promised, but in a looser relation between looking and having.[4] The film experience offered an indirect form of possession.

As the twentieth century drew to its end, the shopping mall and the movie-multiplex carried forth the shared logic of shopping and movie-going. There is now an explicit architectural analogy between the arrangement of stores, windows and displays in shopping mall design and the design of the multiplex movie theatre with its metonymy of screens arrayed like adjacent yet separate shop windows. The multiple-screen movie theatre is often placed as a lure at the end of a route past the maximum number of shop windows, entailing an escalator

Announcement for Frederick Kiesler **The Modern Show Window and Store Front** New York, 1930

tour of several levels of sales space. A shrewd but obvious sales logic appears: the movie screen's virtual shop window is tucked neatly inside the multiplex theater and is accessible only to paying customers.

'The shopping mall has not replaced the movie theater,' it is argued in *Window Shopping*, 'it has become its logical extension.'[5] If malls are virtual cities constructed in the nostalgic image of a clean, safe, legible town centre, multiplex cinemas have become virtual malls, retailing a commodified real. The shopping mall remains what Michel Foucault has called a *heterotopia* – a heterogeneous social space in which 'all other real sites that can be found within the culture are simultaneously represented, contested, and inverted'.[6]

In the shopping mall multiplex, the shopper-spectator tries on different identities in a space that defers external realities, and instead retails a controlled, commodified, pleasurable substitution. In this way, movie spectatorship is not direct consumption. It is a form of identity bulimia where, leaving the movie theatre, the spectator abandons the garment and takes only the memory of having worn it for a few hours – or having been worn by it. And here it is necessary to make an etymological detour: the word *retail* has its origins in tailoring, 'to cut up, to re-tailor; to sell directly to consumer'. Certainly this could describe how the *real* – in its ontological primacy – has been cut up and re-tailored for the consumption and access of the consumer. The cinematic retailing of the real does not just rely on re-telling and re-presenting in pieces – shots that form a visual logic leading the spectator to follow/endorse its 'view'. It is also based on the commodified gaze as already described, where the relation between looking and having is the key switch – a causal circuit where the *specular* is designed as a stimulus to produce/induce the desire to buy.

Of course, there is a larger consequence to examine here as the real itself recedes into its representational other. Jean Baudrillard's theoretical hyperreal is a descriptive diagnosis of our cultural dyslexia, where simulations of the real seem more real than the real itself, where the causal grounding of which came first is lost in a chain of signage. The cultural consequence of the predominant visual forms of the twentieth century – the cinematic and televisual – has been to produce an ingrained virtuality of the senses, where our experience of space, time and the real are removed to the plane of representation.

Shopping in the New Millennium

Perhaps the beginning of the twenty-first century will be remembered as the point where the urban could no longer be understood without shopping.
Rem Koolhas, *Harvard Design School Guide to Shopping*, 2001[7]

To shop without crossing the threshold of a store, to glide electronically through shops in the digital equivalent of an escalator ride, is to enter the virtual mall through the window of the computer or television screen. The shopping mall may have been the key *topos* of postmodern urban space, but as electronic technologies bring information, entertainment, products and services into the home, television and computer screens perform the direct substitution of screen for shop window. In the words of Paul Virilio – the 'pixel replaces the bolt'.[8] Computer and television screens now offer a continuous presence, a 24-hour shop window.

The nineteenth-century *passage* was readable to Walter Benjamin in its decline.[9] Perhaps equally, the contemporary shopping mall now emerges as a comprehensible cultural space as it teeters on the brink of its own obsolence. Unlike Thorstein Veblen's 1899 account of the social and psychic necessities of conspicuous consumption,[10] electronic retailing no longer relies on the pleasures of conspicuous consumption. The privatised public space of the department store and the shopping mall has its virtual competitors. The 'electronic mall' and the 'home shopping network' are technological conduits that supplant the need for physical mobility. While department stores and malls strove to provide a domesticised public space for the consumer, computer and television shopping transform the domestic realm into the locus of consumption. Shopping, once an activity that brought women into the public sphere, is now returning them to the privatised space of the home. Today's home shopper has the mobile gaze of old but (her) urban mobility is replaced with a more virtual gaze: *agoraphilia* (love of the marketplace) retreats to a new form of *agoraphobia* (fear of the market).

In 1991, the futurologist Faith Popcorn predicted these changes when she forecast 'the end of shopping'. 'In the year 2000,' she declared, 'the consumer will control the screen. The computerized shopping screen. The home cocoon will be the site of the future shopping center. Once home distribution takes hold, stores will gradually become obsolete.'[11] Popcorn's apocalyptic foreclosure of shopping in a post-mall world may have overstated the dematerialisation of 'bricks and mortars' as they become replaced by 'e-stores'.

Recent developments in the design and architecture of the retail environment have strategised a commercial retrenchment for this loss of material sales space. Shopping and entertainment complexes intend to take the commodified gaze of the consumer *through* the shop window and place it in an elaborate and immersive *mise-en-scène*. If Baum succinctly emphasised the visual components of the sale and the specular engagement of the consumer, recent retail strategies have not only multiplied the visual targets for this gaze, but have also begun to involve the entire sensorium, appealing to hearing, smell, touch, taste (what has been called 'eater-tainment') – in short, to provide a more fully immersive environment for consumption.

Whereas the cinema demonstrated how sights and sounds can be experienced in a blur of ontological uncertainty, the senses of smell, taste, touch retain their phenomenological primacy. These are the senses that are not easily re-presented, a sensual real that does not get lost in the Möbius strip of sign and referent. Once the consumer is placed in the midst of a visual, auditory, olfactory, haptic stage, every aspect of experience becomes commodifiable. These immersive simulations function as deterence operations, experiences in which the epistemological contours of critical thought (and, it would seem, political action) are lost.

Simulated, 'themed' environments are architecture's disregarded stepchildren in the built environment – descendents of the department store, the theme park and the museum – banal public spaces oriented toward visual display. These theatricalised landscapes are canny commercial syntheses of shopping and tourism where the calculus of goods and experiences multiplies sales. The shopper here is a tourist; the purchase is the souvenir.

Here it is important to remember that Baudrillard began his career as a theorist of consumer society. It was in the shopping mall that he found a sublimation of real life – where work and nature disappear as consumption grasps the whole. 'Individuals no longer compete for the possession of goods,' he wrote, 'they actualize themselves in consumption.'[12] The shopping experience has become what developers of virtual reality systems have only promised: immersion in a 3D realm where sights, sounds, smells and tastes are experienced or simulated in a controlled environment with an interactive illusion of control or choice.

A newly opened shopping and entertainment complex in Hollywood, California – named after the intersection of two key boulevards, Hollywood & Highland™ – capitalises on the innate relationship between cinema spectatorship and shopping.[13] In a calculated invocation of the rite of the Hollywood premiere – its searchlights, limousines, red carpets, screaming crowds – the advertising slogan for Hollywood & Highland™ pitched the spectator-shopper into its immersive realm as it proclaimed, 'Premiere yourself!'

A new monument to the marriage of Hollywood and consumer culture, Hollywood and Highland™ relies on the synthesis of spectator-shopper-tourist. Occupying a central block of Hollywood, the Hollywood and Highland' development was intended to build on the revitalisation begun by the renovation of the Pantages, El Capitan and Egyptian theatres in down-town Hollywood. Starting in the forecourt of Grauman's Chinese – the landmark theatre that opened in 1927 and became the central site for the grand Hollywood premiere – the tourist can step into the cemented immortality of the stars of Hollywood's past and perform a pedestrian reinactment of their footsteps. As the tourist-spectator leaves Grauman's Chinese, the sidewalk that stretches along the Hollywood Boulevard contains embedded 'stars' for those actors and directors whose 'fame' commands a concrete tribute to them on the 'Walk of Fame'.

The new shopping and entertainment complex extends this podiatric identification with the screen star. Entering through the 'Awards Walk', the visitor's stroll through the mall traces the same route as that of Oscar hopefuls on the night of the Academy Awards®. The Awards Walk ends at the new Kodak Theatre, designed to optimise the most telegenic angles for the Oscar telecast (the 2002 Academy Awards ceremony was held there). Accessible to pedestrians year-round, the Awards Walk is linked to Erika Rothenberg's public art work *The Road to Hollywood*. Tracing a red concrete version of a red carpet walk, *The Road* is punctuated by several dozen mosaics containing narratives of those (some failed, some successful, but all left anonymous) who have come to Hollywood. At the centre of the mall is 'Babylon Court' modelled as a homage to the film set of D.W. Griffith's 1916 epic *Intolerance*. Two 33-foot elephants – weighing 13,500 apiece and propped precariously on their hind legs – frame a faux Assyrian portal which frames (perfectly for photo ops) a view of the Hollywood sign. As the *flânerie* of spectator-shopper treads past shop windows, the commodity fetish meets the fetish for feet. Star Shoes – a concept bar/club which retails drinks and 80,000 pairs of vintage shoes – attempts to blur these categories: Have a drink. Try on some shoes. Imagine your feet follow a star's footsteps: *Premiere Yourself!* We have entered into a new commerce with the image – we have tried it on, worn it, walked in it and let it surround us in immersive, commodifiable environments.

Barbara Kruger **Untitled (I shop therefore I am)** 1987

1 L. Frank Baum, 'The Art of Decorating Dry Goods Windows and Interiors', *The Shop Window*, 1900, p.146. Baum's pronoun choice demonstrates his assumption that the 'observer' of the show window was female.

2 Anne Friedberg, *Window Shopping: Cinema and the Postmodern*, Berkeley: University of California Press 1993.

3 Frederick Kiesler, *Contemporary Art Applied to the Storefront and its Display*, New York: Brentano's 1930, p.120.

4 See Charles Eckert, 'The Carole Lombard in Macy's Window', *Quarterly Review of Film Studies*, vol.3, no. 1, Winter 1978; Jeanne Allen, 'The Film Viewer as Consumer', *Quarterly Review of Film Studies*, vol.5, no. 4, Fall 1980.

5 Friedberg, *Window Shopping*, p.120.

6 Michel Foucault, 'Other Spaces: The Principles of Heterotopia', *Lotus*, vols.48/49, 1986, pp.9–17 and 'Of Other Spaces', *Diacritics*, vol.16, no. 1, Spring 1986, pp.22–27.

7 Rem Koolhas, *Project on the City*, 2. *Harvard Design School Guide to Shopping*, Cologne: Taschen 2001, frontispiece.

8 Paul Virilio, 'Impossible Architecture', in *The Lost Dimension*, trans. Daniel Moshenberg, New York: Semiotext(e) 1991.

9 Walter Benjamin, *The Arcades Project*, trans. Howard Eiland and Kevin McLaughlin, Cambridge, Mass.: Harvard University Press 1999.

10 Thorstein Veblen, *The Theory of the Leisure Class: An Economic Study of Institutions*, 1899.

11 Faith Popcorn, 'The End of Shopping', in *The Popcorn Report*, New York: Doubleday 1991, pp.164–8.

12 Jean Baudrillard, 'Consumer Society' (1970), in *Jean Baudrillard: Selected Writings*, ed. Mark Poster, Stanford, California: Stanford University Press 1988, p.30.

13 Built by TrizecHahn Corporation, one of the largest public real estate companies in North America, Hollywood & Highland™ was a $615 million Hollywood redevelopment project which opened in November 2001 (architects: Ehrenkrantz Eckstut & Kuhn). The Hollywood & Highland™ website http://www.hollywoodandhighland.com boasts high concept verbs – EAT SHOP SEE STAY – each of which links to a virtual tour laced with promotional discourse. Click SHOP and the page proclaims that Hollywood and Highland™ 'gives physical presence to the glamour and excitement for which Hollywood has always been known'. 'Visitors can explore the shops and boutiques that set the newest trends in Hollywood fashion and try on everything from classic finery to cutting edge apparel, chic jewelry to up-to-the-moment footwear, and du jour cosmetics, eyewear and health and beauty products.' But the stores that 'set the newest trends in Hollywood fashion' are Banana Republic, GAP, Tommy Hilfiger, Benetton, Ann Taylor and Victoria's Secret – which retail the same merchandise available in Des Moines or Detroit.

OPENING SOON
PRADA

TANYA
BONAKDAR   521 WEST 21 STREET
GALLERY

M.A. Laplanche **Bon Marché** Paris, 1873

Shed, Cathedral or Museum?

Chantal Béret

Give him economic prosperity, such that he would have nothing else to do but sleep, eat cake and occupy himself with the continuation of the species, shower him with every earthly blessing, plunge him in happiness; and little bubbles will rise as through water and break the surface of this happiness …

(Dostoyevsky, *Notes from Underground*, 1863)

Towards the end of the nineteenth century, the luxuriant profusion, accumulation and stacking-up of goods that had come with mass production produced a new urban landscape; one in which this evidence of surplus, a final, magical negation of scarcity, revealed a new Land of Canaan, flowing not with milk and honey, but with commodities glistening in a new light, a flood of plenty whose very excess could be read as symbolising the spectacular and inexhaustible prodigality characteristic of feast and celebration.

The busiest streets of London are crowded with shops whose show cases display all the riches of the world, Indian shawls, American revolvers, Chinese porcelain, Parisian corsets, furs from Russia and spices from the tropics, but all of these worldly things bear odious, white paper labels with Arabic numerals and then the laconic symbols £ s. d. This is how commodities are presented in circulation.[1]

Even the consumer's relationship to goods was changed: he no longer considered an object in its specific utility, but rather contemplated an ensemble of objects, in a coherent vision prompted by the theatre of the shop window, by adverts, manufacturers and brands. Even as the consumer's cold monetary calculation moved on from one object to another, he suffered a dizzying sense of intoxication, a greed to buy, generated by this spectacle of profusion. The marriage of calculation and abundance, the department store – and its irresistible progeny, the shopping centre and later the mall – associated commodity with flirtation, and shopping with diversion, at a site where the myth of equality was transformed into the myth of happiness.

Whatever their status as 'good' or 'bad', considered in terms of architectural typology or as representations of the urban, these new communal spaces, necessarily spectacular if they were to meet the demanding requirements of commercial competition, have in the best of cases provided a laboratory for architectural experiment, in this respect playing a role comparable to that of the private house.

The first department store, the Bon Marché, was opened in Paris in 1852, by Aristide Boucicault. It was an architectural marvel, with a base of brick and stone supporting a superstructure of iron and glass that gave a splendid sense of light and space. Surely the earliest monumental embodiment of bourgeois culture, the first magnet of the new desire, it provided the model for Emile Zola's *Au Bonheur des Dames* (1883). Enlarged by Eiffel and Boileau in 1876, its internal organisation grew more complex, and it gained not only two lifts, but also a buffet, a reading room and an art gallery. Its owner, realising the magical effect of publicity, printed catalogues and posters and published newspaper advertisements; he organised sales and allowed the exchange of goods; and displays in windows and elsewhere exploited effects borrowed from the theatre, promoting the aestheticisation of experience and contributing to the emergence of a 'bourgeois style' that went with the new sense of the domestic interior, the site of intimate relations.

John Wanamaker **Wanamaker Building** Philadelphia

Victor Horta **L'Innovation** Brussels, 1901

The *flâneur*, the urban stroller, would find in the department store, as in the arcades, a pure universe of desire, attraction and seduction. Here he was free to walk about, to look, to touch, to give in, to buy ... or not. The stroller was followed by 'ladies who shop', in thrall to 'the luxury of acquiring things that one can do without' as Edith Wharton put it.[2] This new experience was founded on the desire for mass-produced objects, and the possibility of its satisfaction; in this it was unlike the experience provided by the museum, which the department store so closely resembled, with the same vast spaces, the same division into departments, the same display of objects, for in the museum these remained unique and inaccessible.

From the very beginning, then, the department store rivalled the museum – its model, perhaps – especially in the US, where the power and energy of big business seized on everything, including on art and culture, in the tinsel of kitsch transforming art into trinkets and curios for a conformist middle class. In this respect, the department store was the anti-museum of capitalist production, modern and dynamic, which conserved as such might have served as a fitting memorial for the nine-teenth century.

John Wanamaker, owner of the department stores that bore his name in Philadelphia and New York, did not hide his cultural ambitions: 'The woman who decorates her home ... the man who plants a fine garden ... all these are artists in their own way. I would say the same of the department store, which serves the highest ideals.' In 1892, he would tell his architect that his new store should take its rightful place in the city centre by virtue of four qualities: 'It will be simple, unpretentious, classical and noble, a work of art and a monument for all time.'[3] The building would include a 1,400-seat Egyptian hall for concerts, a Greek hall and a Byzantine hall as well as art nouveau hall; it had restaurants and tea rooms, as well as an art gallery that exhibited and sold (European) works of art, both originals and copies.

These seduction machines, which revolved around women, willing but exploited victims, were fascinating material for the novelist. In France, Zola had written about the *Bonheur des Dames,* and in America, Theodore Dreiser described the eponymous heroine of his *Sister Carrie* (1900), wandering, wanting, through 'the Fair', captivated by all the clothes and fashionable things, by fairy scenes shimmering with light.

Rivals and imitators proliferated, fixing once and for all the economic principles of the stores' operation – admission without obligation, non-negotiable prices, the possibility of exchange, with low prices made possible by a high volume of sales and rapid turnover of stock. The second half of the nineteenth century was the age of the department store, with Paris seeing the opening of the Magasin du Louvre in 1855, Printemps in 1865 and the Samaritaine in 1869. New York had Macy's, Chicago Marshall Field: The lift arrived in store in 1865, the telephone in 1876, electric lighting in 1878 and the recording cash till in 1880. The new iron and glass architecture celebrated the circulation of commodities in these cathedrals of free-market capitalism, while department stores' marketing strategies seized on radical architectural innovations to increase their urban visibility, using these materials not just for roofs, as they had hitherto been employed, but also for façades: the Innovation department store built in Brussels in 1901 is the first great example of this, followed by the Grand Bazar in Frankfurt in 1903.

Their architect, Victor Horta, challenged the historicism of the nine-teenth century, abandoning the tradition of kitsch and pastiche that

Adolf Loos **Goldman & Salatsch** Vienna, 1909–11

Erich Mendelsohn **Department Store Schocken** Stuttgart, 1928

reached its apogee in both Europe and the US at the turn of the century. Developing directly from art nouveau, he lightened the structure, exploiting its decorative potential, amplifying the energy of voids and the sense of virtual depth in a space structured by the rhythm of supports rather than enclosed by a continuous envelope. While the architecture, by now more or less codified, was restricted to commercial and marketing functions, the transparency inherited from the 1889 Universal Exhibition in Paris, and before that from the Crystal Palace in London had become inescapable.

> People today may be inclined to believe that these glass elements, and the angle of their supporting pillars, are simply the fruits of the architect's imagination. Far from it, for this glazing meets the requirements for the maximal exploitation of daylight, in other words of natural light, under which the public prefers to inspect the merchandise, believing the colour of electric light to be misleading.[4]

Horta adapted the execution of the design to the requirements of the bourgeois life of the *belle époque*, breaking with the conventional plan: stairs lead off from a vast central atrium beneath the metal framework of the glass roof, providing a cascading articulation between the fluid spaces, made possible by the flexibility of the floor plan, an arrangement heralded by Adolf Loos' *Raumplan*. Based on the possibilities offered by new materials, the 'Horta line', like something escaped from the work of Dutch Symbolist painter Jan Toorop, unfolds in dizzying exuberance, curling, twining, loosening, as flexible as a jungle liana, yet tamed by geometry, going beyond grim necessity to offer a delicate superfluity, charged with a knowing ambiguity, and introducing a striking and entirely novel poetics of space, opening onto the city.

Ten years later, renouncing the natural innocence of this language, Loos, so-called 'architect of the tabula rasa', built some of the most radical buildings in the history of modern architecture in order to meet the requirements of commercial developments and luxury shops. After the Knize and Steiner stores (Vienna, 1909) came the Loos Haus on the Michaelerplatz (Vienna, 1909-11), built for the renowned tailors Goldman & Salatsch.

The architectural strategy he adopted in order to escape the contradictory cultural heritage of bourgeois society – excluding the vernacular and instrumentalising the classical – allowed him to formulate a new way of thinking about space: 'I don't design plans, facades and sections, I design space.'[5] The facade of the Loos Haus, facing St Michael's Church – and more importantly, the Imperial Palace – expresses the programmatic split between shop and dwelling, and dramatises the relationship between house and city: the Tuscan columns of the first two storeys, the two floors of the shop, contrast with the bare smooth surfaces of the upper storeys, whose vocabulary of indifference and banality is a provocative manifesto for nothingness. Inside, the multiplicity of spaces – salons, workshops and storerooms – are treated in a disaggregated manner, the spatial combinations and interpenetrations of volumes being organised in accordance with Loos' *Raumplan* theory. Clear, abstract spaces, carefully designed furniture, expensive materials, wood veneer and costly marbles; all these characteristics of Loos' style are still with us today. Here there is no continuity between the urban fluidity and banality outside and the structured complexity within. As Karl Kraus put it: 'Loos has built us a thought.'[6]

The inter-war period brought a fundamental change in ideological context. During the 1920s, a whole series of movements set themselves

Erich Mendelsohn **Department Store Schocken** Chemnitz, 1928–30

Victor Gruen **Southdale Shopping Center**
Minneapolis, Cutaway Model, 1956

the problem of integrating architecture with the concerns of the avant-garde, giving it a new and urban dynamic.

While the Russian Constructivists were not interested in the world of commerce, and Le Corbusier had no place for it in his designs, relegating it to the margins of the living areas (*Ville de 3 millions d'habitants*), the 'progressive' architects of the modern movement rubbed shoulders with business only during the heroic phase when the new spirit seized on the signs of the new times to be found outside conventional architectural culture. After the factories and the industrial products, the machinery, the aeroplanes and the silos, it was the turn of the city lights, the medium for all sorts of messages, to provide the space for an emergent mass culture. One example is emblematic of the moment: Oscar Nitschke's design for the Maison de la Publicité on the Champs Élysées (Paris, 1935). Conceived as an information system for the commercial world, the transparent façade serves as an autonomous support for ephemeral adverts, static or cinematic, in random and transient combination.

The question was approached quite differently in Germany. Alongside the work of the Bauhaus architects and those they influenced, who responded less boldly to this type of challenge, the numerous buildings by Erich Mendelsohn stand out. The unbroken enveloping façades of the great stores he built in Duisburg, Stuttgart, Chemnitz, Breslau and Berlin during the 1920s gave the *Großstadt* a Dionysiac aspect. Their fluid and continuous forms, both massive and dynamic, and highly attractive to the metropolitan public, combined the advances of modernism – the modern syntax of horizontal windows, pure volumes, and the assembly of simple geometrical units – with the formal tensions of expressionism and its excesses of profiles, ridges and curves. The

buildings reconciled the organic and a poetics of the line of force to confront, encounter and master a discontinuous, polyphonic and boundless metropolis that dissolved and swept away all form. With an optimistic vision of the city in terms of consumption, what Adolf Behne would call *Reklamearchitektur*, Mendelsohn succeeded in transforming the chaos of stimuli that was the department store into an urban node that exalted the forces at work in the big city.

After the ravages of the Second World War, this contextual approach, typically European, had difficulty in standing against other models in the US. Already in 1935, Frank Lloyd Wright had described in 'Broadacre City' the near future of the commercial world:

> Vast amusement parks, commercial spaces standing alongside the road and made up of enormous and splendid buildings, will be designed as places for the sale not only of commercial products but also of cultural productions … These department stores, standing in the midst of green spaces and open all day, will perhaps be the most attractive, most educational and most diverting feature of the new city.[7]

The changes foreshadowed here would appear first in the US, a development governed by the four principles identified by Elias Canetti in *Crowds and Power:* 'The crowd always wants to grow … Within the crowd, there is equality … The crowd loves density … The crowd needs direction', all these being qualities identifiable in mass culture and consumer society, and expressible as expansion, homogeneity, density.'[8]

With the advent of the shopping centre and the mall (the latter invented by Victor Gruen in 1956), Ebenezer Howard's Crystal Palace became

Victor Gruen **Southdale Shopping Center** Minneapolis, Opera Ball, 1956

Victor Gruen **Southdale Shopping Center** Minneapolis, Parking Legend, 1956

a shed afloat on a sea of parking spaces amid the expanding banality of the North American suburbs. The unreal spectacle of these 'shopping towns', offspring of the consumerist utopia, would soon escape the confines of fiction to become the reality decoded ten years later in Las Vegas: 'An image is worth a million forms.'[9]

The architecturally correct model of the shopping centre developed by the American modernist establishment spread under the auspices of the great pioneering firms of Gruen, Pei and Becket. Organised in accord with functionalist orthodoxy, these sites of consumption, repetitive and homogeneous, are treated in a deeply unmonumental, convivially urban manner. There is an axial pedestrian way flanked by small businesses and terminated at each end by big stores surrounded by vast car parks, the very condition of their existence.

Take 100 acres of suitable flat land. Surround it with 500,000 consumers who have no access to other commercial developments. Prepare the site, and cover the centre with 10 million square feet of building. Fill with the best merchandisers selling quality products at a low price. Decorate the whole with 10,000 parking spaces, and ensure that the site can be reached by excellent, underused expressways. Finish by decorating with bushes, a mixed border, a small sculpture, and serve hot to the consumer.[10]

From the mid-1950s onwards, space found itself changed by the introduction of new technical possibilities. With air-conditioning and artificial lighting, and thus the elimination of windows and openings, the exterior could be interiorised, protected, sheltered and controlled. With the escalator – which controls flow maximising freedom of circulation and hence sales, borders are replaced by supple transitions, unifying

levels and compartments. The escalator, indeed, would become the very symbol of shopping: 'Moving products or people is the same.'[11] This was how Gruen built the first, famous mall in Minneapolis, 'the largest space in the region, and the best protected from bad weather', potentially a 'place for meeting, for night-life, where the most important events could take place'. Since then, the irresistible development of the mall into a self-enclosed public space has replaced the traditional sites of urban experience, the streets, parks and squares: in it, 'everything is included'.

Promoted by consumer society as a pure distillation of the American way of life, the shopping centre has in Europe been the object of ideological suspicion, populism being unpopular amongst elites, and its architecture has been refused any cultural significance. Not only is it vulgar in its conception, not only is it 'ugly and ordinary', a destructuring influence on the urban fabric, implanted on the periphery, but it is part of the market economy and of commercial culture.[12] The empire of signs, or political reality? That is the question: 'As mediaeval society balanced between God and the Devil, ours balances between consumption and its denunciation'.[13]

Hence the recourse to ambivalent metaphors to describe these sites of exchange and hyperabundance: they are formless masses of urban residue, temples to consumerism, new cathedrals, great urban machines, vulgar boxes, sales factories. These 'shoddy warehouses' (Walter Benjamin) have been condemned, yet at the same time have been objects of fascination. In his *Society of the Spectacle*, published in 1967, Guy Debord held them responsible for the self-destruction of the city, precisely in a time of reconstruction:

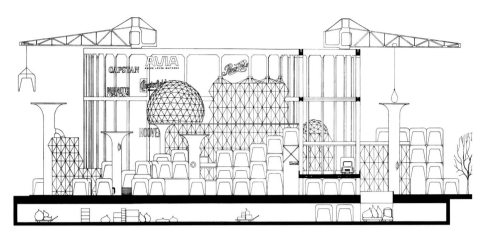

Archigram **Nottingham Shopping Viaduct** 1962

Stages of incomplete reorganisation of the urban fabric polarise temporarily around 'distribution factories', enormous shopping centres built on the bare ground of parking lots; and these temples of frenzied consumption, after bringing about a partial rearrangement of congestion, themselves flee within the centrifugal movement which rejects them as soon as they in turn become overburdened secondary centres. ... The spectacle is *capital* to such a degree of accumulation that it becomes an image.[14]

That same year, Roland Barthes failed to mention the rituals of the shopping centre in his celebrated *Mythologies*. However, its later reputation was indeed made in the English-speaking world: Reyner Banham, historian of the immediate future, began to praise Pop architecture in 1962, in such articles as 'Towards a Pop Architecture' and 'Architecture as Package and Commodity'.

The European appropriation of American poular culture by high culture – ephemeral, disposable, cheap, mass-produced, young, witty, fantastical, glamorous and profitable, according to Richard Hamilton's definition of Pop – was first demanded by the Independent Group, and then, in an entirely different way, by the London group Archigram. They too wanted to exploit the playful misappropriation or diversion (*détournement*) of the technology of the electro-nuclear age, which they associated with the experiments carried out in the name of science fiction, as in the new 'megastructures' which provided the scaffolding for many of the amazing stories invented by 1960s architects. They combined the imperative of consumption with the cybernetic age to produce a metropolitan terrain that was 'obsolescent, disposable, playful, fun, prefabricated, evolving, modular' made up of 'nodes, connections, sockets, networks, flows, cables, lattices, inflatables, containers, caravans,

kits, robots, geodesic domes ...'. The 'Nottingham Shopping Viaduct' of 1962 thus denounced the boredom of the first North American shopping centres. The horizontality dictated by the imperatives of economic function and profitability was replaced by a vertical solution to the problem of the urban, increasing the density of a 'spatial structure' that included the circulation of motor traffic. Adopting the principle of mobility, they stacked the megastructure with capsules for shops, grouped into 'clusters'. With adverts and neon signs on the upper parts, they made the facade into a vast and spectacular landscape, moving and imaginary, juxtaposing the worlds of Campbell's Soup and the mobile home, of Elvis Presley and Cape Canaveral, of Brillo boxes and drive-in cinemas, of Buckminster Fuller and science fiction.

This optimistic utopia was opposed by the dystopian theoretical fictions of the Italian Radicals, whose characteristic tone can be detected in their first manifesto, in 1966: 'Super-architecture is the architecture of super-production, of super-consumption, of super-incitement to consumption, of the supermarket, Superman and super petrol. Super-architecture accepts the logic of production and consumption, demystifying it.'[15] The author, Andrea Branzi, co-founder that same year of the Archizoom movement, gained his degree at Florence with a thesis on 'Recreational Structures at Prato, or Supermarket-Piper-Lunapark'. This resolutely Pop design for a permanent amusement park, derived from the famous 'Piper's', consists of a supermarket located within an immense discothéque, the whole traversed by a big dipper. Another example of this hybridisation can be found among the work of the Italian Radical architect Ugo La Pietra, who in 1968 built a famous boutique in Milan, called 'Altre Cose', combining a fashion shop and a disco.

Victor Gruen **Southdale Shopping Center** Minneapolis, Shops in the Arcade Area, 1956

From: Robert Venturi, Steven Izenour, Denise Scott-Brown **Learning from Las Vegas: The Forgotten Symbolism of Architectural Form** 1977

For the Italian Radicals, 'wherever there are the media, there is the city'.[16] There is no culture outside the urban phenomenon and its models of consumption. Their thinking about the metropolis was influenced by Marshall McLuhan, Andy Warhol and Herbert Marcuse. Mass production had created a new, mobile urban condition, exportable everywhere:

> The commodity circulates the metropolis throughout the territory. Every day, industry produces cubic kilometers of city in the form of mass-produced goods, and every day thousands and thousands of these molecular metropoles are put into circulation, consumed and transformed into waste inside the old towns of immobile stone. The new reality of the metropolis is that of a consumer market.[17]

The one-dimensional isotropic structure of the supermarket, like that of the factory, with their artificial light and their air-conditioning, are now criteria for the definition of spatial and social reality. They provide the matrix of the post-industrial metropolis, disseminated and diluted in an infinite subterranean space, abstract, anonymous, neutral, smooth, hyper-rationalist, cold, featureless and repetitive, a single fluid space of communication, an artificial, temperature-controlled universe, immobile, homogeneous and formless. This theory of fettered urbanism formulated in the fiction of 'the non-stop city' lays down the premises of the new metropolis, anticipating the networked hyper-cities of Virilio's *ulcéro-mondaine*.

The metropolis is no longer a place but a condition, a way of being, a way of behaving, determined by consumer goods, language, clothes and information. The urban artefact is treated as a chemical datum, the laws of whose formation are independent of historical criteria and of

functional or aesthetic judgement. The qualities of isotropy and artificiality ascribed to the subterranean world would much later be taken up in a positive, pragmatic mode in the invisible, subterranean shopping areas that, over the last twenty years, have been grafted onto the networks of underground rail systems in Rotterdam, Shanghai, Tokyo, Zurich and other cities.

Starting from the same observation of the spectacular artificiality of urban networks and their continuous transformation under the sway of commerce, Robert Venturi and Denise Scott Brown drew a diametrically opposed conclusion: 'Main Street is almost perfect.'[18] Following Ed Ruscha, they observed and decoded the Las Vegas Strip and its invasive kitsch. In *Learning from Las Vegas*, they make a scholarly inventory of this loud and disorderly succession of hamburger joints, motels, hotels, service stations, drive-ins and shopping centres, and of the jubilant, demanding clamour of the signs – all these ephemeral, spontaneous, inventive, uninhibited architectural expressions – analysing their devices, defending their picturesque everydayness and reclaiming the rights of decoration, vulgarity and roadside culture. The rights, in fact, of popular culture: 'Less is bore, more is more.'

Pragmatic, they simply theorised a state of affairs coining their famous concepts: the theory of the duck, 'the special building that is a symbol', and the decorated shed, 'the conventional shelter that applies symbols'; the replacement of space by image; the dualism of front and back, the façade with its seductive masks and eye-catching icons, a spectacle as free and unconstrained as competition, and the other with its rubbish; neither, in contravention of all modernist theory, having any organic relation to the plan. Construction is practical, inconsistent, designed on the basis of the client's values, cheap and boring: 'Boring architec-

Hans Hollein **Retti Candleshop** Vienna, 1964–65

Richard Gluckman **Helmut Lang Boutique**
New York, 1998

ture is interesting.' Neither heroic nor original, the ideal prototype is the '$10,000 roadside stand with the $100,000 sign ... Like the archetypical grain silo some generations ago, the sign of the Flamingo Hotel will be the model to shock our sensibilities towards a new architecture ... the sign is more important than the architecture ... take the sign away, there is no place.' They quote Pugin, who said, 'It is all right to decorate construction, but never construct decoration.'

Answering to the identity principle of the silent majority – the middle class – Venturi's conservative revolution nevertheless introduced such experimental concepts as 'light architecture' or 'electrographic architecture' as Tom Wolfe would say, media buildings whose screen-façades juxtapose the real and the illusory. Architecture disappears, realising in its going the ambitions of Oscar Nitschke. Exploiting the breach opened by Venturi, the SITE (Sculpture In The Environment) group of New York inaugurated a 'de-architecture' with their iconoclastic designs for the 'Best Products' chain. With images of catastrophe, narrative games and the dissolution of the building into the landscape, their projects in the 1970s were intended to destabilise 'idiot culture' and its cynicism, and even the conditions of its emergence, through a distantiation both critical and inclusive. Hence the images of deconstruction that were ironically reactivated by the project titles: peeling, tilt, indeterminate, notch, fragment, float, split. Fractures and landslips, terrariums and glasshouses were all anomalies designed for specific sites, making the 'Best' shops successors to the *objet trouvé* and the 'poetically evocative' objects of the Surrealists. Paradoxically, they became at the same time an architectural and symbolic manifesto for 'unproductive expenditure'[19] and a seductive and insidious encouragement to perfectly real spending. Their bold theatrical devices disintegrate and destructure the anonymous, smooth box, meeting the Venturian challenge in the way they privilege the signifying function 'complexity and contradiction' to confer on them the artistic aura that makes them 'non-uments,' to use Gordon Matta-Clark's terminology.

In the quantitative escalation characteristic of the development of 1960s consumerism, quality was rare. One modest example stands out and remains relevant: the Retti candleshop built in Vienna by Hans Hollein in 1964–65, relying on no tricks to create an erudite space, a conceptual object that privileges the experience of space rather than purchase. In declaring that 'to build is always a devotional act' (1962), Hollein was saying not only that the practice of architecture is essentially artistic, but that it is connected to a mythological vision in which perceptual psychology, ritualisation and the poetics of the object all play a role in bringing the spirit that animates it to an expressive sublimation.[20]

The sense of metamorphosis that always haunts his work certainly suggests that architecture is a matter of 'continuous transformation'. Hence the recourse to the art of the illusionist, to mirrors and reflective surfaces, in the design of the Retti shop, where space is as virtual as it is real, and limits are always evanescent. The space plays on physical and psychological experience from the start, the narrow entrance provoking a sense of liberation as one arrives in the wider space beyond. This symbolic transition gives access to an intimate, closed and delicate space, whose treatment – exploiting symmetry, perspective, the regular succession of spaces, the use of dematerialising materials, and the play of light and dark – suggests a sense of ceremony, transforming a simple candleshop into a chapel, a particularly appropriate symbolic displacement. With the dissolution of geometry in this different road, that of reality as construction, the logical premise of these implacable transformations.

Rem Koolhaas **Prada** Soho, New York, 2001

With the 1980s began a Golden Age of retail architecture, as in the world of fashion a business culture emerged that reacted immediately to the new architectural trends born from post-modernity and the crisis in the language of the modern. Marketing and advertising strategies seized on this moment in the socio-cultural significance of architecture to strengthen brand images and their media impact, giving a cultural aura to financial ambitions. Inevitably, they followed the architectural fashion, itself unstable, ephemeral and governed by the same economic principles of novelty and planned obsolescence. The only difference being that in architecture the cycle lasted rather longer, and the demand was for something more consensual that avoided risk or scandal, thus avoiding too, with very few exceptions, the need for any real effort of choice or discrimination. From New York to Tokyo, from Milan to Paris and London, retail fashion saw a relatively homogeneous phase of construction and reconstruction, marked by the same 'fig-leaf' aesthetic. The shops designed for Armani, Calvin Klein and Jil Sander by Gabellini and Claudio Silvestrin all resemble each other, sharing the same orthodoxy, transposing the new minimalist idiom like a Donald Judd ready-made. These architects made lack of decoration into a new genre, characterised by the central role of the staircase, the use of daylight, the valorisation of traditional openings, screen-effects with glass of different textures, the use of costly, highly-polished wood, marble and metal. The effect is always modish, reassuring and culturally correct.

Although in the same minimalist idiom, the new Helmut Lang perfumery in New York, designed by Richard Gluckman stands out from this normative good taste for its more radical approach that makes play with figures of excess. Predominantly white and black, extremely bare, except for a subtly integrated work by Jenny Holzer, whose words celebrating the presence/absence of perfume advance discreetly across the top of a wall. With dematerialisation and disappearance effects produced by the use of reflective materials (such as the excessively long counter in white glass), and a geometry that accentuates the illusion of height and depth – a narrow staircase plunging vertiginously towards a mysterious basement – its concept is based on a brilliant reinterpretation of the traditional layout of the European apothecary's shop.

Very different is the universe of Rei Kawakubo, as expressed in the Chelsea (New York) branch of her Comme des Garçons chain, built in 1998 by English architects Future Systems. An ethereal place, withdrawn from the sound and fury of New York, a hidden, inturned pocket of space bathed in 'luxury, calm and delight'.

The Future Systems group, combining organic references with high-tech processes, have placed various pods and blobs so as to structure the space in almost random fashion. These digital forms, fluid and organic, alluding to the form of the human body, serve to display clothes, to shelter counters and changing rooms, and form and reform in changing compositions as one moves through them. Following on entirely naturally from the age-old function of fabric and clothing taken as paradigmatic expression of the firm's identity, and playing too with the fabric/skin and body/architecture analogies, the architects have given 'dermic' qualities to the surface of the pods: smooth, supple and white. Here there is no spectacle, no voyeurism: the architecture suggests rather a state of symbiosis and intimate acquaintance with one's body, the sense of choosing a 'new skin', a moment to oneself in a supernatural, magical universe that embodies Rei Kawakubo's own style: asymmetry, monochromy, deconstruction and devotion to materials.

Future Systems **Comme des Garçons** New York, 1998

Jon Jerde **Mall of America** Minneapolis, 1992

Finally, there is the long-awaited Prada shop on the old site of the Guggenheim Soho in New York. The work of Rem Koolhaas, it opened in December 2001, at the same time as the enormous Toys'R'Us in Times Square to which it is often compared, with the same void, the same loss of the sense of space – here the means to a feeling of luxury. To express the Prada image Koolhaas has made use of the quality/quantity contradiction in a reversal of the conventions of the luxury shop. Not only does he introduce non-commercial elements into commercial premises, for instance a stage, disguised by its steep slope for performances, fashion parades or conferences. To accentuate its singularity he treats the shop in the manner of an art gallery or museum. This immense space onto three streets, is the site for an installation in the artistic sense of the term: structures and display units are 'hung' like artworks, while the immense wallpaper pasted right along one wall (the width of the block) can also be changed like an artwork. Koolhaas is playing with the associations of the site, the memory of the museum, and just as in a museum, 'You go, you look, you leave.'[21] There is no pressure on the consumer, only the goods vie for attention as one moves from one level to another, the consumers' passage discreetly organised to introduce them to the seductive charms of mystery and heterogeneity in a big space, rhythmically structured by the multiple sequences that succeed each other, each different and surprising. Another feature of luxury, borrowed from the world of art, is the rough surface – 'Commercial is smooth, art is rough'[22]. Used especially in the basement, a bare, raw counterpoint to the technological refinements of the fitting rooms and the lift, a nod towards Dan Graham. Hence, too, the not inconsiderable cost, some $50 million dollars, the price of such 'artistic' ambitions. The store fuses apparently antagonistic models, the business and the museum, an association that accentuates the similarities between museums and department stores already emphasised

by Walter Benjamin – the shared accumulation and display of artefacts in quantity. Rem Koolhaas is applying concepts developed in his submission for the MoMA competition, where he turned to the airport for his model of circulation and to the shopping centre for his model of consumer behaviour.

A symptom of globalisation, the gradual invasion of the entire field of the social by generalised market relations, is determining the space of its structures: the airport becomes a mall, the museum a shopping centre, while the shopping centre becomes a city or fragment of a city. 'Shopping is doubtless the last form of public activity'.[23] The trend is clear in the Euralille development, which Koolhaas was also responsible for planning. Its 'centre' is a retail zone, sheltered beneath an enormous four-hectare roof, after the model of a subterranean city. This shopping centre, called the Triangle des Gares, was built by architect Jean Nouvel. Structured on a grid and designed as an urban plan, it is a model of this type of hybridisation. The city and its structures have penetrated the space of the shopping centre, while the shopping centre replaces the city, taking the place of the traditional, symbolic, spatial markers, the iconic monuments and other now obsolete manifestations of power.

Another example of hybridisation, on an even larger scale, is the Mall of America, built near Minneapolis airport in 1992. A hybrid of commerce and amusement, like Disneyland, it simulates the city in its combination of the spectacular and the communal. A Goliath among shopping malls, it has 40 million visitors a year. Its floor plan of 4.2 million square feet (more than seven times bigger than the Yankee Stadium) accommodates 400 shops, 71 restaurants and a complex of 14 cinemas, together with Camp Snoopy, America's largest indoor themed enter-

Jean Nouvel **Euralille** Lille 1991–94

Gordon Kipping and Frank Gehry **Issey Miyake Store** New York, 2001

tainment park. This new type of entertainment-shopping-centre had an immediate effect on the urban chain stores: to attract consumers and win them away from shopping on the Net, they now ensure a strong link between brand and place of purchase. Shoppers at Nike Town in New York spend their money in a festive atmosphere that evokes the football or athletics stadium, turning buying into a playful, participatory experience.

Consumption has become a planetary tribal rite. Shopping is everywhere, grafted onto all kinds of public activity, colonising every aspect of urban life. The income it provides ensures the survival of the museums: since 1992, American museums have increased their exhibition space by 3% and the floor area of their shops by 29%. At airports, revenues from shopping are higher than from services provided in support of transport proper. London Heathrow is ten times more profitable than the average shopping-centre and 60% of the British Airport Authority's income comes from shopping.[24]

Every citizen is unrelentingly treated and reborn as a consumer. Benjamin's *flâneur*, has become Banham's consumer, Marcuse's one-dimensional man, and no-one escapes the 'hunger for today'.

[1] Karl Marx, *Contribution to the Critique of Political Economy*, London 1859.

[2] Edith Warton, *A Backwards Glance*. New York, London: D. Appleton-Century, 1934

[3] Quoted by Rémy G. Saisselin, *The Bourgeois and the Bibelot*. New Brunswick, New Jersey: Rutgers University Press, 1985.

[4] Victor Horta. *Mémoires, Archives du musée Horta*, Brussels

[5] Adolf Loos, *Ins Leere gesprochen, 1897–1900*, Paris, Zurich: Edition Georges Crès, 1921.

[6] Karl Kraus, *Die Fackel*, nos. 313/314, 1913, p.4. Quoted after *The Architecture of Adolf Loos*. London: Arts Council of Great Britain, 1985, p.48.

[7] Frank Lloyd Wright, *The Disappearing City*, New York: W. F. Payson 1932.

[8] Elias Canetti. *Crowds and Power*. Trans. Carol Stewart. Harmondsworth: Penguin, 1973.

[9] Robert Venturi, Denise Scott Brown and Steven Izenour, *Learning from Las Vegas* Cambridge, Mass.: MIT Press, 1972.

[10] Victor Gruen. 'Recipe for the Ideal Shopping Center', *Stores*, January 1963, p.21.

[11] Victor Gruen and Larry Smith. *Shopping Towns USA. The Planning of Shopping Centers*. New York: Reinhold Publishing Corporation, 1960.

[12] Venturi et al. *Learning from Las Vegas*.

[13] Jean Baudrillard, *La societe de consommation*, Paris: Denoel, 1970.

[14] Guy Debord, *The Society of the Spectacle* (1967). Exeter: Rebel Press 1987, n.p. Section VII, paragraph 174; Section I, paragraph 34.

[15] Andrea Branzi and Adolfo Natalini, 'Manifesto for "Superarchitettura"'. Exhibition Gallery Jolly 2, Pistoia 1966.

[16] Andrea Branzi, *Moderno, Post Moderno, Millenario*. Milan: Studio Forma / Alchimia 1980.

[17] Andrea Branzi, 'La categna di montaggio del sociale: ideologia e teoria della metropoli', *Casabella*, nos. 350–351, 1970.

[18] Venturi et al. *Learning from Las Vegas*.

[19] Georges Bataille, *La Part maudite essai d'économie générale*. Paris: Minuit, 1949.

[20] Hans Hollein, 'Negozio a Vienna: la sigla è la facciata'. *Domus* no. 456, 1967.

[21] Rem Koolhaas in *OMA/AMO Rem Koolhaas. Projects for Prada; Part 1*. Milan: Fondazione Prada, 2001. [22] Ibid.

[23] Chuihua Judy Chang, Jeffrey Inaba, Rem Koolhaas, Sze Tsung Leong (eds.), *Harvard Design School Guide to Shopping*. Cologne: Taschen, 2001, inside cover.

[24] Sze Tsung Leong, '... And Then There Was Shopping', in: Chang et al. (eds.), *Harvard Design School Guide to Shopping*, pp.128–155.

Evolution of Shopping

Sze Tsung Leong

- 7000 B.C.E.: City of Çatalhöyük founded for the trade of commodities
- c. 1500 B.C.E.: Market at Thebes
- c. 400 B.C.E.: The Greek agora conflates public forum and marketplace
- *Seventh century B.C.E.: Lydians invent retail shops*
- Several centuries B.C.E.: Chains of retail stores are known to have operated in China
- c. 110: Trajan's Market
- Middle Ages: Marketplace as civic center
- 1100–1300: Rise of trade causes significant growth of shops

agora shop marketplace

• Lock-up stalls

• **1566–68: Royal Exchange, London**

• Late 16th century: Fabric bazaar, Isfahan

• Early 17th century: Growth of markets in Europe
• 1606: New Exchange, London
• 1608: Amsterdam Exchange

exchanges

• 17th century: Explosion of shops due to rise in credit

• 1657: Boston Town Hall and Marketplace

• 1667–71: Second Royal Exchange, London

• 18th century: Rise of bourgeoisie

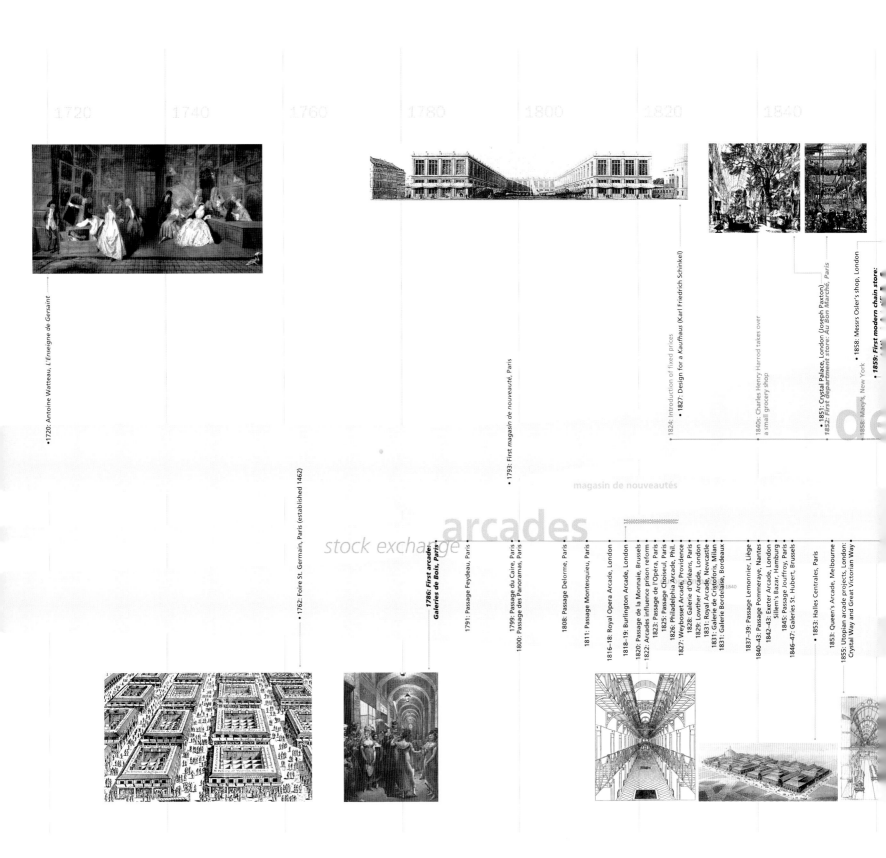

1720   1740   1760   1780   1800   1820   1840

• 1720: Antoine Watteau, *L'Enseigne de Gersaint*

• 1762: Foire St. Germain, Paris (established 1462)

• 1793: First *magasin de nouveauté*, Paris

1824: Introduction of fixed prices

• 1827: Design for a *Kaufhaus* (Karl Friedrich Schinkel)

1840s: Charles Henry Harrod takes over a small grocery shop

• 1851: Crystal Palace, London (Joseph Paxton)
1852: *First department store: Au Bon Marché, Paris*

• 1858: Messrs Osler's shop, London

• 1858: Macy's, New York

• 1859: *First modern chain store:*

de

magasin de nouveautés

arcades

stock exchange

1786: *First arcade:*
Galeries de Bois, Paris

1791: Passage Feydeau, Paris

1799: Passage du Caire, Paris
1800: Passage des Panoramas, Paris

1808: Passage Delorme, Paris

1811: Passage Montesquieu, Paris

1816–18: Royal Opera Arcade, London
1818–19: Burlington Arcade, London
1820: Passage de la Monnaie, Brussels
1822: Arcades influence prison reform
1823: Passage de l'Opéra, Paris
1825: Passage Choiseul, Paris
1826: Philadelphia Arcade, Phil.
1827: Weybosset Arcade, Providence
1828: Galerie d'Orléans, Paris
1829: Lowther Arcade, London
1831: Royal Arcade, Newcastle
1831: Galerie de Cristoforis, Milan
1831: Galerie Bordelaise, Bordeaux

1837–39: Passage Lemonnier, Liège
1840–43: Passage Pommeraye, Nantes
1842–43: Exeter Arcade, London
Sillem's Bazar, Hamburg
1845: Passage Jouffroy, Paris
1846–47: Galeries St. Hubert, Brussels

• 1853: Halles Centrales, Paris

1853: Queen's Arcade, Melbourne

1855: Utopian arcade projects, London:
Crystal Way and Great Victorian Way

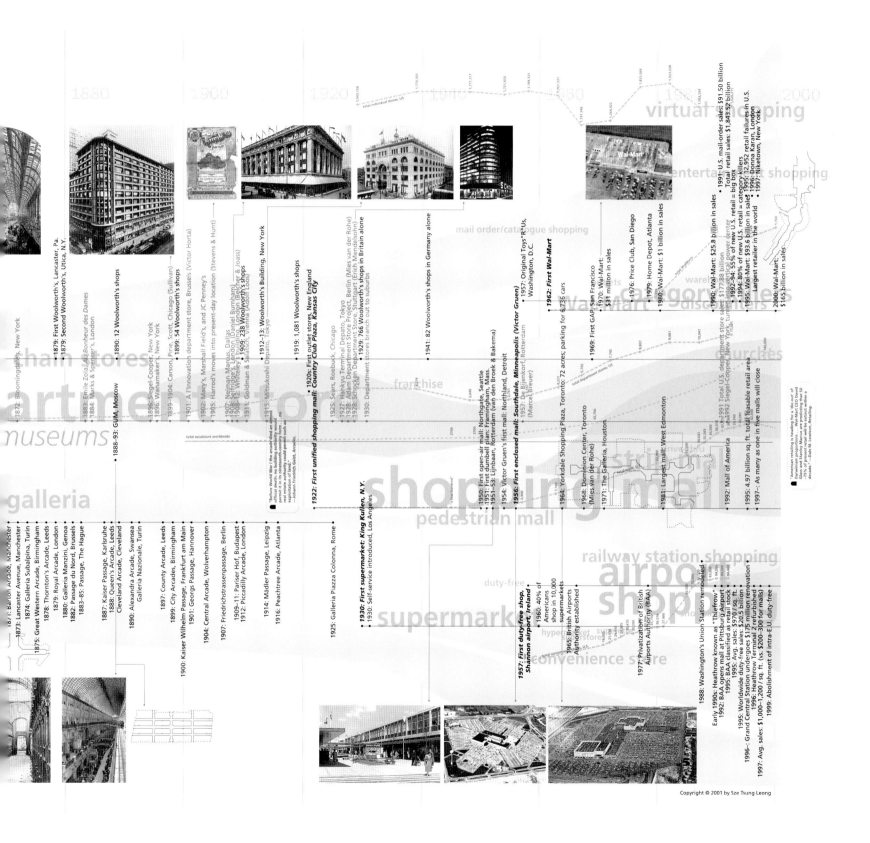

Défense d'afficher: Posters, Women and Modernity

Rachel Bowlby

At the start of the twenty-first century, the complaint within Western Society that consumer culture – advertising, shopping, marketing – is coming to occupy every last space sounds a familiar note. And we hear it, generally, as something quite new. Only now, we think, has it gone this far, got this bad; until recently, or not so long ago, there was a clear separation between what was shopping and what was not; between the best part of life and its contingent consumerly aspects. But now, we may believe, we are rapidly entering a different stage of things. The language of the market has infiltrated what used to be our public services, ever more and larger superstores are opening, international chains of stores and cafes abolish the differences between localities, in sum, our leisure and our work are becoming commercialised as never before, and we are surrounded by a sameness that we are individually powerless to resist.

But in 1890, in Paris, there appeared a small cartoon of a woman bather whose back bears a placard marked with the words 'DEFENSE D'AFFICHER' ('No Bill Posting'). To a lecherous male apparently staring at the board, she is saying, 'You do have to take precautions, these days advertising is taking over every surface.' The French cartoon may act as a salutary corrective to present despondency: evidently it is nothing new to protest that we are drowning in a sea of shopping. It is over a century, it seems – perhaps longer – since this complaint was first made. Does this mean it's always mistaken, always an exaggeration? Whether nothing or everything has changed since the end of the nineteenth century, the claim that shopping is about to engulf us can't be true for both times.

But perhaps, instead of dismissing these claims as being in error, we ought rather to be thinking about what lies behind such forceful and fearful declarations about the modern world. Something about consumer culture seems to present itself in the form of a colonisation that is just about to be completed: we are (always) the last to protest, impotently, just before the floods finally wash over whatever is left of pre-commercial civilisation. In this connection, the interesting question is not so much whether a claim of this kind has ever been true, or is finally true this time. For one thing, that would be difficult to test: the goalposts, or shopfronts, are always moving, so that now there are infinitely more available 'surfaces' for commercial display than there were in 1890. These range from the new media that emerged in the first half of the twentieth century – radio and cinema in particular – to the computer and TV screens of the past few decades, all of them presenting more and more rentable spaces and times for selling. Apart from assuming a finite number of surfaces, the complaint significantly bemoans an encroachment over which the speaker (and, by implication, whoever may be listening) has no power. In this kind of declaration, commercial culture is an invader: of nature, of genuine culture, of people – particularly, of women.

In the 1890s, the announcement of imminent surrender to a ubiquitous market culture, that of *la publicité*, may have been expressed as a joke, as it is in the cartoon, but it was also a pressing political issue, just as it is today. First of all, we might draw attention to the 'Défense d'afficher' notice which can still be seen imprinted on the walls of public buildings in Paris, followed by the words 'Loi du 29 juillet, 1881' ('Law of 29 July, 1881'). In 1890, this marking of urban surfaces as not for poster advertising was a relatively new feature of the cityscape. To set aside spaces in this way paradoxically has the effect of ratifying the

Cartoon **Défense d'afficher** 1890

Cartoon advertising **Le Bon Marché Department Store** Paris, 1915

presence of advertising: just as non-smoking railway carriages imply that smoking is the default mode and can take place anywhere else, so a designated non-advertising space suggests that every other surface *is* available for postering. And it also, perversely, turns the non-advertising space into an advertising space in spite of itself: the wall is no longer a wall, but a space for advertising the fact that it is not an advertising space, or still a wall.

At the end of the 19th century, there was much talk about how the city was coming to look like a kind of outdoor poster display, and much argument about what that meant. Commerce was everywhere, or art was everywhere, depending on how you looked at it. Either the city was becoming more beautiful through its free picture gallery or it was being contaminated through the ugly crudeness of its advertising hoardings. Either the bright colours of poster art covered the greyness of the climate and the buildings with the gaiety of modernity – think of all those swirling reds and oranges on the posters promoting the girls of the Folies Bergères or Moulin Rouge in the 1890s – or else tattiness and tackiness were being installed where only the bricks and stone of ancient buildings should be. In the French context, the positive angle is beautifully specified in Baudelaire's famous essay of 1863, *Le Peintre de la vie moderne* (*The Painter of Modern Life*), in which he celebrates the modern urban pleasure of looking every day at what is new, of enjoying fashion. The ephemeral has its place in art.

While it evokes these arguments about urban aesthetics, the beach cartoon also takes us away from the city. In the 1890s and 1900s, objections to advertising in the countryside and on the coast led in several countries, notably Britain, France and the United States, to well-organised campaigns, some followed by legislation. Motoring was becoming a

new leisure activity for those who had the means, and with the help of a billboard or two, that little run out into the country might well be enlivened by timely reminders of all the things you were leaving behind you in the city. This was probably the first form of what today gets called ambient advertising, meaning the sort that is all around, that pops up just where you least expect it: on petrol pumps, supermarket carts, litter bins. In the same way, a hundred years ago, posters were erected in farmers' fields – conveniently visible from the railway line or the road, or positioned dangerously to catch your eye just as your dust-scattering motor rounded a particularly tough bend.

The cartoon jokes about advertising taking over every single space, and the setting on the beach suggests very neatly the way that this issue had already migrated beyond cities by the end of the nineteenth century. But its overt point has to do with the takeover of another kind of space: the woman's body. At one level, this is presented as though it were the last frontier, the very last possible space for commercial conquest. At the same time, the comedy also depends on an established complicity between women and shopping. This goes back a very long way, in terms of both mythology and history; and the mythical connections have been rampantly exploited by advertising. In particular, there are associations with the biblical Eve, the original consumer who ate the forbidden apple offered to her by a tempter figure. In this connection, the woman presented oscillates between innocence and corruption, between paradisiacal nakedness and shameful cover-up. If women are 'naturally' shoppers, it is never quite clear whether that nature requires the supplementary manoeuvres of a (male) initiator, or whether they are driven to take the transgressive shopping initiative themselves, against the better, more modest judgement of their menfolk. The cleverness of this cartoon is that it doesn't, as usual, show the woman seduced

Exterior of a Department Store Paris c. 1900

Liberty's Sale London, 1920s

by the advertiser or store manager taking the place of the serpent, but instead has her resisting the use of her own body as a medium for advertising or a dummy on which to hang the latest fashions. She is not a fashion victim, she seems to be saying, nor is she in the business of promoting consumer culture. But in order to make this point dramatically, the body has to be advertised as an ad-free zone – to announce its refusal of posters in a way that can only seem to be disingenuously provocative. There is a further irony to the cartoon in the light of what has changed since 1890. Then, the 'label' was something tucked out of sight, perhaps a mildly embarrassing indication that the garment was not custom-made but off-the-peg. But a century later, our beach-girl's great-granddaughter is seen proudly sporting T-shirts stamped with the name of the store where she bought them and, if she can afford them or wants such things, more expensive 'signature' items linking her identity to an exclusive, rather than a mass-market brand. She willingly makes herself into a sign, an unpaid advertising support for the store where she bought her clothes – or would like to be seen to have bought them. She is more than happy to be branded.

The blend of comedy, coquettishness and critique in this picture becomes still more complicated when we consider the space in which it appeared itself. First published in a weekly called *L'Illustration*, it was reprinted in an annual desk diary for the year 1891 issued to customers of the Bon Marché department store. It is not known exactly how or to whom the diary was distributed: it may or may not have been offered gratis or restricted to customers with a credit account at the store. Whatever the precise circumstances, it seems clear that when it was reprinted the principal readers of the cartoon's critique or pseudo-critique of shopping culture, and of its protest or pseudo-protest against the exploitation of women within it, were none other than ladies who

shopped regularly at one of the largest stores in town. Are they being invited to laugh at or even condemn themselves? Alternatively, is the store having a laugh on them, as if they might not be expected to be bright enough to make the connection between the issue of public advertising and the prevalence of shops and shopping in modern culture? The second of these would seem to be excluded because this and others of the diaries also include numerous cartoons that show advertisements for the Bon Marché store itself appearing in the midst of rural or coastal beauty spots. The Bon Marché diaries have a field day, as it were, with this kind of advertising, their cartoons showing ads for the store's own sales emerging unexpectedly into the view of customers getting away from it all, but presumably relieved to be reminded of the real meaning of their urban lives. At the same time, there's a kind of anxious pride in the cartoons' recognition of the way that commerce is engaging in the colonisation of spaces that are partly defined by their very exemption from its presence: you go to the country for an image of a slower, pre-commercial way of life. And though the country is seen as 'nature', it is nature aestheticised, as though in a frame. The windows of the train and later the car, the modern forms of transport from which the image of the country is unrolled before the eyes of the effortless spectator, make this literally true. Rural poster advertising thus superimposes one picture on another, the picture of nature. There is something in common here with the way that the department store's regular sales events are marked on the pages of diaries along with traditional religious days, staking out a new kind of seasonal ritual to be meshed in with the existing one.

The surprising statement of the 1890 cartoon and its multi-sided ambiguities may serve to indicate some of the intricate complexities of trying to think about the relation of women and shopping culture since

Eugène Atget **Rue des Petits Pères**
Paris, c. 1900

the nineteenth century. Shopping is habitually presented as a phenomenon that is gradually and inexorably coming to dominate the other
parts of culture. This encroachment may be shown as full-blown
aggression, sometimes with identifiable invaders: the advertisers and
store managers who plan and promote the attack. Sometimes, as in
this particular cartoon and its analogues showing Bon Marché hoardings in the middle of the countryside, the takeover is shown as being
literally one of territory and virgin spaces, from pastoral retreats to
modest femininity. Almost always, the woman is the paradigm of both
the victim and the compliantly cooperative ally in this dubious enterprise. She participates in her own appropriation, even as she may
gesture towards protesting against it. In these kinds of critical description, moreover, it is not only the woman but also shopping itself that is
two-faced. On the one hand, shopping is a threatening phenomenon,
on the way to making a complete conquest after which there will be
nowhere left free from its imprint. On the other hand, it is literally superficial – in other words, it occupies only surfaces and so perhaps leaves
intact some profounder place or space to which it fails to penetrate,
and which remains unaffected by it.

The superficiality of surface is also important in less pessimistic representations of the place of shopping culture in modern life. In these,
shopping as fashion is not damningly associated with cultural decline,
but instead with the playful and pleasurable ephemerality of the present
moment: what's new, what's in. Fashion is to be celebrated not dis-
missed for being a sign of the times – for being in its essence mutable,
transitory, superficial. Baudelaire's wonderful manifesto argues power-
fully for the equal importance in art of the temporary modes of the
present to the eternal, classical forms hitherto thought of as the only
source of value. His 'painter' of modern life is an enjoyer of all that the

changing modern city has to show; he is eager to consume it, to take
it all in and get it all down on paper as fast as possible. He is a consumer of modernity in its daily variations. Baudelaire's text includes a
chapter with the wonderful title 'In Praise of Make-up' ('Eloge du
maquillage') in which he mocks what he regards as the eighteenth-
century tendency to value the natural over the man-made, when nature,
so he claims, is brutal and ugly in the raw and so can only benefit from
the artificial embellishment that make-up, like civilised behaviour, may
supply. Women in Baudelaire's text are not very active in this process;
they are not themselves imagined as artists – or even as artist-con-
sumers – but more as being among the aesthetic images that make
up the spectacle of modernity. Yet even so, his association of women
with fashion and make-up has helped to forge a connection that links
all three with the cutting edge of modernity in art and life.

In our present postmodern days, with a new critique of global consumer
capitalism and a new celebration of the ephemeral perfections of the
contemporary, the position of women in relation to arguments for and
against shopping culture has somewhat altered from what it was in the
nineteenth century and for much of the twentieth. Women are no longer
regarded as the sole shoppers (in actual fact, they never were the sole
shoppers, but men shoppers, those that there were, did not count symbolically and so until recently were never counted in the statistical surveys of shopping practices). This is not to say that sexual differences in
shopping have ceased to be promoted; the fact that men now have their
own style magazines suggests more that the concept of masculinity
has been modified to include certain kinds of disposition that would
previously have been thought of as only feminine. But the fact that men
are doing it too, or at least that we are asked to believe that they are,
cannot fail to have effects on how both shopping and men are regarded:

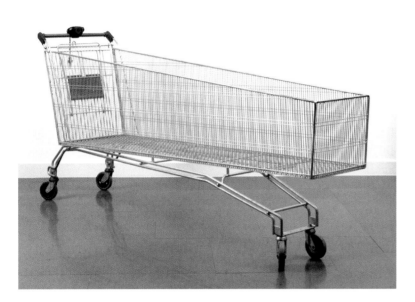

Maurizio Cattelan **Less than Ten Items** 1997

Marko Lehanka **Untitled (Cigarette Vending Machine)** 1990

more seriously in the first case, and possibly less so in the second. At the start of the twenty-first century, with the welcome softening of some of its gender associations, perhaps we can move beyond the demand that shopping be seen in starkly alternative terms – as either politically deplorable and exploitative of both workers and consumers, or else fashionably artistic and enjoyable. It ought to be possible to combine the ethical rightness of fair trade, all the way from production to retail, with the pleasures of contemporary beauty. And that will include the new and always changing beauties found on or by today's painters of modern life.

Consumption is the sole end and purpose of all production, and the interest of the producer ought to be attended to only so far as it may be necessary for promoting that of the consumer.

Adam Smith, 1776

... commodities are in love with money but 'the course of true love never did run smooth'.

Karl Marx, 1867

At first glance, a commodity seems a commonplace sort of thing, one easily understood. Analysis shows, however, that it is a very queer thing indeed, full of metaphysical subtleties and theological whimsies.

Karl Marx, 1867

Art in retail business serves the same function as colour for flowers andplumage for birds: it's the means of attraction.

Friedrich Naumann, 1905

Art lies in the street and it is to be found on the shelves of the department stores.

Marcel Duchamp, 1913

But the furnace-like heat with which the shop was ablaze came above all from the selling. There was the continuous roar of the machine at work, of customers crowding into the departments, dazzled by the merchandise, then propelled towards the cash-desk. And it was all regulated and organised with the remorselessness of a machine: the vast horde of women were as if caught in the wheels of an inevitable force.

Emile Zola, 1883

The store can be considered one of the fine arts, for it is majestically dressed by a thousand hands that daily make and remake the modern stores' pretty scenery.

Fernand Léger, 1928

If the passageway is the classical form of the interior, which is how the street appears to the flâneur, the sign of its decline is the department store. The department store is the flâneur's last haunt.

Walter Benjamin, 1938

Shop windows are still lifes not history paintings.

Karl Ernst Osthaus, 1913

The objective world of human beings assumes ever more relentlessly the characteristics of the merchandise. At the same time publicity sets about softening the merchandisable nature of the things. Its distortion into the allegorical opposes the deceptive transfiguration of the world of merchandise. The article tries to look itself in the face. It celebrates its incarnation in the prostitute.

Walter Benjamin, 1938

Among low-priced, factory-produced goods, none is so appealing to the senses as the really good tool. Hence, a hardware store is a kind of offbeat museum show for the man who responds to good, clear, undesigned forms.

Walker Evans, 1955

Because you see the main thing today is — shopping. Years ago a person, if he was unhappy, didn't know what to do himself. He'd go to church, start a revolution — something. Today you're unhappy? Can't figure it out? What is the salvation? Go shopping.

Arthur Miller, 1968

Looking at store windows is great entertainment because you can see all of these things and be really glad it's not home filling up your closets and drawers.

Andy Warhol, 1985

What thoughts I have thought of you tonight, Walt Whitman, for I walked down the sidestreets under the trees with headache self-conscious looking at the full moon. In my hungry fatigue, and shopping for images, I went into the neon fruit supermarket, dreaming of your enumerations! What peaches and what penumbras! Whole families at night! Aisles full of husbands! Wives in the avocados, babies in the tomatoes! – and you, García Lorca, what were you doing down by the watermelons?

Allen Ginsberg, 1955

Buying is more American than thinking and I'm as American as they come.

Andy Warhol, 1975

I've found out it's fun to go shopping.
It's such a feminine thing to do.

Marilyn Monroe

Lock up a department store today, open the door after a hundred years and you will have a Museum of Modern Art.

Andy Warhol, 1985

I'm all lost in the supermarket

I can no longer shop happily

I came here for that special offer

A guaranteed personality

The Clash, 1979

It was the first female-style revolution: no violence and we all went shopping.

Gloria Steinem on the fall of the Berlin Wall, 1989

Shopping malls are liquid TVs for the end of the twentieth century.

Arthur Kroker und David Cook, 1989

They came, they saw, they did a little shopping.

Graffiti on Berlin Wall, 1989

For me, shopping is like masturbating public.

Slavoj Žižek, 2002

At some point we have to face the certain reality:
despite all the good the world seems to offer,
true happiness can only be found in one thing – shopping

Ally McBeal

**In a world where everything is shopping…
And shopping is everything…
What is luxury?
True luxury is NOT shopping.**

Rem Koolhaas, 2001

Eugène Atget **Au Soleil d'Or, Place de l'Ecoles** 1902

Eugène Atget **Au Port Salut** 1903

Circumstantial Evidence

Shops and Display Windows in Photographs by
Eugène Atget, Berenice Abbott and Walker Evans

Ingrid Pfeiffer

Vases and containers with lids, arranged in tidy rows near the shop entrance, from which the owner peers out almost timidly. His face cannot be recognised and his white apron blends in unobtrusively with the exhibited goods. It is not the portrait of the shopkeeper that forms the subject of the photograph Eugène Atget took in 1902, but the delicatessen itself. In an overall view of the shop the Parisian photographer documents the extreme orderliness of the packages on display, stacked in regular, horizontal rows from the display windows to the glazed showcases. Factually, almost head-on and without any drama, the photographer directs his gaze at his city, at Paris at the beginning of the twentieth century.

Atget always arranged his exposures thematically and by subject matter. In his album *Métiers, Boutiques et Étalages* (*Trades, Shops and Shop Windows*), spanning a period of almost thirty years, there are numerous shop fronts and business window displays, all kinds of goods in baskets or on shelves, display windows with dummies and corsets, every aspect and almost every kind of everyday consumer article customary in his period. Completely lacking in his work, however, are the well-known representative views as well as all signs of modernity in the Parisian metropolis, which, from the second half of the nineteenth century, was famous for its sumptuous arcades and huge department stores, such as Le Bon Marché. Emile Zola's novel *Au Bonheur des Dames*, which appeared in 1883, was to a large extent set in this paradise of goods and reflected the new rising class of bourgeois society. To all intents and purposes Paris around 1900 was the European capital of luxury, inhabited by the *flâneur* and proud of its leading role in the

fields of economics, science, engineering and art. Instead of making a photographic copy of the self-assured and sparkling Paris of the *belle époque*, Atget, in the tradition of topographical photography of the nineteenth century,[1] cast a retrospective, melancholy look 'at a culture that was foundering, at narrow streets threatened with being pulled down, tiny shops and trades that were dying out and, without having any public or private commission to do so, portrayed the most unusual pictorial inventory of a city – Paris – ... which an individual person has ever accomplished.'[2]

'Documents for Artists' was how Atget himself described his collection of approximately 10,000 photographs, selling appropriate subjects to painters and illustrators such as Braque, Derain and Utrillo as well as, later, to museums and archives in Paris. In spite of his thoroughness, which at first sight seems encyclopedic – as previously mentioned, Atget arranged his photographs in thematic groups – his photographic series differ from the romanticising images of many other street photographers in Paris, who sought the purely picturesque.[3] He always retained a certain distance and objectivity of perception, totally independent of the subject being photographed. People were photographed at the same range and with the same detached and precise perception as baskets of vegetables. Atget's analytical visual angle was always the same, and in the course of time human individuals almost vanished completely from his repertoire.

To a large extent Atget's personal style is attributable to the photographic technique he preferred and which was quite normal at the start of his career. This consisted of a comparatively old-fashioned, heavy, wooden camera, which forced him always to work with a tripod, which in turn meant he always had the same visual angle at 'eye-level'. In

Eugène Atget
Avenue des Gobelins 1926

Eugène Atget **Rue Mouffetard**
(Boutique de fruits et legumes) 1925

addition Atget used a lens guaranteeing little variety in aperture but considerable depth of focus, an outstanding attribute of his photographs. Atget remained faithful to his camera to the end and declined lighter, more manageable and more modern models, no doubt because he was too well accustomed to his own camera, which provided him with precisely the results he sought to achieve. Typical of his photographs are the neutral, uniform daylight and the scenarios without humans, often taken in the early hours of morning, which together created the unmistakable, documentarily direct, yet also very mysterious and ambiguous impression, for which Atget was then esteemed in the 1920s by the Surrealists in Man Ray's circle.[4] Like 'police photography at the scene of the crime' was how, in 1930, Camille Recht first described the humanless scenarios in one of the first monographs on Atget, and Walter Benjamin subsequently paid homage at some length to Atget's work a year later in his *Kleine Geschichte der Photographie* (*Short History of Photography*) speaking of it as seeming to provide 'circumstantial evidence'.[5]

In his shop window series from the years 1925–27, which Man Ray later acquired for his collection, themes are tackled that were central for the Surrealists: reflections in the glass panes – allegory for interior and exterior, for transcending boundaries – and display dummies as female objects of desire, simultaneously symbolic of what is for sale.[6] In this group of photographs taken shortly before his death – an earlier part of which dates from a phase before the First World War – Atget photographed for the first time the display windows of the 'magasin du Bon Marché', that is to say, in contrast to earlier work, the explicitly bourgeois Paris, but even here without representative views of the department store as a whole. In the absurd manner of their presentation the smiling display window dummies, which look peculiarly similar to

each other, produce the effect more of 'chimeras of luxury'[7] than of seductresses enticing one to purchase goods.

Berenice Abbott, who, as Man Ray's colleague, got to know Atget (resident in the same quarter in Montmartre) shortly before his death in 1927 and acquired his estate, described his shop window photos as 'bizarre, delightfully naïve, relentlessly individualistic'.[8] In a comprehensive investigation of Atget's *Seven Albums*, Molly Nesbit describes his visual angle as even being that of the 'shopper': only someone directly engaged with purchasing would normally look so precisely and intensively at all these goods.[9] The lining up in rows of consumer goods in everyday use, such as shoes, corsets, fruit and vegetables, vases, dummies and clothes, which obviously fascinated Atget, is in addition compared with serial structures in the works of the Bauhaus member Albert Renger-Patzsch.[10] In fact the 'massed' goods in rows act as precursors for many artists of the twentieth century, who, in the display windows and aesthetics of goods, were able to discover an entirely new artistic theme world, still current today, and to develop it further.

From the 1920s to the present day Atget's work has undergone many interpretations and continues to reflect the view of the generation of onlookers and their specific questions. Walter Benjamin emphasised the 'emptiness' of the photographs, the visualisation of the 'estrangement of human being and environment', which could provide 'full scope for the politically schooled point of view'.[11] In his celebrated analysis of the cultural value of the art of the past compared with the display value apparent in (his) modern day, Benjamin cited Atget's photographs as symptomatic examples of display value. Considering the extreme *cultural* value that banal things like fashion items and consumer goods have acquired during the course of the twentieth century and up to the

Berenice Abbott **Blossom Restaurant** 1935

Bernice Abbott **Bread Store,
259 Bleecker Street** New York, 1937

present day, in both art and everyday life, the contrast that Benjamin affirmed in 1931 appears to have been cancelled out. Atget's direct and factual view of his world was not, however, a chance decision but an artistic one, for 'what matters is the result', as Benjamin stated to the photographer Gisèle Freund when the latter drew attention to the simple technique that Atget had used.[12] The photo series of shops and display windows certainly form only a small part of Atget's total work, but they document an interest, unusual for his generation, in the seemingly banal things of everyday life. Under the analytical glance of the indefatigable street photographer revealed specific formal structures that were also sociologically informative. Among the most interesting examples of Atget's effect upon later generations of artists is an example from Pop Art: Claes Oldenburg referred to Atget's famous photograph of corsets lined up in a display window in his book *Store Days*, published in 1961.[13] The series of headless mannequins in underwear with extremely tightly laced waists, which in Atget's earlier version from 1912 look more like a collection of underclothes, has the effect in the second version of 1926 of being like an absurd design made from female body parts. Individual legs, composed as vertical shapes, alternate with old-fashioned girdles and the whole window exhibits the morbid charm of a spare parts store for female bodies. The inscription on the shop front, 'PLUS REDUIT' (further reduction), acts as a commentary to this impression. If one considers the highly individual 'alienation' that Oldenburg's painted plaster objects underwent in his *Store*, his fascination with Atget's photographs of corsets swiftly becomes apparent.

It is not merely the personal contact with Berenice Abbott, whose series *Changing New York* (1935–38) provides a similar photographic inventory of her city and who, in 1930, published the first book on Atget and made

him known in the US, that connects the two photographers. There were matters of common interest concerning their typical photographic viewpoint as well as subjects. Abbott and another American, Walker Evans, are today considered to be prominent representatives of the trend towards documentary photography that developed at the beginning of the 1930s, and that developed in the US during the depression era. Atget was regarded by the American photographers as a spiritual forerunner of their specific form of modernity in photography. The genuineness and authenticity that Abbott and her contemporaries believed to have discovered in Atget's work that retained its integrity in spite of a kind of detachment towards the subject, was esteemed by the American photographers who adapted to their own work.

Berenice Abbott's photographs of shop windows and businesses as part of her *Changing New York* series are not only stylistically reminiscent of Atget's series. Her statement, 'I wanted to record it, before it completely changes'[14] documents a retrospective look and assigns the role of preserver of the past to the photographer in a similar manner. Abbott's photographic exploration of specific parts of Manhattan was undertaken on behalf of the Federal Art Project and appeared first in 1939 as a book and guide to the city of New York, accompanied by a text by the art critic Elizabeth McCausland.

Abbott even modelled her photographic technique on Atget, in that she exchanged her handy small camera for a large-format professional camera, with which she was able to capture the greatest detail.[15] In her choice of subjects Abbott shared Atget's interest in the less glamorous sides of the metropolis: she preferred to photograph south of the 14th Street in Greenwich Village, East Village, the Bowery, and in South Manhattan not only skyscrapers under construction but also a row of

Berenice Abbott **Newsstand, 32nd Street and Third Avenue** 1935

Berenice Abbott **Chicken Market** 1937

typical small businesses and window displays and her neighbourhood in New York. In her photographs of baker's shops and ironmongers, drug stores, newspaper stands and a Jewish poultry shop Abbott combined delightful contrasts of goods, letters and figures. The price boards and advertisements, produced during that period by the shop owners themselves, illustrate vernacular typography and were appreciated by the photographer because of their individuality. Only one business belonged to a newly-emerging supermarket chains – in 1937 A & P, founded back in 1859, already had more than 119 branches and 15,000 supermarkets in the US as a whole[16] – but the display window of this new type of shop is scarcely distinguishable from the small retail shops, merely having a larger collection of price tags. The accentuation of the painted figures such as '5 c' in the window of the bread shop (which still exists today and in which Abbott's photo is hanging) or the many price tags in A & P's display window (of varying sizes and typographically quite different) are forerunners of Andy Warhol's *Giant Size $1.57 each* lithographs of 1963, elevated to 'picture' status.

'My photos should be documentation and art at the same time', said Abbott. 'They will report facts … but these facts are appended as an organic part of a whole, as living, expressive details of the overall picture of society.'[17] The socio-political background for Abbott's photo-documentation – and also that of Walker Evans – was only one part of their conception of themselves as both documentary photographers and photographic artists. Their specific attitude and new style were successful because of photography's special ability to reach a wide public.

Walker Evans's photographic series on themes from the southern states of America during the years 1936–38 also arose at the behest of

an American organisation: the FSA (Farm Security Administration). Simultaneously documentary evidence and photographs with artistic pretensions, Evans' series depict, amongst other things, a succession of shop fronts and businesses in small settlements, that is to say set pieces on the daily life of the population in an economically little-developed area. The series of exterior and interior shots of shops and window displays in villages and small towns in Alabama and Mississippi are characterised by their piercing clarity and detail, and as a whole have a decidedly 'un-posed' and direct effect: 'The gaze is directed neither upwards nor downwards, it is straight ahead at eye level; the angle of vision is neither particularly wide nor particularly narrow. We see the objects depicted as if we were looking through a window.'[18] This description is again strongly reminiscent of Atget's view, who always photographed at eye-level. About twenty years after Atget, Evans took the conscious decision to choose a similar quasi-human, yet detached visual angle because of the explicitly realistic impression that his photographs were intended to evoke. Evans was seeking to achieve the most 'un-affected' view, which he himself described as 'documentary in style'.[19]

Although the camera's viewpoint cannot correspond with the human visual experience (even from exactly the same angle of vision), photographs like those by Evans create for the observer the illusion of having been taken straight from the front and without additional dramatic effects. Thus, in Evans' case, the style met with the photographer's objective regarding content, namely to document the actual life of the American rural population at a specific period of time and archive it in a quasi-sociological manner. Not without good reason does the considerable esteem for Evans' photographic work owe a very great deal to the investigations of sociologists and historians.[20] Nevertheless,

Walker Evans **The Old Reliable House Mover** 1936

Walker Evans **Storefronts** Moundville, Alabama, 1936

Evans' photographs resist adopting any clear political position – in contrast to other contemporaries, such as Margaret Bourke-White or Dorothea Lange, who photographed in an intrinsically direct, socially critical manner – and avoid social commentary in an obvious manner: 'NO POLITICS whatever' was his comment on the subject.[21] Current political or social references are indirectly present in some images, for example through the price tags of the goods, which Evans frequently photographed. He had a fundamental interest in literature, language and typography, and therefore shop and display window inscriptions were among his most important themes. He intentionally combined the visual and the linguistic, the abstract and the illustrative in a single photograph.[22]

Three of the most important documentary among the photographers of the twentieth century chose not only a similar style and visual angle but also very similar themes in quite different locations. A comparative analysis of the shops and shop windows portrayed by Atget, Abbott and Evans shows that all of them directed a nostalgic look at the details of everyday life. In their choice of subjects they provided almost a *negation* of shopping in the sense of 'pleasurable purchasing': away from the sparkling arcades, department store palaces and luxury worlds of Paris and New York, they photographed their unspectacular neighbourhoods in 'old Paris' and Greenwich Village or impressions from the small towns of Alabama and Mississippi. With all three photographers the interest is quite consciously directed towards a more personal world, condemned to extinction perhaps for that reason, in that one is primarily concerned not with the glittering staging of consumption but with the necessary purchasing of everyday items. Nothing is exaggerated in their photographs; their accurate observance of the obvious is the only spectacular and (given the period) unusual act.

While Abbott and Evans operated in a particular phase of American documentary making, clearly defined from a photo-historical point of view and determined by their public commissions as well as the political situation in the depression era, Atget's work appears to be significantly more complex. As a precursor of the style later declared to be documentary, and as an individual working without a commission, his photographs allow much more room for interpretation. In spite of renouncing all dramatic art, photographic tricks and manipulations, such as light and shadow effects, over- or under-exposure, and spectacular subjects – in spite of great formal proximity to the display windows of Abbott and Evans, and a shared objectivity and freshness of view – there are some 'empty spaces' remaining in Atget's work, mysterious atmospheres and surreal moments in the otherwise normal, petit-bourgeois everyday life.

Susan Sontag has asserted that photography is by its very nature the only surreal art, for 'what could be more surreal than an object, which in practical terms creates itself and with a minimum of effort? … Photography has best brought to our attention the coexistence of sewing machine and umbrella, that chance meeting, which a great Surrealist poet has praised as the essence of beauty.'[23] With Atget there is always such a 'coexistence', and it is precisely this 'empty space' in the interpretation of his apparently everyday themes that makes a study of this early 'shopper' among photographers an appropriate starting point for tracing the fascination of the world of goods in the history of photography.

Walker Evans **Household Supply Store** 1935

1 In 1851 five French photographers (Le Gray, Le Seq, Baldus, Bayard and Mestral) were commissioned by the French state to undertake a 'mission héliographique' and for the first time photographed systematically the historical monuments in various regions of France. Hans Georg Puttnies, 'Atget', in *Atget*, exh. cat., Rudolf Kicken Gallery, Cologne 1980, p.6.

2 Romeo E. Martinez, 'Eugène Atget 1857–1927', in *Eugène Atget, Das alte Paris*, exh. cat., Bonn 1978, p.12.

3 Cf. Colin Westerbeck and Joel Meyerowitz, *Bystander: A History of Street Photography*, London, Boston, New York: Little Brown 1994, pp.105–114.

4 Man Ray published some of Atget's photographs (anonymously at the latter's request) in the June and December 1926 editions of the periodical *La Révolution surréaliste*.

5 Walter Benjamin, *Das Kunstwerk im Zeitalter seiner technischen Reproduzierbarkeit*, Frankfurt 1977 (1963), p.21.

6 Cf. this volume: Katharina Sykora, 'Merchandise Temptress'; John Fuller, 'Atget and Man Ray in the Context of Surrealism', *Art Journal*, vol.36, no.2, Winter 1976–77, pp.130–138.

7 Andreas Krase, 'Archiv der Blicke – Inventar der Dinge: Eugène Atgets Paris', in *Paris: Eugène Atget 1857-1927*, Cologne 2000, p.140.

8 Berenice Abbott, 'Eugène Atget', *Creative Art*, vol.5, Sept. 1929, quoted in Beaumont and Newhall (eds.), *Photography: Essays & Images*, New York: Museum of Modern Art 1980 p.237.

9 Molly Nesbit, *Atget's Seven Albums*, New Haven and London: Yale University Press 1993, p.161.

10 Jean-Claude Lemagny, 'Atget, le prophète', in *Atget, le pionier*, exh. cat., Paris and New York 2000, p.16.

11 Walter Benjamin, *Das Kunstwerk*, p.58.

12 Gisèle Freund, 'Wie Atget wiederentdeckt wurde', in *Eugène Atget: Das alte Paris*, p.14.

13 Claes Oldenburg, *Store Days: Documents from* The Store *(1961) and* Ray Gun Theatre *(1962)*, selected by Claes Oldenburg and Emmett Williams, photographs by Robert R. McElroy, New York: Something Else Press 1967, p.26.

14 Quoted in Susan Sontag, 'Melancholy Objects', in *On Photography*, London: Penguin, 1979 (New York 1977), p.70.

15 Bonnie Yochelson, *Berenice Abbott: Changing New York*, Munich, Paris and London: Schirmer /Mosel 1997, p.12.

16 Ibid. p.377

17 Ibid. p.22.

18 Joel Snyder, 'Sehen Darstellen', in Wolfgang Kemp (ed.), *Theorie der Fotografie*, vol.3. *1945–1980*, Munich: Schirmer und Mosel 1999 (1983), p.277.

19 Leslie Katz, 'Interview with Walker Evans', *Art in America*, vol.59, no.2, Mar.–Apr. 1971, p.87.

20 Michael Brix and Birgit Mayer 'Vorwort der Herausgeber', in *Walker Evans Amerika: Bilder aus den Jahren der Depression*, exh. cat., Munich 1990, p.7.

21 *Walker Evans at Work, 745 Photographs together with Documents: Selected from Letters, Memoranda, Interviews, Notes*, ed. with an essay by Jerry L. Thompson, New York: Harper and Row 1982, p.112.

22 Andrei Codrescu, 'Modernism was in awe of the Word', in *Walker Evans: Signs*, London: Thames and Hudson 1998, p.31.

23 Sontag, 'Melancholy Objects', p.55.

Eugène Atget **Rue de Petit Thouars** 1910–11

Eugène Atget **Boulevard de Strasbourg** 1912 100

101 Eugène Atget **Boulevard de Strasbourg** 1926

Eugène Atget **Avenue de l'Observatoire** 1926

Berenice Abbott **Rope Store** 1936

Berenice Abbott **Whelan's Drug Store** 1936

Berenice Abbott **A & P (Great Atlantic & Pacific Tea Co.)** 1936

Berenice Abbott **Hardware Store** 1938

Walker Evans **Roadside Fruit**
Ponchatoula, Louisiana, 1936

Walker Evans **Auto Parts Shop**
Atlanta, Georgia, 1936

Walker Evans **Seed Store Interior** Vicksburg, Mississippi, 1936

Nigel Henderson **Wig Stall** Petticoat Lane,
London, 1952

Nigel Henderson **W & F Riley, Newsagents
and Confectioners** London, 1949–53

Nigel Henderson **Barber's Shop Window**
London, 1949–53

Nigel Henderson **Roman Road Street Market**
London, 1949–53

Stewart Bale **F. W. Woolworth & Co. Ltd.** London Road, Liverpool, 1931

Stewart Bale **F. W. Woolworth & Co. Ltd.** London Road, Liverpool, 1931

Stewart Bale **Lewis's Ltd.** Ranelagh Street Liverpool, 1949

Stewart Bale **Blacklers Store Ltd.** Great Charlotte Street, Liverpool, 1954

Hannes Meyer **Co-op Vitrine, Basel (Second Version)** 1925

Picturing Collective Consumer Culture: Hannes Meyer's Co-op Vitrine

K. Michael Hays

Modern society does not recognise itself as an ideological construction, so it must be represented as such. To show the 'real' as construct, to 'de-conceal' the arbitrary structures and operations behind what appears given, natural, even fixed – this is the vocation of any political-ly engaged modern art and part of its performance criteria. Hannes Meyer's *Co-op Vitrine* project of 1925 directs our attention not only to the practical, formal problems of representing modern industrial-consumer society, but also and more fundamentally to the question of the ideological nature and function of that representation.

Meyer developed a body of work, including linocuts and screened prints, photographs, assemblages, rooms, buildings and other projects, all designated by the name 'cooperative' or 'Co-op', a locution that he would use throughout his career to signal a type of form he conside-red 'adequate for our times'.[1] The *Co-op Vitrine* was designed for the *Internationale Ausstellung des Genossenschaftswesens und der sozia-len Wohlfahrtspflege*, an exhibition of Swiss cooperative consumer products in Ghent and Basel in 1924 and 1925 under the direction of Bernhard Jäggi, one of the founders of the Swiss cooperative movement with whom Meyer had worked on the Freidorf cooperative housing estate since 1921. Meyer himself was a member of the cooperative and a resident of Siedlung Freidorf from 1921 to 1926 (about which more later), as well as the chief of its building commission. In the latter capacity he designed not only the buildings but also the graphic logo for the cooperative – which appears, for example, on the coupons used in place of Swiss marks for exchange of everyday goods – as well as the packages and window displays of the standard products of the

magasin d'alimentation, at which all members of the cooperative were obliged to shop. The international cooperative exhibition gave Meyer the opportunity to develop his design ideas, bringing together issues of industrial production, commercial advertising and artistic reception in a new relation that he would polemically announce in his essay 'Die neue Welt' ('The New World') as a high-speed, boundary bursting deli-rium of art becoming reality through the embrace of an aesthetics of standardisation, repetition, mechanised media, advertisement and nomadic impersonality.

In the *Co-op Vitrine*, thirty-six standard consumer products, packaged in various shapes and sizes of cartons, tins, bottles, tubes and bags, appear at first gloss as the very images of commodity production and exchange, distanced from their producers and users by the abstract conditions of their display, bracketed off from the physical space of the consumer and rendered – exactly and merely it seems – as distantia-ted, reified images. Arranged as the repetitive components of so many mechanical processes of stacking, extruding and aligning, they bear no traces of human manufacture, no evidence of an individual produ-cer's control. But Meyer seems to celebrate rather than lament this fact, for it is the collective rather than the individual that interests him. He comments,

The demands we make on life today are all of the same nature regardless of social stratification. The surest sign of true communi-ty is the satisfaction of the same needs by the same means. The upshot of such a collective demand is the standard product ... The degree of our standardization is an index of our communal produc-tive system.[2]

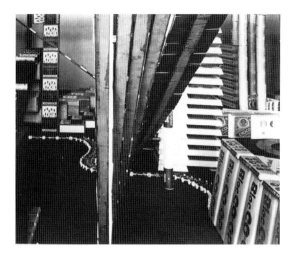 

Hannes Meyer **Co-op Vitrine, Basel (Second Version)** 1925   Hannes Meyer **Co-op Vitrine, Basel (Second Version)** 1925

Thus, the disenfranchisement of individual manufacture in modern industrialisation finds its aesthetic correlate in the destruction of the aura of modern products. But if the aesthetic structure of the *Vitrine* is determined first of all by the repetitive and serially structured formation that is the very nature of mass-reproduced commodities and their distribution, what we have here is, nevertheless, no conventional display of commodities. For the repetition, seriality, diagonal and frontal layering and circumnavigable space are also all compositional strategies constituent of a modernist formal practice already evolved to its most advanced stages in postcubist and elementarist pictorial and sculptural practices such as suprematism and constructivism. That Meyer intends to take full advantage of the visual impact of such strategies is confirmed in his *Lino Co-op* of 1925, a kind of deep structural diagram of the *Vitrine* that is also part of a series of projects Meyer referred to as 'abstract architecture'. Without sacrificing the formal rigour and self-referentiality of a thoroughly modern art form, Meyer introduces into this work a new *iconic* potential based on the very loss of aesthetic aura – in the sense that the Model 'T' Fords, Havana cigarettes, and Gillette razors that so fascinate him in 'Die neue Welt' are icons of the secularised, deterritorialised nomad of the socialist future – that seeks to engage a wholly different audience in wholly different terms than those routinely associated with modern art, terms closer to the instrumentalised factographic and cinematographic researches of productivism and even dadaism – the punctual experience of objectification itself – than to the valorisation of autonomy, abstraction and hermetic withdrawal of 'high' modernism.

But there is yet another reference, for rather than the familiar arrangement of isolated individual products in a shop window, the Co-op articles are presented here as an image or facsimile of the industriali-

sed manufacturing process itself, each series of products configured as if having issued from the various conveyor belts of an assembly line, in a metropolis worthy of Fritz Lang or Dziga Vertov or even of Jean-Luc Godard, who presented packages of detergents, cigarettes and crackers strikingly similar to Meyer's, arranged as a *grand ensemble* or housing project, in the last shot of *2 ou 3 choses que je sais d'elle* (1967). We must read Meyer's project on two scales simultaneously: the picture of the commodity-producing industrial city is itself framed as the overall scene of collective reception and consumption of the standard product; the final, finished product to which the consumer has the most direct access is the constituent element of the overall pictorial device that the 'pictorial consumer' must apprehend. More than just making the mechanisms of representation and mode of address part of its actual content, the work also stresses the site and process of commodity production and reception, as well as the reification and abstraction that that commodity must undergo in its transmutation into an image, an advertisement of itself.

In the mid-1920s the most politically committed artists recognised that those artistic forms, procedures and conditions of reception received from bourgeois society and its aesthetic institutions would have to be systematically dismantled and redefined in an effort to establish the new conditions of what Walter Benjamin called 'simultaneous collective reception', and that those latter conditions would involve changed perceptual conventions for mass products as well as objects of art, thus eroding the boundary between the two. The *Co-op Vitrine* adheres to, but refunctions the formal strategies of the modernist avant-garde even as it folds into itself those images of industrialised production and mass consumption on which its representation is born. This doubled circuit of signs is an imaginary projection, a picture of an as yet

Hannes Meyer **Lino Co-op Diagram of the vitrine** 1925–26

unattained condition of collective production and reception, and should be seen as part of a general attempt by Meyer in his Co-op work to devise such aesthetic apparatuses as quasi-material transmission or commutation systems that would help produce, even force, a new, corresponding collective subjectivity. The forms of the consumer products are, for Meyer, what Benjamin called *Wunschbilder* (wish-images), which contain transformative expressive potential and appear in anticipation of genuine social change.[3] Meyer provides his own summary of the expressive potential of mass products:

In the display window of today psychological capital is made of the tensions between modern materials with the aid of lighting. It is display window organization rather than window dressing. It appeals to the finely distinguishing sense of materials found in modern man and covers the gamut of its expressive power: fortissimo = tennis shoes to Havana cigarettes to scouring soap to nut chocolate! Mezzoforte = glass (as a bottle) to wood (as a packing case) to pasteboard (as a packing) to tin (as a can)! Pianissimo = silk pajamas to cambric shirts to Valenciennes lace to 'L'Origan de Coty'![4]

Along with advertisements, product logos and photographs of the mass industrial and mass cultural landscape, a photograph of the *Co-op Vitrine* was reproduced as an illustration to Meyer's essay 'Die neue Welt', in a section significantly entitled 'Die Propaganda'. It does not simplify Meyer's enterprise in either this essay or the *Vitrine* project to insist that he attempts to conjure up wish-images, to picture a new collective modern culture. For what we understand by the significance of Meyer's project has less to do with the picture as a source of sheer aesthetic experimentation than it does with the picture's claim to cognitive and practical as well as visual and aesthetic status. The

appropriation and presentation of the wish-images testify to Meyer's preoccupation not only with the industrialisation process, but also with the forms of experience that are the subjective consequences of such a process. The images seek to satisfy not only the appetite for form, but also the appetite for *matter*. The picture stands as a fact of experience, as the actual form of our knowledge of things. And its richness may therefore be recognised in terms of its ability to assimilate material and productive values as well as visual and psychological effects, to convert the qualities of one into the forms of the other, and thereby to reunite the two levels of subjective mental labour and the objective realities of production. Co-op form attests to the possibility that forms of simultaneous collective reception, by linking the structure of subjectivity directly to the inexorable movement of mass production, can afford a kind of proto-political and practical apprenticeship for the collective society to come. The emphatic assertion of the visual products of mass consumerism – which, understood in terms of received theories of alienation and reification, would have to stand condemned – when understood as affording epistemic access to, or a symbolic and psychological mapping of, the now vivid and tractable consequences of modernity, may be reconceived as a functional diagram for cognitive retooling and social change.

And so now to the compass of significations in the *Vitrine* developed so far must be added another register: the sign system organised by the *Co-op Vitrine* is class-directed; a viewer's affiliation with a workers' collective consciousness, as opposed to middle-class individualism, confers an additional capacity to apprehend its signification. This apprehension is not merely a matter of finding class signals added to the work (Meyer referred to the colour of the *Vitrine*, for example, as 'signal red'), but also of understanding the context of its emergence,

Jean-Luc Godard during the filming of **One or Two Things I Know About Her** 1966

for behind all of Meyer's Co-op work lie the sedimented experiences of Siedlung Freidorf, the community facility built by Meyer between 1919 and 1924 for the Swiss Co-operative Union, under the direction of Bernhard Jäggi and Henry Faucherre, professor of political economy at the University of Zurich, along with Karl Mundig, who coined the name Freidorf, and Rudolf Kündig. The promoters of Freidorf found the inspiration for their patronage in two figures directly related to the international and Helvetic cooperative movements: Heinrich Pestalozzi and Heinrich Zschokke. Faucherre cited the eighteenth-century educational reformer Pestalozzi as the veritable source of the 'Freidorf adventure'.[5] In his novel *Leonard and Gertrude* (1781), Pestalozzi pays particular attention to collective self-help and self-determination, as well as to family education and the key role of the mother, whose common sense, sound judgement and liberating suppleness contrast to patriarchal, authoritarian strength, influencing first her family, then her village and finally the state. Faucherre credited Pestalozzi as the initiator of the modern cooperative movements and the principal influence on later town planners like Robert Owen, who had visited Pestalozzi in Switzerland. On the other hand, Zschokke's didactic novel *The Goldminer's Village* (1817) – which narrated the systematic transformation of a village toward collectivity and described in detail the benefits for all, emphasising that different forms of behaviour are reflections of tensions between a humanising possibility and specific social situations – was, for its founders, nothing less than a prototype of Meyer's Siedlung. It is from these early experiences of the specific economic situation and way of life in the workers' cooperative that the *Co-op Vitrine* derives.

In the Ghent exhibition, along with the *Co-op Vitrine*, Meyer presented his *Co-op Theater*. In one of the short plays, *Der Traum* – staged simply with a phonograph recording, life-sized puppets and local actors – there initially appears a poor mother and two children sleeping as a black spider descends, horrifying the mother and upsetting the children. Enter the father who pulls a sandwich from its wrapper to share with his family. The is 'stillness and anticipation'. The wrapper, it turns out, is a Co-op poster, which the father then places on the wall to the excitement of the family. The family returns to their sleep and the dream commences: Co-op packages descend, containing food and products of daily use. An apparition of an outstretched hand appears, laden with refunds and reimbursements from the commune. As the dream ends, Meyer writes, 'the picture of the future advances'.[6]

In its investigations of commodity sign production and reception, and its positing of a continuum in the life of the commodity product from the factory to the shop window to the city itself, Meyer's *Co-op Vitrine* similarly pictures a collective consumer culture. But if it is repetition, seriality, banality and the like that the *Vitrine* seems to recommend as the valid conceptualisation of the totality of our experience of modern society, it is not because Co-op form betrays a legitimation of the already existing order, but rather because it identifies the transformatory potential of that order out of which an authentic collective life and a single international culture of the future might be developed. The *Co-op Vitrine* seeks to recode the reified objective content of mass culture and to make it available for simultaneous collective reception. At the same time, however, such a transmutation must be understood as an anticipatory representation of a future society and a future mode of production that seek to emerge from the present.

Hannes Meyer **Theater Co-op** 1924   Hannes Meyer **Theater Co-op** 1924

1 Hannes Meyer, 'Die neue Welt', *Das Werk*, vol.7, Bern 1926, pp.205–24, trans. 'The New World', in Claude Schnaidt, *Hannes Meyer: Buildings, Projects and Writings*, Teufen: Verlag Arthur Nigggli 1965, pp.205–24.

2 Meyer, 'The New World', p.222.

3 Walter Benjamin, 'Paris, Capital of the Nineteenth Century', in *Reflections*, New York: Harcourt Brace Jovanovich 1978, p.148.

4 Meyer, 'The New World', p.223.

5 Henry Faucherre, 'Vom inneren Aufbau der Siedlungsgenossenschaft Freidorf', in *25 Jahre Siedlungsgenossenschaft Freidorf*, Basel: Buchhandlung VSK 1943.

6 Hannes Meyer, 'Das Theater Co-op', *Das Werk*, vol.11, no.12, Bern 1924, pp.329–32.

Hannes Meyer **Coop Virtrine,
Gent (First Version)** 1924

Hannes Meyer **Co-op Vitrine, Basel
(Second Version)** 1925

Albert Renger-Patzsch **Aluminium Pots Schocken Department Store** Zwickau, 1926

Albert Renger-Patzsch **Boot-trees in the Fagus Factory** Alfeld, 1926

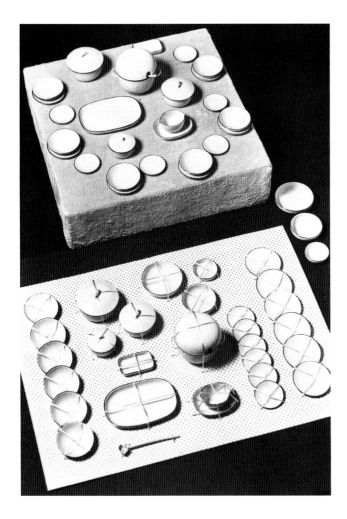

Hans Finsler **Praline Selection** 1927–28

top left: Hans Finsler **Dinner Service, Two Arrangements** 1930–31
bottom left: Hans Finsler **Coffee Service I** 1930

László Moholy-Nagy **Store Alexander Simpson** 1936

László Moholy-Nagy **Model for Courtaulds** 1936

Friedrich Vordemberge-Gildewart **Window for de Bijenkorf Department Store** Amsterdam, 1950

Frederick Kiesler **Study for a Façade Design for a Department Store** 1927–28

Contemporary Art Applied to the Store and its Display

Thoughts on Frederick Kiesler's Show Windows

Eva Christina Kraus

Why doesn't the show window hold instead of a display – a play? A stage play. Where Mr Hat and Miss Glove are partners. The window a veritable peepshow stage. Let the street be your auditorium with its ever-changing audience. Has nobody tried to conceive plays for merchandise?[1]

Frederick Kiesler's artistic view was influenced by the European avant-garde and the removal of the boundaries between the disciplines of theatre, painting, sculpture, design and architecture.[2] He understood how to continue to realise his radical and visionary concepts in new areas and to adapt to the needs of the time – be they commercial, perceptual, psychological or aesthetic. Like many other European immigrant artists, Frederick Kiesler brought an enormous artistic background with him to America and – in spite of financial difficulties – was able to develop his ideas and concepts further and move, initially, into the area of furniture design and the discipline of show-window dressing, which at that time was still in its infancy.

In 1930 when Kiesler published his book *Contemporary Art Applied to the Store and its Display*[3] on the role of contemporary art and its effect upon consumer culture, the American economy was at a low point and the adoption of European art was still afforded little publicity. In the years of the Great Depression after 1929, increasing competitive pressure compelled trade and industry in America to have an intense preoccupation with the needs and wishes of their consumers, and creative concepts and new strategies were demanded in the areas of production, presentation and marketing.[4] In 1925 the *Exposition Internationale des Arts Décoratifs et Industriels Modernes* took place in Paris. This uncovered the incongruity between the achievements of the art of the avant-garde and the artistic forms of expression in the related arts, which had up to that print been lacking and which Kiesler had criticised. According to his view the most important aim must be to integrate production processes and aesthetic demands uniformly in the production and presentation of goods, as well as to redefine the relationship between the observer/consumer and the goods/displays.[5]

Even if the art deco style, widespread in America, developed after the Paris exhibition, the aesthetic of the modern trend, based upon reduction, at first only slowly took hold. In the introduction to *Contemporary Art Applied to the Store and its Display* Kiesler declared, 'The arts – Painting, Sculpture, Architecture – are the sources of the "applied" arts', and 'careful consideration will show that the "applied" arts are the link between daily life and the fine arts'.[6] He talks about the importance of the commercial market for art and defines their relationship to one another as walking together so that 'Contemporary Art reached the masses through the Store. The department store was the true introducer of modernism to the public at large.'[7] Later he expounds, 'The Department store acted as the interpreter for the populace of a new spirit in art. Here was the art gaining acceptance not through slow fostering of its theories and principles in academies and art schools, but simply by planting its creations down in the commercial marts.'[8]

The first chapter of the book is also dedicated to art. Kiesler gives a pregnant summary of the important representatives from different sectors – painting, sculpture and architecture – of the European avant-garde. He calls for the aesthetic principles of contemporary art to be applied to the design and dressing of show windows, recommends that show windows be created like pictures and argues, 'Asymmetry is

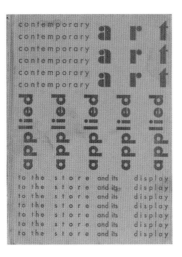

Frederick Kiesler **Contemporary Art Applied to the Store and its Display** 1930

dynamic – The rhythm which results from asymmetry is mobile and kinetic. Therefore if rightly composed, it directs the eye straight to the point to which you wish it directed. In this case it would be to your merchandise.'[9]

In addition there are examples of European and American shop entrances as well as show-window displays or presentations of goods by Mies van der Rohe and Lucie Rie,[10] by Norman Bel Geddes, Donald Deskey, Bruno Paul, the Reimann school from Berlin and the London Arundell Studios. Also exhibited here are Kiesler's show-window displays for the New York fashion house Saks-Fifth Avenue. His pleading for the use of modern means of presentation, which he acquires from analysis of abstract art, is manifested in two quite different but, at the same time, very innovative displays: asymmetry, radical reduction in shape and colour, simplicity of means and a minimum of articles on exhibition.[11] One is an extremely elegant display in which Kiesler shows nothing more than a fur coat and a pair of gloves, draped on a chair – in the background there is an enormous, monochrome wall, which moves rhythmically through the normally partitioned show window.[12] For the other display window, a *Junior Apparel Display*, Kiesler designed a flexible wall out of right-angled, square and round shapes, in which articles were placed – similar to a seed tray – or whose sections were opened to and exhibit the display window dummies behind.[13]

Going beyond the formal criteria, in *Contemporary Art Applied to the Store and its Display* Kiesler analyses important aspects of perceptual psychology as an introduction for designers and managers. In his concepts Kiesler always seeks complete solution arrangements, which place the human being in the centre and take his needs into account. He concerns himself with the human's 'psychological function' and

seems to pursue the same ideals that he had wanted to make possible in his theatre concepts of the 1920s:[14] the dissolution of the boundaries between stage and auditorium; the inclusion of the spectator in the scenery.[15] Kiesler re-defines the relationship between art and the beholder, and at the same time draws advantages from it for consumer culture. His marketing thoughts anticipate our modern advertising strategies: it is no longer a question of products but – freely interpreted – of the philosophy of a world of goods, which becomes acquired during the purchase: 'Create Demand. You must stimulate desire. That is why show windows, institutional propaganda, and advertising were created and why their importance is continually increasing.'[16]

Kiesler's conception for the department stores of the future were interactive, kinetic show windows, which should present selected articles to the passer-by by means of a push-button. He had in mind mechanical sales devices – 'Sales Robots'[17] – which would show the customer short films about the articles and expound upon their qualities and advantages. The window display transmitted in this way works 'with sensitized panels which will act as receiving-surfaces for broadcasted pictures'.[18] This idea stems from the concept of the *Telemuseum* for a model apartment, which Kiesler put to the Société Anonyme back in 1926.[19] In it he conceived the idea that 'through the dials of your Teleset you will share in the ownership of the world's greatest art treasures'.[20] Friedrich Kiesler succeeded in outgrowing early techniques of window display and in transferring the aesthetic principles and achievements of contemporary art to the area of window dressing. With his vision of the show window as a kinetic theatre or as an interactive projection cinema, he created whole concepts, the strategies of which still work innovatively today, indeed even in an utopian manner.

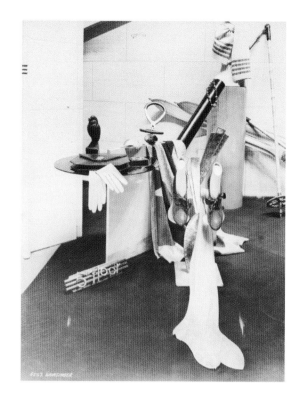

Frederick Kiesler **Window Display** 1927–28

1 F. Kiesler, 'Some Notes on Show Windows', undated typescript, Austrian Frederick and Lillian Kiesler Privat Foundation. Vienna, p.3.

2 For Kiesler's biography, see Dieter Bogner et al., *Friedrich Kiesler 1890–1965*, Vienna: Löcker Verlag, 1988.

3 *Contemporary Art Applied to the Store and its Display*, New York: Brentano's 1930 (1939), p.130.

4 'The competition for customer attention among the shop owners in New York was perhaps more intense than in any other major city … Even during the Depression, new shops were continually opening and the old ones were redesigned. Fifth Avenue maintained its prestige as a shopping street through the interwar years, yet its character changed dramatically', R.A.M. Stern, G. Gilmartin and T. Mellins, *New York 1930: Architecture and Urbanism between the Two World Wars*, New York: Rizzoli 1994, p.293.

5 Nina Schleif, 'Künstlerschaufenster, Eine Untersuchung am Beispiel Friedrich Kiesler', unpublished.

6 Kiesler, *Contemporary Art*, p.14

7 Ibid. p.66.

8 Ibid. p.66.

9 Ibid. p.106.

10 Lucie Rie was not mentioned by name and her presentations were frequently falsely published under the name of Mies van der Rohe.

11 Typologically one can establish a reference to De Stijl and Theo van Doesburg's contra-compositions.

12 'In this window of Saks-Fifth Avenue, the rule of simplicity is realized in a high measure. One sees only a chair, over which a coat and a pair of gloves have been thrown, displayed against a vast background. The background is of a neutral uniform gray, the coat is black velvet with a white fur collar, the gloves are also white, the cushion of the chair red, the wood of the chair gray', Kiesler, *Contemporary Art*, p.25.

13 Frederick Kiesler, *The Modern Show Window and Store Front*, New York: Bretano's 1929, as a short advertisement for the publication of *Contemporary Art*, pt.2, ch.5, Austrian Frederick and Lillian Kiesler Privat Foundation, Vienna.

14 *W.U.R.* 1922, *Raumbühne* 1924 and *Leger-und Trägersystem* 1924.

15 Kiesler was concerned here not only with a formal interpretation of the auditorium as theatre stage, but much more with the conversion of dynamic display windows, designed in accordance with the latest technical achievements, in order to create direct contact between the passer-by and the show window. 'The direct contact between

Frederick Kiesler and Display Furniture 1927–28

such a display stage and the passerby has been anticipated by the newest stage

direction where contact between actor and audience is sought', Kiesler,

Contemporary Art, pp.110–11.

[16] Ibid. p.79.

[17] Ibid. p.120.

[18] Ibid.

[19] Kiesler reports (ibid p.121) that he put forward the *Telemuseum* in 1926 to the

Société Anonyme (Katherine Dreier and Marcel Duchamp) for an exhibition in

the Brooklyn Museum.

[20] Ibid.

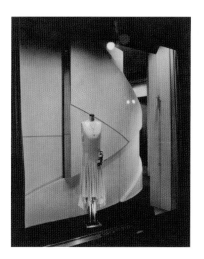  

Frederick Kiesler **Window Displays for Saks Fifth Avenue** 1927–28

Umbo **Untitled (Slippers)** 1928–29

Merchandise Temptress:
The Surrealistic Enticements of
the Display Window Dummy

Katharina Sykora

Light and colour and glamour radiate from thousands of display windows. Like invisible galleries of a gigantic exhibition, an uninterrupted series of huge plate glass windows, behind which luxury, fashion and taste have laid out their enticing advertising material, accompanies the pedestrian.[1]

According to Georg Simmel, the metropolis of modern times is shaped by an imperceptible movement: the circulation of money. Calculable only superficially, this movement remains abstract. It expresses itself only in part and indirectly through the outward merchandisable character of objects and human beings.[2] Jacques Boulanger describes how the metropolitan passers-by slowly began to adapt to this economic control circuit during the 1920s and 1930s: 'With the *flâneur*s mingled passers-by in a hurry, people going about their business, who were only there to sell, to buy, to do business.'[3]

Walter Benjamin also observes how the *flâneur* of the nineteenth century, with his unfocused longing for an unexpected (erotic) encounter, gives way to the modern phenomenon of the passer-by. For the latter the street is a place for doing business.[4] Yet here, too, the seductress is in evidence. The display windows of the cities, those entrance doors to the world of goods, transparent to the street, are populated by ideal embodiments of femininity: the display window dummies. They signal availability, but only for money. And what they promote are the goods, which they themselves symbolise. The display window is not only the threshold but the visual model of the merchandising machinery and the artificial mannequins its agents. They transport the smart passers-by into a very special form of street intoxication: a buying frenzy.

In the context of the modern metropolis, display windows are developing into a specific space configuration. They gradually replaced the wooden display cases fitted with small windows, which were once placed in front of open sales arches, and they now draw the attention through large glass windows directly into their stage-like displays, 'peopled' by the artificial mannequins. They thus become competitive with other places of visual desire, like the museum and the theatre. 'One no longer enjoys spectacles of applied art solely in the exhibitions of our salons, in the stage settings of our theatres,' it was stated back in 1906, 'but on the streets of the major cities. The street walls, in times past a strongly isolating bulwark, have now become transparent, vitreous, permeated with light, presenting colourful stages, changing panoramas.'[5]

Perviously it was the sales ladies themselves who promoted the goods. Now the display window dummies have replaced them. While the display window was perfected to be the 'mirror of reality, as the mirror of the passer-by',[6] its protagonist, the tailor's dummy, was developed into the naturalistic wax mannequin with real hair and languishing gaze from blue, brown or green eyes. The indirect potential for seduction transfers itself from the real woman to her artificial double. The attraction of these artificial seductresses is invoked in countless essays and novels of the period. It is due to an illusionistic approximation to reality, which bonds the dummies back to their model, the real woman. For the figures in the display windows are the spitting image of their doubles in the street:

The fashionable display window plagiarises life, only by so doing can it nowadays teach what is to be worn and how it is to be worn, only thus tempt one to purchase, which makes the imitation possible ... It should, however, also entertain. Therefore the dummies must be

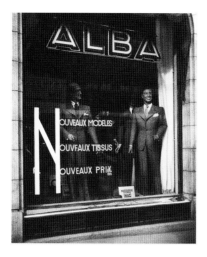

Germaine Krull **Untitled** Paris, 1927–28

interesting in the sense of the current ideal of beauty, be interesting also ... in the charm that they breathe and exude. True, as with all standardisation, which production necessitates, they are copies of some individual reality and, therefore, many a fashionable lady ... certainly finds her counterfeit in the display window. But the crowd sees merely the type and thinks that to look like that is the ideal – and, consciously or unconsciously, it copies the copy. The display window dummy as educator, the display window as a creative institute ... thus do humans, who accompany it, come into being![7]

Since the 1920s photography has made itself an accomplice of this seduction in that it increases the potential of both the iridescent status of the artificial mannequin; between 'genuine' woman and deceptive double, and the ambivalent topography of the display window. If the decoration of the display window itself draws the genuine gaze through the pane of glass towards the dummies and the goods, whilst denying haptic contact, the photographic picture of the display window has a similarly confusing game for the observer with the transparency of its camera lens. What is exhibited also seems to be within reach in the photographic picture and to stand in front of our eyes as if it were alive, however, at a second glance the commodity or figurine 'reveals itself' to be merely a reference to something absent. If the aesthetic staging of the display window and photography combine together, their potential for seduction can thereby be twice as great:

But there is also something uncanny about these dummies, which are so similar to humans, that, *photographed, for example*, one can hardly distinguish them from a living being, from flesh and blood ... One ought not to approach them too closely mentally, not allow one that they offer and their function of becoming the means to an end.[8]

Such literary incantations are clear indicators that for the male passer-by a new female figure of fascination has developed – the modern display window dummy – as dangerous as the unknown woman was to the *flâneur* in the nineteenth century.

It is not only the ambiguous figure of the display window dummy that imparts its economic and erotic seductive power to the display window, but also its ambiguous position. The display window marks the threshold over which the city's interior – equivalent to the private interior of a bourgeois dwelling, with all its feminine connotations, where, according to Benjamin, things escape from the circulation of goods[9] – is crossed by the urban exterior of the street, previously reserved for the artistic *flâneurs* and sexually ambivalent, potentially available women. In the modern metropolis the display window feeds alternately on both layers of space and meaning: the erotic promise of being available for purchase and the protected, intimate idyll, where things and humans apparently lose their mercantile character. The display window makes possible the fading in and out of both illusions: an allegedly better world of the private one and the direct financial availability of the public one. That is to say that in the display windows of the large cities the gazes of the passers-by are constantly pulled between the promise of an intimate sphere, which in the act of purchase signals exclusivity, and a public act of exhibition, which shows what is being purchased and at what price.

In the inter-war period numerous male and female photographers in the large European cities, such as Germaine Krull, Otto Umbehr, Josef Albers or Jindřich Štyrský, reflected this ambivalence of the display window aesthetically. In the photographic medium, through their frontal camera positions and depth of focus settings, they adapt and double

Denise Bellon **Mannequin by Marcel Jean** 1938

the fading effect between interior and exterior. The glass of the display window and the camera lens become indistinguishable and the camera simultaneously negates itself and the showcase glass. The optical lens replaces the display window and makes the glass dividing-pane invisible. This is only possible on account of their shared visual transparency. Thus photography itself becomes part of the threshold area and takes over the function of the invisible membrane of glass, which promises direct seizure of the desirable goods/woman and, at the same time, makes this impossible. The display window dummy and the goods for which it acts as an intermediary thus become an increasing source of stimulation through photography. On the one hand the eye is drawn infinitely closer, for nothing pushes its way between the observer and the object being observed. On the other hand dummy and goods are all the more withheld from the spectator. For we can still overcome the barrier of the display window by stepping through the shop door; faced with photography, however, and the pretended availability of the goods, their real absence is all the more evident. Although photography thus replaces the display window and at the same time negates it, it refers back all the more forcefully to the real place of potential fulfilment. In this intricate manner photography becomes the accomplice of the circulation of goods. It absorbs and intensifies the ambivalence of seduction and denial of the display window and of its female figures, yet it also detaches from the real place of happening and itself becomes a mobile substitute for the display window, expanding and refining the rotation of the machinery of desire and purchase.

By placing the seductive display window dummies with the goods offered for sale as pictures in the illustrated magazines, which appear in massive numbers, they become transportable and pass from hand to hand. Their images reach the passer-by everywhere: at the street kiosk, in the café and at home. In so doing the display window photography occupies all urban spaces uniformly, the intimate and the public alike. It no longer simulates the static membrane between interior and exterior, but itself becomes the mobile agent of the osmosis between the two urban areas. Thus display window photography stands at the end of a progression that commenced with the promotion and sale of goods, mostly by women, from the archways, balconies and doorways of the houses. Now, through photography, the apparently true-to-life, ideal sales lady, the modern display window dummy, returns to the houses. Photography becomes a Trojan horse in two senses: under an imperceptible, technical guise it makes the presenter of the goods alive and the goods themselves all the more seductive, while it is also the vehicle with which these enticements are smuggled into spheres of the city previously closed. Thus window-shopping is slowly being subjected to competition, now also in the home.[10]

The Parisian Surrealists, themselves notorious metropolitan *flâneurs*, have sharp-sightedly recognised the seductive potential of the display window dummies and their spatial shifting between interior and exterior, and integrated them in their aesthetic cosmos. The major Surrealist exhibition that opened on 17 February 1938 in the Georges Wildenstein Gallery represented a highpoint in their obsessive dealings with these object-beings, the *êtres-objets* as Dalí described them. In addition to a taxi in the courtyard filled with display window dummies and a main room, which was changed into a 'world in reverse' with pictures, objets d'art and everyday items, a long corridor, lined by sixteen artificial mannequins, entitled *The Most Beautiful Streets of Paris*, attracted particularly widespread attention. Each dummy was transformed by an artist into a surrealistic chimera.[11] In each case a

Denise Bellon **Maurice Henry and his Mannequin** 1938

Denise Bellon **Mannequin by Paul Eluard** 1938

street sign was appliqued onto the walls behind them, which referred to real or fictitious worlds. Alongside these hung placards, drawings and postcards, announcing surrealistic exhibitions and projects. It was the Surrealists' aim to release the 'grand mannequin' from the cages formed by the sales windows and give her back her genuine freedom, about which René Crevel wrote admiringly:

Certainly you know her well, the grand mannequin, this Iris, shimmering with violet, powerful strength, too violet, too powerful to accept bourgeois flattery … She needs gardens other than the flat enclosures of the streets and be they ever so roomy. She is too untamed to submit to the role of innocent presentation of unresponsive attitudes. The exploiters wished to condemn her to a term of imprisonment. But in vain did the icy window panes and the effusive decorations of the façades seek to put a stop to her momentum. Instead of that she is free …[12]

By transporting them into the fictitious area of the 'most beautiful streets of Paris' the Surrealists sought to release the dummies from their function as a fetish of merchandise. At the same time it was precisely this nature of the goods that made the display window figures into erotic, ideal creatures of an unconditionally available femininity and thereby into surreal artistic fetishes. In the eyes of the Surrealists the mannequins' origin in the twilight threshold area of the display window was akin to that of the streetwalkers, who were for sale, and so it is not surprising that Man Ray describes the 'encounter' of the Surrealists with the display window dummies as analogous to a sexual orgy. Their arrangement and preparation become an imagined ravishment and the photographic pictures, which still bear witness to the exhibition, become voyeuristic acts of self-gratification:

In 1937 nineteen young women were abducted from the display windows of the department stores and handed over to the whims of the Surrealists, who immediately began to ravish them, each in his own and unmistakable way and without in the slightest heeding the feelings of the victims, who, however, suffered, with the most charming goodwill, the offensive displaying of their honour that was forced upon them there and this in such a pure way that it increased the stimulation still further, which one of the most active of the partners, a certain Man Ray, realised, who, unbuttoning himself, fetched his apparatus and recorded the orgy, less out of historic interest than in order to succumb to the burning desire.[13]

Thus, in the Surrealism exhibition of 1938 and in its photographic pictures, the 'twilight' function of the display window dummies itself becomes a theme. While the gesture of 'liberating' the artificial mannequins from their cage and releasing them onto the fictitious streets of Paris is tied up with their banishment to the gallery's corridor, the exhibition room itself becomes simultaneously a large display window and a psychic interior. As such it reveals the artificial female bodies to be both commodity and art, that is to say surrealistic and merchandisable objects in equal measure. The threshold area created here, together with the figures that inhabit it, thereby becomes doubly ambivalent, for the male and female visitors share the same terrain as the dummies, a terrain that changes from display window to street strip and gallery.

The lighting that Man Ray devised for the opening of the exhibition heightened the surreal, puzzling nature between interior and exterior, the real and the artificial human being, observers and object-beings, voyeurism and exhibition. It changed the scenery into a daydream and

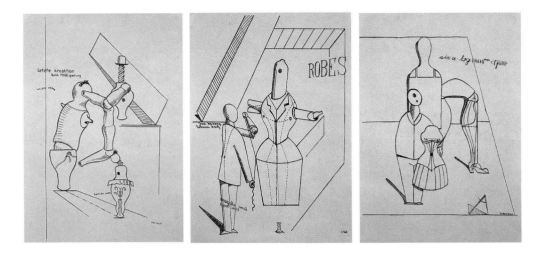

the visit into a peculiar cinematic experience. The exhibition remained unlit and the visitors had to find their way with the aid of a torch. The result was that beams of light, flitting about like will-o'-the-wisps, skimmed over and illuminated the street signs and placards, the display window dummies and visitors indiscriminately. The gallery as inward-facing street and its inhabitants – the dummies/young girls and the visitors/suitors – 'materialised' only incidentally during the short moment that the flashlight was directed upon them. They thereby became pure effects of individual (light) projections. The photographs of the 'nightly encounter' between display window dummies and passers-by became, in the world of the Surrealists, the continued realisation of *beauté couvuesive* and its paradoxical function, *explosante fixe*. Not unlike photography, the wandering spotlights released from the dark time-space continuum of the exhibition – one might also say from the unilluminated world or the optically unconscious – picture segments, that provided more information about the psychic inner worlds of the participants than about an objective exterior world. During the course of their transient 'emanation', the dummies, signs and placards thus acquired a suggestive animation, while the other visitors – blinded by the beam of light from the torches – were frozen for a moment, like waxwork figures.

Numerous male and female photographers have followed this practice of *explosante fixe* and have created whole picture sequences of the surrealist mannequins.[14] In his series of full-length photographs, Raoul Ubac transports the dummies into a kind of parade, which files past before our eyes. The uniform, upright, rectangular cadre surrounds the dummies, as if they were standing in a homogenous row of display boxes. Photography appears as a translucent pane of glass, a two-dimensional display window, in which the artificial woman once again

appears spellbound. Separated from us by the invisible photo membrane, the encounter becomes less threatening. The 'grand mannequin' has apparently returned to her enclosure. And yet her latent mobility remains present, for with her photograph she passes from hand to hand, from exhibition to exhibition, and addresses us with her magic eye again and again.

Unlike Ubac's photographic sequence of the isolated mannequins Man Ray, Denise Bellon and Josef Breitenbach the photographs reproduce the area immediately surrounding the display window figures as if they were dealing with well-furnished living rooms and not with a street. Man Ray's portrait of Dalí's mannequin, for example, with its old-fashioned commode, *aphrodisiacal telephone* and the latter's lobster-shaped receiver, is photographically fitted into its surroundings as if into a surrealistic interior. The 'introversion' of the dangerous street and its erotically seductive inhabitants, however, in no way evokes the appearance of a comfortably ordered bourgeois living room. Instead, the bourgeois order tilts towards bizarre unions of incompatibles and they in their turn tilt in the photographic room towards the claustrophobic. That is to say, when – as in Man Ray's photo of the Dalí dummy – the mistress of the house appears half-naked, half-hidden behind a primitivist mask, it is not merely the telephone but every part of the bourgeois living room that is in danger of becoming a cutting tool, that turns itself against its owner. The photographic picture reveals its mediating function here. Like Snow White's coffin it provides objects to be seen, which – however fantastic they may be – can change directly into something living. Thus, things are placed on display that can be objects of libidinous projections and objects animated for purchase. The photographic copy as 'container of the uncanny' becomes a similarly ambivalent place to the display window. The consistently small

Franz Hessel **'A Dangerous Street'** in **Das Illustrierte Blatt**
no. 24, 15 June, 1929; photographs by Umbo

Germaine Krull **Untitled, Passages – Paris** 1928/1980s

formats of the photographs contribute to this. The turning inwards of the public street area to the interior – also meant as psychic internalisation – is accompanied by a reduction in size. Like two-dimensional doll's houses, the photographs become mirrors of the inner life of their bourgeois beholders. This inner life reveals itself as an invisible prison, which attempts to restrain an unbridled fantasy. This time, however, the beholder is himself sitting in the glass case. There – as exhibited by the Surrealists – he is now also to be seen as an ambivalent and uncanny figure. Fallen prey to the enticements of the merchandise temptress, the surrealistic dummies have finally drawn him into that intermediate world where he is totally lost: into the world between desire and reality, which keeps the imperceptible circulation of art – and the economy as well – in motion.

1 Hans Ostwald, *Kultur-und Sittengeschichte Berlins* , n.d., p.349.

2 Cf. Georg Simmel, 'The Metropolis and Mental Life' (1903), in Simmel on Culture, ed. David Frisby and Mike Featherstone, London: Sage 1997, pp.174–185; Peter Weibel, 'Schaufenster-Botschaften', in *Künstler-Schaufenster*, Graz: Steirischer Herbst 1980, pp.5–17; Katharina Sykora, *Weiblichkeit, Großstadt, Modern: Ernst Ludwig Kirchners Berliner Strassenszenen 1913 bis 1915*, Berlin: Museumspädagogischer Dienst 1996, p.50.

3 Jacques Boulanger, *Sous Louis Phillippe le Boulevard*, Paris 1933, p.11, quoted in Eckhardt Schön, *Strassenrausch, Flanerie und kleine Form: Versuch zur Literaturgeschichte des Flâneurs von 1890–1933*, Berlin: Das Arsenal 1989, p.30.

4 Walter Benjamin, 'Paris – the Capital of the Nieneteenth Century', in Idem., *Charles Baudelaire: A Lyric Poet in the Era of High Capitalism*, London, New York: Verso 1997, p.170.

5 Felix Poppenberg, 'Schaufenster-Regie', in *Arena*, Dec. 1906, p.963.

6 *Schaufenster: Die Kulturgeschichte eines Massenmediums*, ed. Tilman Osterwold,

Stuttgart: Württembergischer Kunstverein 1974, p.8.

7 Ludwig Sternaur, 'Puppen wie Du und ich', in *Velhagen und Klasings Monatshefte*, vol.47, no.1, 1932/3, p.522.

8 Ibid., p.525 (italics are my own).

9 Walter Benjamin, 'Louis Phillippe or the Interior', quoted in 'Paris', pp.167–169.

10 This development away from the display window to the 'private' circulation of goods has increased still more with the development of mail-order catalogues and, particularly, with shopping on the Internet.

11 Only one female artist, Sonia Mossé, exhibited a dummy.

12 René Crevel, 'La Grande Mannequin cherche et trouve sa peau', in *Minotaure*, no. 5, 1935, p.19.

13 Man Ray, *Les Mannequins – La Résurrection des Mannequins*, Paris 1966, quoted in Nicole Parrot, *Mannequins*, Berne: Erpf 1982, p.151.

14 See Katharina Sykora, 'Fotoparade 1938: Die Mannequins des Internationalen Surrealismus-Ausstellung', Idem. in *Unheimliche Paarungen: Androidenfaszination und Geschlecht in der Fotografie*, Cologne: Walther König 1999, pp.168–194.

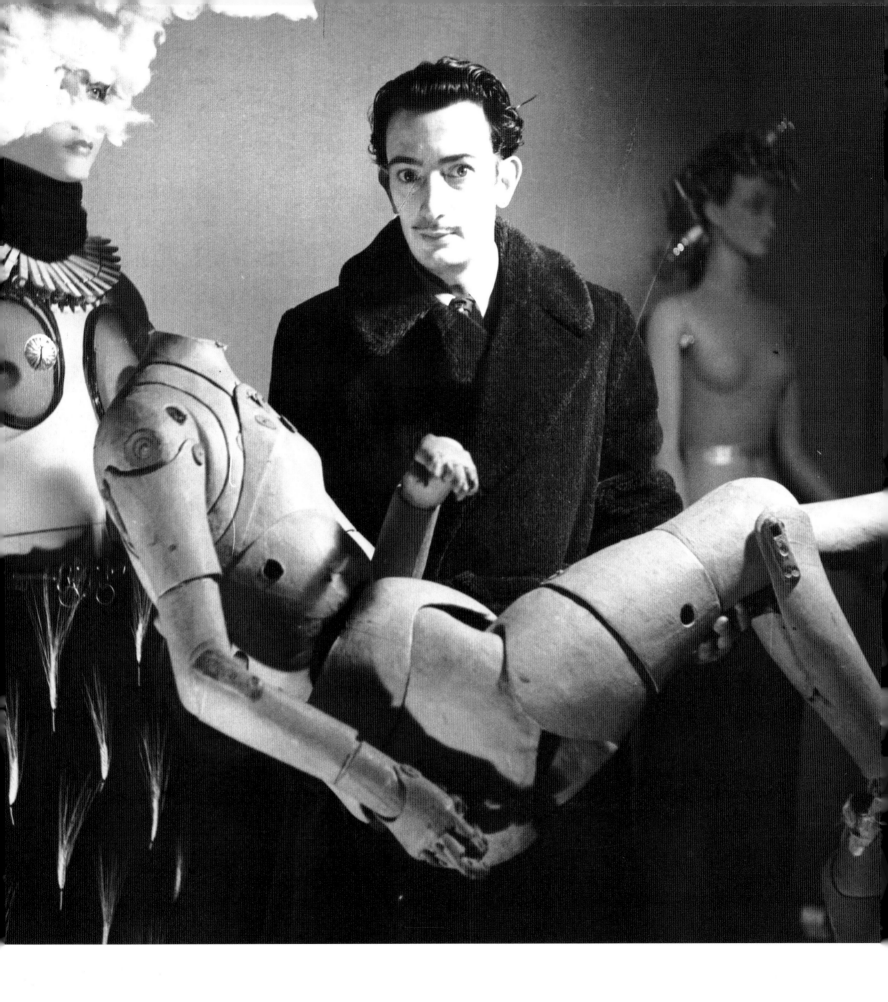

Denise Bellon **Salvador Dalí and his Mannequin** 1938 136

Denise Bellon **Mannequin by Sonia Mossé** 1938

Denise Bellon **Mannequin by Oscar Dominguez** 1938

Man Ray **Mannequin by Espinoza** 1938

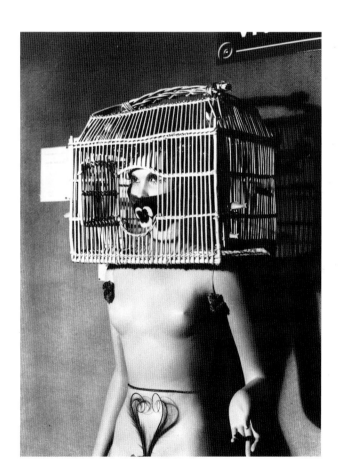

Man Ray **Mannequin by André Masson** 1938

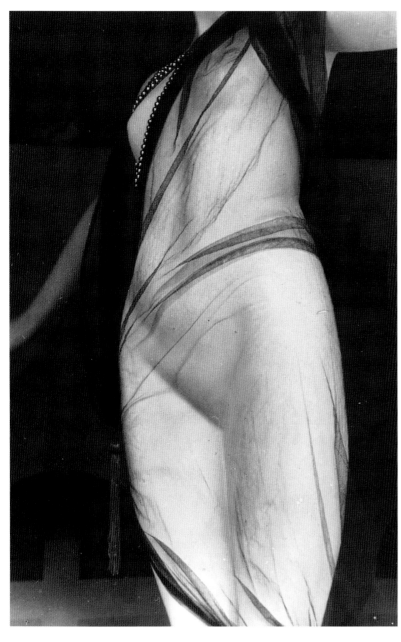

Josef Albers **New Nike** c. 1929

Josef Albers **Silent Gesture** c. 1929

Josef Albers **Untitled (Mannequins)** c. 1930

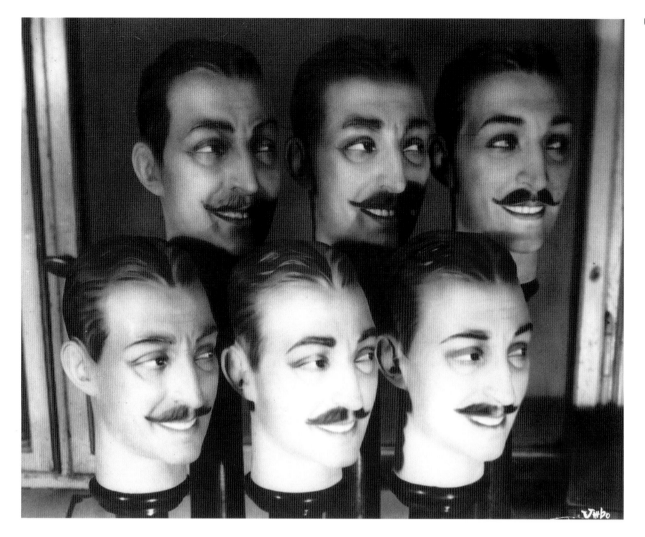

Umbo **Menjou en gros** 1928–29

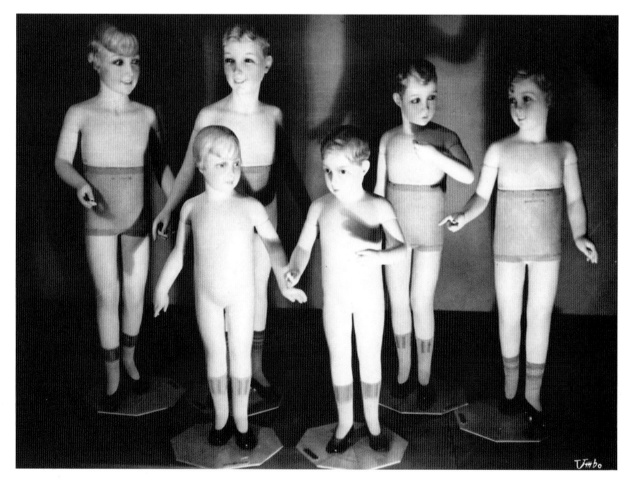

Umbo **Children** 1928–29

Marcel Duchamp, Window display for Breton's **Le Surréalisme et la Peinture**
New York, 1945

Those Objects of Obscure Desires: Marcel Duchamp and his Shop Windows

Thomas Girst

The question of shop windows:.

To undergo

The interrogation by shop windows:.

The necessity of the shop window:.

The shop window proof of existence of the world

outside:. –

      When undergoing the interrogation

by shop windows, you also pronounce

your own ~~judgment~~ Condemnation.

In fact, the choice is a round trip. From

the demands of shop windows, from the

inevitable response to shop windows,

the conclusion is the making of a choice.

No obstinacy, ad absurdum,: in hiding

this coition through a sheet of glass

with one or more of the objects in the

shop window. The penalty consists in

cutting the glass and in kicking yourself

as soon as possession is consummated.

q.e.d. –

Neuilly, 1913

Marchel Duchamp

Note from *À l'Infinitif*, 1967[1]

Marcel Duchamp always did things for a reason. In Rouen, on New Year's Day in 1913, he discovered in the window of the Gamelin confectioner's shop a gigantic 'Broyeuse du Chocolat' dating from the middle of the previous century. After numerous preliminary studies this chocolate grinder reappears as the central point of the lower part of *The Bride Stripped Bare by Her Bachelors, Even* (1915–23). There is no doubt as to why the imposing piece of equipment rears up so dominantly in the area around the bachelors. 'The bachelor grinds his chocolate himself'[2] is what Duchamp previously wrote in his notes accompanying the *Large Glass*, and who can be surprised that the bachelor machinery sets itself in motion to the oscillating noise of the grinder's 'litanies', which also owe a great deal to 'onanism'.[3] The desired bride of the upper region is separated from the nine eager bachelors by three narrow, horizontal panes of glass. A shop window of a wholly special kind, according to Duchamp's notes, it also marks the interface, the horizon between the third and fourth dimension. In a note from 1913, and much later, in 1935, in a first essay by André Breton on the *Large Glass*[4], Duchamp described the three panes of glass as the bride's clothes. However, whether intercourse ultimately takes place between one or more of the bachelors and the bride remains obscure in the highly complicated course of events. For it is only as 'mirrorical return'[5] that the original illuminating gas from the 'eros' matrix'[6] of the bachelors can succeed in penetrating the panes of glass in the form of 'images'[7] of individual drops (rather than the drops themselves!).

We come across Duchamp's reference to the 'mirrorical return' again in an etching from 1964, in which can be seen his urinal *Fountain*, the scandal-evoking 'ready-made' from 1917. The black letters of the French text on the etching – 'An Original Revolutionary Faucet / "Mirrorical return"? / A faucet which stops dripping when nobody is listening to

Marcel Duchamp, Study for
Given: 1. The Waterfall, 2. The Illuminating Gas c. 1947

Marcel Duchamp
Given: 1. The Waterfall, 2. The Illuminating Gas 1945–1966

it'[8] – are intermixed with single red letters, which, read together, spell out the words 'Urinoir' and 'Urine'.[9] Three years prior to the *Fountain*, in his *Box of 1914*, Duchamp recorded, 'one only has: for female the public urinal and one lives by it'.[10] With the exception of the reference to the 'mirrorical return' , the text on the etching refers to a play on words from his film *Anémic Cinéma* of 1926 – produced jointly with Man Ray – in which Duchamp uses the jargon of advertising to offer for sale the product 'lazy hardware' . The text, laid out in a spiral, is printed on a disk revolving in front of the camera: 'Among our articles of lazy hardware we recommend a faucet which stops dripping when nobody is listening to it'.[10] In April 1945, in a shop window of the Gotham Book Mart, New York, designed by Duchamp for the publication of André Breton's volume of poetry *Arcane 17*, he attaches a cast-iron faucet on the right thigh of a headless shop window dummy.[12] The installation's caption was 'Lazy Hardware' . A well-known photograph shows Duchamp's image reflected in the glass of the shop window, his face turned towards the faucet at about the same height. Only about two years later we encounter a comparable portrayal in Duchamp's work: a headless nude, raising her left thigh, stands in the middle of a natural landscape, a waterfall rushing down between her legs. The collage is a preliminary study for Duchamp's last great major work, *Given: 1 The Waterfall / 2 The Illuminating Gas* (1945–66), an installation on which he had secretly worked for more than two decades and which was first revealed in the Philadelphia Museum of Art a year after his death. Looking through two peep-holes in a massive Spanish wooden door, the observer discovers in the foreground a headless, naked woman with legs wide apart lying on branches; in the background a turbulent waterfall murmurs as if reflecting the rays of the sun. References to the shop window for *Arcane 17*, to his early note on the 'public urinal' and to the *Fountain* etching of 1964 all make it clear that the waterfall does not necessarily

have to do with water.[13] After all, back in 1913 Duchamp had described his *Large Glass* as 'a world in yellow'.[14]

Another shop window from 1945 contains clear allusions to *Given*. In November Duchamp designed the display for André Breton's book *Le Surréalisme et la peinture*, which had just appeared at Brentano's in New York – an enlarged edition of a collection of essays on Surrealist painters, first published in 1928 by Gallimard in Paris. Duchamp collaborated on the shop window with the artists Isabelle Waldberg and Enrico Donati, but, as Waldberg informed her husband in a letter dated 10 November 1945, 'Naturally Marcel has done everything, the whole design and the whole execution.'[15] An attached sketch specifies the individual objects in the shop window: on the left a 'mannequin made of wire netting, bought ready-made'; on the right a 'boot with toes painted on by Donati'; and above the 'books' in the middle, 'something of mine under the tent', the tent consisting of 'old strips of paper from Marcel's studio'('papier ... en chute' as it appears in the original).[16]

All the component parts listed by Waldberg are indispensable for a comprehensive discussion of this complex arrangement.[17] Let us, however, confine ourselves to the object in the shop window most neglected so far by research: the sculpture by Isabelle Waldberg, made from twisted wire or branches and found directly under the tent-like paper strips from Duchamp's studio. Less an allusion to the wedding veil of the bride of the *Large Glass*,[18] the 'paperfall' anticipates the waterfall in Duchamp's late work, particularly since the more accurate view of Waldberg's freely suspended sculpture as a skeletal model corresponds in its pose with the preliminary studies and final torso for *Given*. Playing with two pieces of pliable wire during a crossing from America to France back in 1927, Duchamp confided to Julien Levy that he wanted

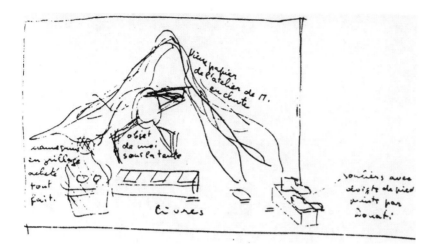

Isabelle Waldberg, drawing of the shop window of André Breton's
Le Surréalisme et la peinture 1945

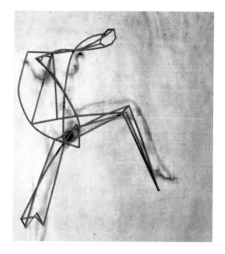

Robert Slawinski, 3-D computer design of Isabelle Waldberg's
sculpture (1945) and Marcel Duchamp's **Given...** (1947) 2001

to construct a 'mechanical female apparatus', a 'soft anatomical machine'.[19] The whole thing, continued Duchamp, should be a 'life-size, articulated dummy', a 'mechanical woman, whose vagina ... [is] possibly self-lubricating and activated from a remote control, perhaps located in the head':[20] his 'machine-onaniste'.[21]

Marcel Duchamp always did things for a reason. If he began work on his assemblage *Given*, kept secret for so long, with two shop windows, which, observed retrospectively, anticipated the programme of his late work, then that must also have had a connection with the early note quoted at the beginning of this essay. For the 'desire' directed at the objects lying behind, there is only 'coitus through a pane of glass'. In the *Large Glass* this dividing wall consists of narrow, horizontal panes; in *Given*, completed four decades later, it is a Spanish door with peepholes, determining the observer's viewpoint. Dating from exactly between the two and providing a critical link are the shop windows of 1945.

[1] From *Marcel Duchamp: In the Infinitive – A Typotranslation by Richard Hamilton and Ecke Bonk of Marcel Duchamp's White Box*, Northend: The Typosophic Society 1999, pp.5-6 (translated from the French by Jackie Matisse, Richard Hamilton and Ecke Bonk).

[2] Michel Sanouillet and Elmer Peterson (eds.), *The Writings of Marcel Duchamp*, New York: DaCapo 1989, p.68. *The Bride Stripped Bare by Her Bachelors, Even* is the title both for the work referred to as the *Large Glass* and for the *Green Box* of 1934, a collection of just under a hundred notes, photos and sketches, intended to explain the mechanisms of the *Large Glass*.

[3] Ibid. p.56.

[4] André Breton, 'Phare de la Mariée', in *Minotaure*, vol.2, no.6, Winter 1935, p.48.

[5] Sanouillet and Peterson (eds.), *The Writings of Marcel Duchamp*, p. 65.

[6] Ibid. p.56.

[7] Ibid. p.65.

[8] Ibid. p.106.

[9] In the same year Duchamp produced the deluxe edition for the *Marcel Duchamp: Ready-mades etc. (1913–1964)* touring exhibition held in Milan. His sketch for *Fountain* appears on the leather binding for each of the 100 volumes, as do the words that later appear on the etching. However, in this instance the letters forming 'Urine' and 'Urinoir' are highlighted not in red but in gold.

[10] Sanouillet and Peterson (eds.), *The Writings of Marcel Duchamp*, p.23.

[11] Ibid. p.106.

[12] Apart from the two shop windows to which reference is made in this essay, Duchamp was employed on the design of at least two others: in January 1943, for Brentano's in

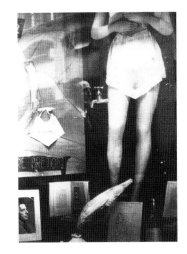

Marcel Duchamp, Shop Window for André Breton's
Arcane 17 New York, 1946 (detail)

New York, he designed, together with André Breton and Kurt Seligmann, the shop window for the publication of *La Part du Diable* by Denis de Rougement (see Arturo Schwarz, *The Complete Works of Marcel Duchamp*, New York: Delano Greenidge 2000, p.768). And on 29 January 1960 Duchamp completed his work on the shop window for Bamberger in Newark, New Jersey, which for the next fortnight advertised the first edition in English of Robert Lebels's *Sur Marcel Duchamp*, published by Grove Press, New York (see Jennifer Gough-Cooper and Jacques Caumont, 'Ephemerides on and about Marcel Duchamp and Rrose Sélavy', in Pontus Hulten (ed.), *Marcel Duchamp: Work and Life*, exh. cat., Cambridge, Mass.: MIT Press 1993. I am indebted to Nina Schleif for the information relating to this last shop window.

[13] I am grateful to Herbert Molderings for drawing attention to the figure of the 'Pisseuse' as a possible connection between 'Lazy Hardware' and the study of *Given* (1947).

[14] Sanouillet and Peterson (eds.), *The Writings of Marcel Duchamp*, p.44.

[15] Patrick Waldberg and Isabelle Waldberg, *Un Amour Acéphale, Correspondance 1940–1949*, Paris: Editions de la Différence 1992, p.331.

[16] Ibid.

[17] See Thomas Girst, 'Duchamp's Window Display for André Breton's *Le Surréalisme et la peinture* (1945)', in *Tout-Fait: The Marcel Duchamp Studies Online Journal*, vol.2, no.4, January 2002 http://www.toutfait.com/issues/volume2/issue_4/articles/girst/girst1.html; also published in German by the Hessisches Landesmuseum in Darmstadt as part of its publication to mark the conference on Duchamp held there on 23–25 November 2001.

[18] See Arturo Schwarz, *The Complete Works of Marcel Duchamp*, New York: Delano Greenidge 2000, p.782.

[19] Julien Levy, *Memoirs of an Art Gallery*, New York: Putnam 1977, p.20.

[20] Ibid.

[21] Ibid. (italics in original).

Marcel Duchamp, Shop Window for André Breton's **Arcane 17** New York, 1946

The Consumer Article in the Art World: On the Para-Economy of American Pop Art

Michael Lüthy

In the 1960s art appeared to rid itself in an offensive manner of everything that up until then could have been regarded as part of its concept. Beauty, exclusiveness, individuality, significance, artistry, complexity, depth, originality were at a stroke no longer mandatory categories. It was not the defence of artistic autonomy, which immediately before was still held in esteem by American and European Abstraction, but its abandonment that was promoted to the artistic programme. American Pop Art manifested the radical shift in position in a particularly striking manner. As art in this sphere began to approach its 'other being'– consumption and its banal products – an important taboo seemed to be broken. Both appeared to merge into one another, not only by reason of their choice of subject but also because of the production of pieces in large numbers, as happened in the case of the so-called 'multiples'. Nevertheless, Pop Art was only truly 'popular', as its name suggests, to a limited extent. 'Popular' was an iconographic reference to the everyday phenomena of the modern world of goods; what remained 'unpopular' about it, however, was the fact that the phenomena acted thematically against its own matter-of-factness. Pop Art was in no way a mere reflection of reality, but a transfer operation that took place between thing and likeness – or, as Roy Lichtenstein formulated it, a 'significant interaction'.[1] Something was becoming visible for Pop Art to combine with the contemporaneously emerging conceptual art: artists not only regarded themselves as producers of artefacts, but simultaneously questioned the cultural, institutional and discursive 'frameworks', in which the production and reception of art took place. Thus, the apparent convergence of art and consumer goods in no way caused the old differences between art and non-art – between appearance and being, the aesthetic and the functional, the 'superficial' and the 'profound' – to disappear, but allowed them to break out anew and in a particularly explosive manner. It was precisely Pop Art, which appeared to strip art of its attributes, that, because of its reflexivity and conceptuality, contributed significantly to the fact that art could assert itself in a period of change and even radically renew itself. But this took place only through a radical shift of paradigms. If Cézanne, according to his famous dictum, worked in parallel with nature, the Pop artists did so in parallel with contemporary consumer culture. At the same time they recognised that the argument with it required not only a new spectrum of themes, but above all a decisive new definition of artistic production, one that transcended the traditional craftsman's trade. To that end, however, they needed to retain a pre-requisite significant for art, the equivalence of what was portrayed and the method of portrayal, content and form.

'I find it quite natural', said Claes Oldenburg, 'to work under the conditions of American technical civilisation. I know every effect, every result of the technical working processes and I believe I can control them.'[2] However prosaic it may sound, Oldenburg at the same time believed obstinately in the old dream of a reconciliation between art and life. He wished to attain it through the reconciliation of human being and thing. 'This elevation of sensibility above bourgeois values will (hopefully) destroy the notion of art and give the object back its power. Then the magic inherent in the universe will be restored and people will live in sympathetic religious exchange with the objects surrounding them. They will not feel so different from these objects, and the animate/inanimate schism will be mended.[3] Oldenburg criticised the alienation of everyday life in general just as much as the specific alienation of art from everyday life. In exchange he offered a 'shapeless'

Claes Oldenburg, Business Cards for **The Store** 1961

universalism, which placed everything in a relationship with every-thing else, his ideal picture of an 'erotical-political-mystical' art, as he described it.[4]

In 1961 he opened a shop, *The Store*, in his workshop in New York's Lower East Side, in the wider context of which the 'Lingerie Counter' also came into being.[5] The shop was not only the point of sale, but also the place of production. Its stock covered the whole spectrum of everyday needs, just like the items in the over-filled shops in the neighbourhood, from foodstuffs through clothes and shoes to writing materials. Everything was made from the same material – plaster-covered muslin – and painted in strong colours, as if in an Expressionist style.[6] Oldenburg's portrayal of reality worked on several levels. First of all it related to the everyday object itself, but of greater importance to him, however, was the 'imitation' of the different fields of activity, which allowed him to become one with the pastry-cook, tailor, bridal wear designer, butcher, sign-writer and shoe-maker. As salesman it also fell to him to distribute what had been produced. The 'political' dimension, on which he set his sights, consequently lay in a return to the non-alienated craftsman's existence of a pre-capitalist economy in the midst of an American society based on the division of labour. In the art world of *The Store* there was not a single thing that he could not potentially have been able to produce and sell – though at the price of the transference of the things into art, of the individual arti-cles into non-consumable and dysfunctional statues, of the shop as a whole into an 'environment'.

As has already been mentioned, all objects were made from the same material, whether it was a question of an envelope, a sausage or a gym shoe. The surfaces were also exactly the same; everything exhibited the same fissured surface, smoothed by the glossy paint; everything appeared slightly deformed, melted on and lumpy. Some of the objects depicted Oldenburg in relief. They shared part of an unspecified back-ground, in front of which they presented themselves and appeared as if broken off from a larger, imaginary context. The continuum, which began to evolve between the things, did not originate from the objects themselves – what have gym shoes and sausages in common after all – but from the unchanging three-dimensional treatment. It trans-formed the variance of the objects and materials into a cosmos 'of the same flesh'. *The Store* was, as Oldenburg said, a 'super texture super-collage', a far-reaching and encroaching, pulsating organism.[7]

Oldenburg's osmotic world of goods loosened the relationship between signs and the designated, in their uniform shapelessness, the individ-ual things were suddenly several things at once. The notices and drawings about *The Store* contain lists of form-analogies, which imme-diately allow the order that they purport to create, to collapse. According to Oldenburg the following 'equate with each other': 'Hair and Bacon; Earrings, Airplane Wheels, Brassiere and Breasts; Obelisk and Ironing Board; Frankfurter in Bun, Airplane and rolled Newspaper; Hat, Lips, Banana Split and Gun; etc.'[8] The 'de-formation' of individual objects and the dissolving of their utilisation connections open up novel connec-tion possibilities for totally disparate things. 'The erotic or the sexual is the root of "art", its first impulse', said Oldenburg. 'Today sexuality is more directed, or here where I am in America at this time, toward substitutes, for example, clothing rather than the person, fetishistic stuff, and this gives the object an intensity and this is what I try to project.'[9] The desire of the mythical sculptor Pygmalion was directed towards his marble sculpture of a young woman; Aphrodite took pity on him, animated her and gave her to Pygmalion as his wife.

Claes Oldenburg, Interior of **The Store**
(Sketch for a Poster, Not Executed), 1961

Oldenburg's desire is directed towards ice-cream cones and micro-phones, towards swimwear and pieces of roast meat. The 'bride', also on sale in *The Store*, was neither more physical nor more desirable than the gym shoe, the same sexual energy being present in everything. Thus, not only did Oldenburg bring about the collapse of the capitalist system in terms of the division of labour but also the pointed fetishi-sation of the world of goods, which for marketing purposes enhances saleability. His occupation of the object world was as complete as it was consistent in its intensity. 'Store: 1. Eros. 2. Stomach. 3. Memory. Enter my Store', is how he invites us in *Store Days*.[10]

Oldenburg approached his goal of the convergence of art and life by allowing their energies to merge into one another. His 'animism', which gives life to things, follows in the tradition of sculpture, which since time immemorial has worked with the dialectic of inanimate material and living, 'animated' effect. He coupled this energy, along with the desire structure of the fetishism of goods, to his 'erotical-political-mystical' art. Oldenburg's *Store* neutralised the tradition of plastic art in that he retained it and at the same time liquidated it. The 'anthro-pomorphising' of the world of things continued the tradition of plastic art, which for centuries had dedicated itself almost exclusively to the human figure. At the same time it was released from this thematic fixation, which, from the point of view of a living world shaped by things, had begun to become outmoded.

Together with other artists in 1964, Oldenburg participated in a New York gallery project, *The American Supermarket*. Like his *Store* it was based on the idea of transferring the irritating closeness between art and goods to a presentation and sales context, but aimed at the cool, hygienic 'look' of a modern outlet. Here, too, the transfer affected the room itself, as it oscillated between art and non-art. It was entered through a turnstile built by Richard Artschwager, and the 'wares' of dif-ferent 'producers' were available from freezers and shelves. On offer, among other things, were Tom Wesselmann's oversized turkey-cock relief made from plastic, a picture by Roy Lichtenstein of the same subject matter, and Robert Watts' chrome steel eggs, wax tomatoes and plaster pumpernickels. Warhol used the situation for if not his best, in the light of the borderline between art and non-art, produced and made problematical by Pop Art, certainly his most pertinent work. Under a silk-screen diptych of two Campbell's cans was a stack built with original cans of soup, signed and declared to be art or 'Warhols', costing many times the normal price. Anyone who decided to buy such a can had – exaggerating slightly – to be schooled in concept art and already to have passed the acid test of endorsing Duchamp's ready-mades. Warhol split the artificial production up into the separate production of a non-artistic object and its subsequent transformation, without alteration, into a work of art. While the signing de-functionalised the can of soup and while, conversely, enjoyment of the soup would have meant 'destruction of art', it was clear that the production of goods and the production of art were counterbalanced. Thus Warhol's trans-formation affected the thing itself to a lesser extent and the thinking about it to a much greater one – through notions of art, institutions, authorship etc. It was precisely the indistinguishableness of art and non-art that allowed the differences between artworks and goods to be set against each other in such an intransigent manner.

If *The American Supermarket* blurred the boundary between the dis-tribution of art and goods in an amusing and playful manner, Christo's *Store Fronts*, shown in the same year and for the first time in New York, gave rise to another, 'darker' form of functional subversion: an abrupt

Claes Oldenburg **Sketch for a Scene in a Performance** 1961

Claes Oldenburg, Notebook page **Suspended Bi-plane** 1962

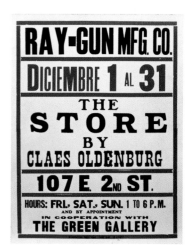

Claes Oldenburg, Poster for **The Store** 1961

stop to the movement of goods. The first wooden *Store Fronts* were created from pieces that Christo had found on demolition sites in the Lower East Side, where the old hardware shops had given way to more rational and more profitable sales structures. The new compilations of debris for *Store Fronts* in gallery rooms led to a complex spatial-functional de- and re-contextualisation. The paradox of the presentation of an architectonic exterior in an inside room was made even more pointed by the fact that the interior of the exterior in question was hung across it – whereby the situation became still more complicated since it was merely a question of façades and the interior did not actually exist. Thus, what was hanging was not something but nothing, and it became less a question of screening than of visualising, in order to produce the seam between what was present and what was absent. The hanging revealed first of all the necessity for the displays of long-vanished shop windows to remain invisible. At least Christo's early work – which decisively oversteps the context of Pop Art, possibly does not even belong to it – has to cross the 'tragic' trend reminiscent of Surrealism, the hiding and burying of things and the desire to see death and Eros.

Not hung of necessity, however, was the shop-window front of the New York department store where Warhol staged his first 'art exhibition' in 1961 – which, nevertheless, remained totally unnoticed. Here he presented five of the first works produced following his decision to give up his successful career as a commercial artist. They were based upon advertisements and comic strips, and provided, since no gallery would show them, the background for clothes dummies. It was a transitional moment in several respects. The art exhibition in the display window marked precisely the interface between Warhol's two lives as a commercial designer and free artist, the precarious intermediate stop between

department store and gallery. The pictures not only stood behind the dummies, which were presenting the latest 'costumes', but themselves revolved around the theme of metamorphosis. In two of them were painted advertisements for nose operations, hair colouring and muscle building, in three the comic figures Superman, Popeye and Little King – fantasy figures, all of which possessed the potential to rise from a humdrum and petit bourgeois persona to an ideal, bursting with vigour.

While Warhol's success as a commercial artist rested upon a pointedly intimate and characteristic trade style, he found his artistic style exactly the reverse and thoroughly paradoxical in its apparently impersonal approach. It led him to the pictorial language of the serialised, reproductive silk-screen pictures. Here Warhol tested the tension between the singular and the mass-produced, repetition and difference. The themes that interested him were things, which no individual had made and yet which possessed individuality, which were 'unique' although they existed in large numbers: Campbell's soup cans, regarded as 'classical' because their label design had remained unchanged for decades, or the flashy boxes in which 'Brillo' pads were packaged. Warhol's first method of dealing pictorially with such phenomena was the elimination of everything handwritten, which the first pictures definitely still showed. It gave way to a method of production that adjusted to the manufacture of the things to such an extent that the printing of a packaging carton only differed from the printing of Warhol's reproduction in that the former was undertaken by a machine while for the latter Warhol was himself the 'machine'. Not only did the object assume a reproductive and serial identity, Warhol's pictures and sculptures matched this.

How essential this parallelism of subject matter and production form was becomes clear when one compares Warhol with, for example,

Andy Warhol **Del Monte** 1964

Andy Warhol **Brillo** 1964

Wayne Thiebaud. Thiebaud, who considered 'painting is more important than art',[11] attempted in pictures such as the *Cake Counter* of 1963 to continue a great painting tradition in the light of contemporary aesthetic phenomena – and thus acquired the nickname 'the Chardin of the cake shops'.[12] To call him a Pop artist because of his choice of motif would be to do justice neither to Pop Art nor to Thiebaud, as his pictures would then have to appear as variants of earlier work, though inevitably backward in their handiwork. Down to the individual brush stroke, Thiebaud's reverence for Morandi reveals itself, an artist with whom no one from Pop (or Proto-Pop) wished to speak because of the fact that he painted banal bottles. Like Morandi, Thiebaud created an atmosphere of contemplative peace, which sought to capture the 'quiet life' of things, while the pastose brushwork round the objects served to evoke both their materiality as well as their 'fraternal' togetherness. The contrast with Warhol's diptych on *Campbell's Soup Cans (Chicken with Rice, Bean with Bacon)* of 1962 could not be more distinct, not only on account of the absence of the painted object but also from the point of view of composition. The two cans, one on each table, float without any atmospheric embedding on the white primed surface. Even the most miniscule indication of location, which no still life omits, is left out: the horizontal line, which depending upon the picture means a desk or the edge of a room. Whilst every connection relating to situation is missing, there still remains the question as to why the right can is so much smaller than the left one. Without place or time, without reference to the picture surface and the beholder and without making any determinable statement, the simultaneously banal and epiphanic cans remain encapsulated in nothingness.

The ambivalence between singularity and mass-production that Warhol sought has left the argument still unresolved as to whether his view of the new world of things turned out to be subversive or affirmative, pessimistic or optimistic. The question ought for that reason to be unanswerable, because Warhol in a 'scandalous' manner seemed to find no difference between free choice and necessity, subjectivity and standardisation. 'I'm just the opposite,' said Warhol, ' I don't want it to be essentially the same – I want it to be *exactly* the same.'[13] The Campbell's cans and the Brillo boxes announced that Warhol wanted it just as it already was and wanted to make it just like it had already been made. That was Warhol's caustic test of subjectivity and, simultaneously, what made him 'American' in such a provocative way.

1   Bruce Glaser, 'Oldenburg, Lichtenstein, Warhol: A Discussion', *Artforum*, vol.4, Feb. 1966, p.22.

2   Friedrich Bach, 'Interview with Claes Oldenburg', *Das Kunstwerk*, vol.28, no.3, 1975, p.13 (translation my own).

3   Claes Oldenburg, *Store Days, Documents from* The Store *(1961) and* Ray Gun Theatre *(1962)*, selected by Claes Oldenburg and Emmett Williams, photographs by Robert R. McElroy, New York: Something Else Press 1967, p.60.

4   Ibid. p.39.

5   The 'Lingerie Counter' was created in 1962 as a display window item for the New Realists' exhibition at the Sidney Janis Gallery in New York, the first general display of the nascent Pop Art; see letter from Oldenburg to the Schirn Kunsthalle in Frankfurt, dated 17 April 2002.

6   In so doing Oldenburg crossed Abstract Expressionism with Pop Art: 'Lately I have begun to understand action painting, that old thing, in a new, vital and peculiar sense – as corny as the scratches on a New York wall and by parodying its corn I have (miracle) come back to its authenticity. I feel as if Pollock is sitting on my shoulder, or rather crouching in my pants!' *Store Days*, p.13.

7   Ibid. p.54.

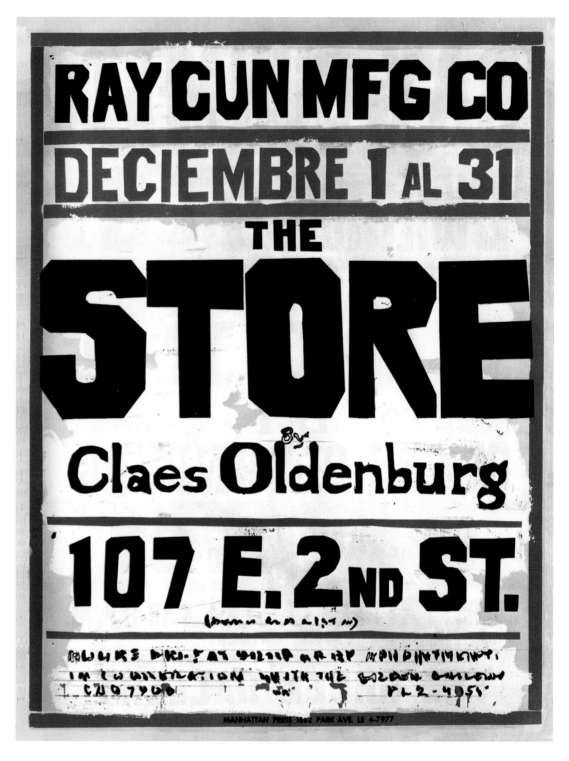

Claes Oldenburg, Poster design for **The Store** 1961

8   Ibid. p.137.

9   Ibid. p.62.

10 Ibid. p.44

11 Wayne Thiebaud, quoted in Adam Gopnik, 'An American Painter', in *Wayne Thiebaud:
    A Paintings Retrospective*, exh. cat., Fine Arts Museums of San Francisco 2000, p.40.

12 Paul Richard, 'Luscious Realism: Thiebaud, Making the Mouth Water', *Washington
    Post*, 16 Dec. 1992, quoted in Steven A. Nash, 'Unbalancing Acts: Wayne Thiebaud
    Reconsidered', in *Wayne Thiebaud*, p.12.

13 Warhol Andy and Pat Hackett, *POPism: The Warhol Sixties*, New York:
    Harcourt Brace Jovanovich 1980, p.50.

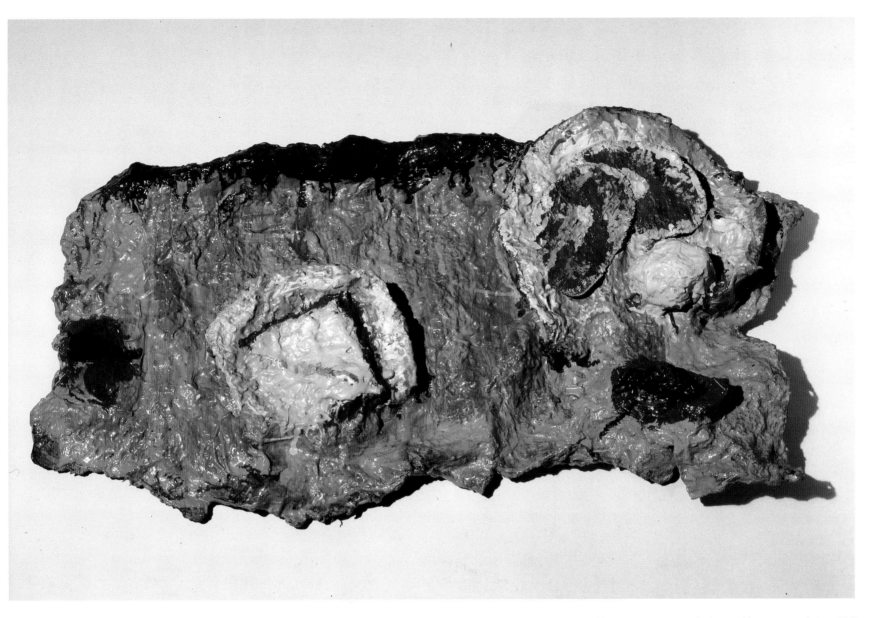

Claes Oldenburg **Counter and Plates with Potato and Ham** 1961

Claes Oldenburg **Lingerie Counter** 1962

Claes Oldenburg **Meats** 1964

Claes Oldenburg **Banana Splits and glaces en degustation** 1964

Wayne Thiebaud **Cake Counter** 1963

Erró **Foodscape** 1964

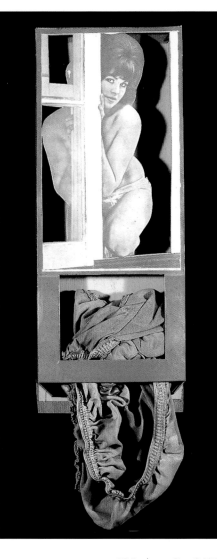

KP Brehmer **Display 15** 1965

KP Brehmer **Box 3** 1966

KP Brehmer **Display 'Advertisement for Miss F'** 1965

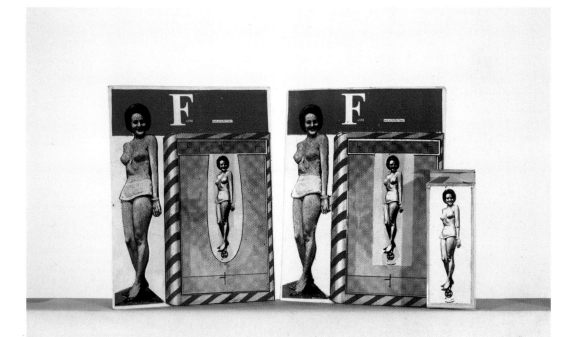

Peter Blake **Toy Shop** 1962

Christo **Pousette (Packed Supermarket Cart)** 1963

162

Christo **Four Store Fronts Corner** 1964–65

Richard Estes **The Candy Store** 1969

Don Eddy **Hosiery, Handbags and Shoes** 1974

Andy Warhol **Giant Size $1.57 Each** 1963

Andy Warhol **Skeletons** 1986

Andy Warhol **Window Display, Cookout Supplies** 1986

Andy Warhol **Drugstore Shelves** 1985–86

Andy Warhol **Hellmann's Mayonaise** 1987

Andy Warhol **Window Display, Last Eight Days** 1984

Andy Warhol **Window Display, Mona Lisa** c. 1985

Andy Warhol **Store Signs** 1984

Andy Warhol **Window Display, Jewelry** 1986

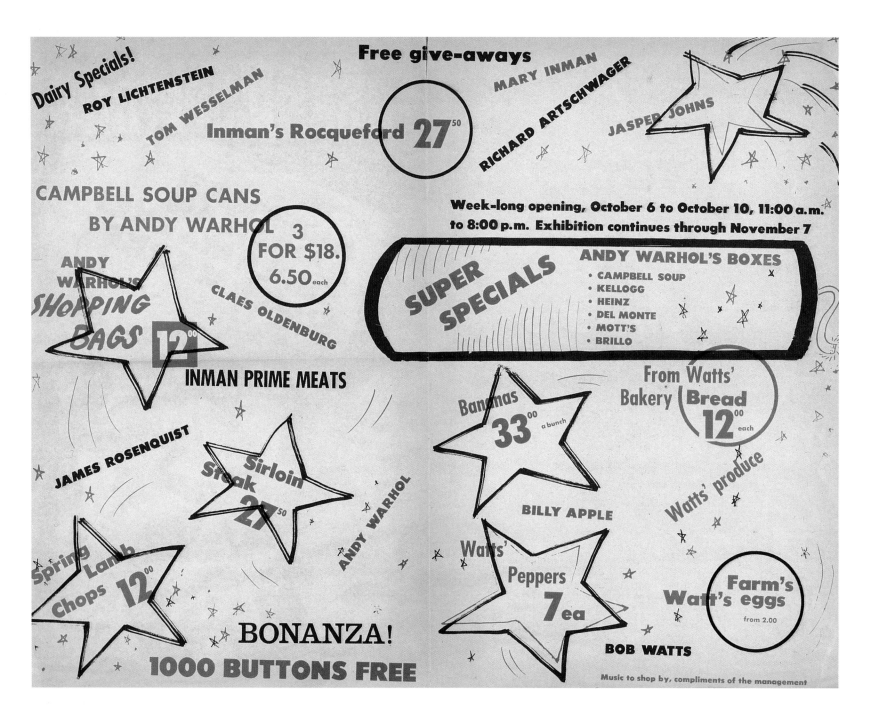

Invitation to **Grand Opening of the American Supermarket** New York, 1964

The American Supermarket

Christoph Grunenberg

On 6 October 1964 a new supermarket opened in a modest space at 16 East 78th Street in New York.[1] Customers entered from the street through a turnstile by Richard Artschwager. The supermarket featured stacks of Campbell's soup cans (signed by Andy Warhol) and Ballantine beer (not signed by Jasper Johns).[2] A neon sign advertised Ballantine beer and illuminated signs directed the customers to the Egg, Canned Fruit, Bread and Fruit aisles. In the rear of the store a large variety of apples, pears, melons and bananas as well as lettuce, tomatoes, peppers and zucchini by Robert Watts were displayed on coloured paper in wooden crates. Muzak played in the background while Paul Bianchini took orders on his grocery pad: '"Pick me out a fresh one, Paul," Robert Fischer, an advertising executive man, said pointing to a box of $12 chrome eggs by Bob Watts.'[3] As the *New York Times* reported, prices were rather 'horrendous', starting with $2 for an egg, $12 for a paper bag with a silk-screened Campbell's Tomato Soup motif by Warhol or a turkey motif by Roy Lichtenstein, $27 for a fake sirloin steak by Mary Inman and going up to $125 for one of Watts' chrome cantaloupes.[4] Business nevertheless was brisk as customers snapped up 'Specials', such as actual Campbell's soup cans signed by Warhol for only $18, occasionally disrupted by shoppers confused about the distinction between real supermarket and art gallery: 'Chic neighborhood women walking by, with or without little dogs, have kept sticking in their heads and asking, "May I come in for a minute?" They hardly ever managed to leave without wanting at least a $15 piece of fruit.'[5]

The driving force behind *The American Supermarket* was artist Ben Birillo, partner with Paul Bianchini in the Bianchini Gallery, who in a four-month period devised the installation, approached artists and produced many of the objects on display. Working closely with him was Dorothy Herzka who met her husband Roy Lichtenstein during the preparation for the show.[6] As Birillo recalls, the idea for *The American Supermarket* originally emerged out of an exhibition planned with Robert Watts at the Bianchini Gallery.[7] Watts featured prominently in *The American Supermarket* with a whole corner given over to his flocked and chromed fruit and vegetables as well as vacuum-formed and wax eggs and plaster and chrome breads.[8] Birillo had a knack for publicity and staged a week-long 'Grand Opening' which closely followed 'the increased promotion and ballyhoo techniques of supermarket operators'.[9] As announced on the invitation, 1,000 buttons with soup can, turkey or apple motifs were given away free, while a hot-dog stand outside the gallery provided nourishment. The exhibition attracted widespread press attention including a full-colour feature in *Life* magazine. *The American Supermarket* celebrated the spectacle of consumption with a happening-like event in which shopping was elevated to an art form, the art dealer turned grocer, and serious art collectors became ordinary supermarket shoppers.

The success of *The American Supermarket* was based on the clever fusion of real and fake elements, realising Pop Art's ambition of blurring the boundaries between art and everyday life. It was conceived as a complete environment in which the paintings and objects that celebrated consumer products were disconcertingly returned into the space of their origin, reversing the distancing authority of the white cube that had made their elevation to works of art possible in the first place. 'Someone left a couple of real chocolate cookies on the bread counter. They looked fake', the *New York Times* reported. 'The gifts – boxes of genuine frozen blintzes donated by an advertising agency – caused some

Andy Warhol in the **American Supermarket** Bianchini Gallery, New York 1964 (Photograph and © Henry Dauman/Dauman Pictures, NYC, 2002)

Ben Birillo and Paul Bianchini in the **American Supermarket** Bianchini Gallery, New York 1964 (Photograph and © Henry Dauman/Dauman Pictures, NYC, 2002)

confusion. "I'd rather have make-believe blintzes," one woman said.[10] The show not only mixed art, real and reproductions of real objects but also so-called fine and commercial display artists – such as Mary Inman who owned a company in Long Island City that produced deceptively real wax replicas of food. *The American Supermarket* presented contemporary commodities as art and sold art like commodities, operating, as Calvin Tomkins stated in *Life* magazine, 'in the no man's land between art and life'.[11]

The American Supermarket was radical in its appropriation not only of contemporary products but also of contemporary strategies of display and exchange. While Claes Oldenburg's *Store* (1961) presented an almost abject shopping environment with entropic and garishly painted products that seemed to disintegrate rather frustratingly in front of the customer's eyes, *The American Supermarket* was an unambiguous celebration of new forms of consumerism and shopping. It followed the Pop artists in their recognition of the pivotal importance of aesthetics in modern consumer capitalism and its energising effect on all aspects of the cycle of exchange.

The event was a celebration of a particularly American form of consumption which, at the time, had become a dominant form of retail and reflected the sociological changes and relative post-war affluence with its higher disposable incomes, a lifestyle dominated by the automobile and the related suburban sprawl.[12] Supermarkets occupied large areas of land with ample parking space outside town centres and featured all the latest conveniences: 'More elaborate interiors and exteriors became the vogue, with services such as music and air conditioning added.'[13] The display techniques applied in supermarkets cleverly enforced the desirability of the products: glaring neon lights

intensified the bright colours of the packaging; the stacking of endless rows of identical products emulated the illusion of boundless abundance and ready availability; the generous layout and absence of sales staff encouraged customers to freely roam the aisles, examine merchandise and compare brands and prices.[14] The name supermarket in itself conjured visions of fast, clean and modern ways of consumption: 'But who can deny that a supermarket is more efficient than even the most charming small speciality shop?'[15]

The celebration of the unique American way of shopping was an important underlying formal and iconographic theme of *The American Supermarket*. 'Bananas with an all American flavor' and pears similarly flocked in the colours of the American flag featured in one of Bob Watts produce crates.[16] Wesselmann's *Still Life no. 45* (1962) featured a giant, vacuum-formed turkey – the most patriotic of American foods alluding to the seasonal anticipation of Thanksgiving. Billy Apple's variations on the apple theme also referenced New York City, the US' unofficial capital also known as the 'Big Apple'.[17] The triad of red, white and blue also appeared in the ribbons decorating the plastic straw boater hats and the Ballantine's neon sign, and can even be detected in Warhol's Brillo boxes (which might have been included as a pun on Ben Birillo's name). American food and brands were as much a reflection of national identity as George Washington, the Star-Spangled Banner, the Declaration of Independence and Liberty Bell. National commodities, shopping and, by extension, Pop Art, were celebrated as innately American and deeply patriotic activities: 'With the pop movement, American art becomes truly American for the first time and thus becomes universal', deriving 'its unique vision and inspiration from the mythogenic forces generated by a new social and economic reality'.[18]

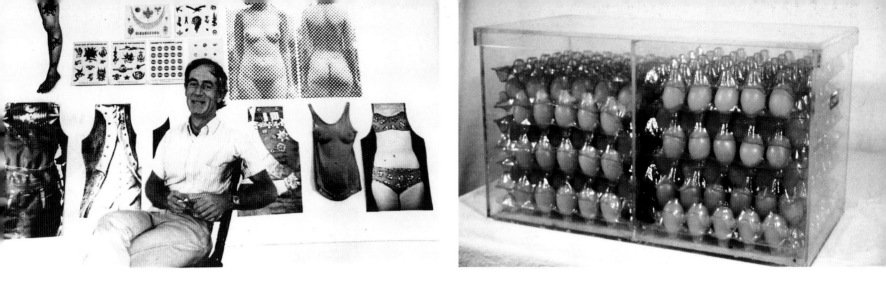

Robert Watts in front of **Products by Implosions, Inc.** and **Fluxus** 1964–66

Robert Watts **Case of Eggs (with Rainbow Wax Eggs)** 1964

1 *The American Supermarket* opened with a week-long event, from 6 to 11 October, 11am–8pm, as the exhibition invitation fashioned after a supermarket flyer announced. It continued until to 7 November 1964. The space is now occupied by the Ubu Gallery.

2 Jasper Johns' *Painted Bronze* (1960), consisting of an empty and a full Ballantine beer can, was removed on the opening night by the prominent collectors Robert C. and Ethel Scull, fearing for the safety of the work. 'When the gallery makes a protective covering for them, I'll bring them back ... After all, we lost that sausage at the Venice Biennale.' Quoted in Grace Glueck, 'Gallery Market Hawks Art on Rye', *New York Times*, 8 Oct.1964, p.51. Following the removal, Ben Birillo recalls, the *New York Times* managed to arrange a picture of Ethel Scull touching Tom Wesselmann's turkey which was published in the above-mentioned review.

3 Glueck, 'Gallery Market', p.51.

4 Ibid.; Eugenia Sheppard, 'The Two Dollar Egg', *New York Times*, 8 Oct. 1964, p.51. Claes Oldenburg is also mentioned on the invitation and, according to John Rublowsky, he presented 'a jar of pickles, a slice of pie and a candy bar display'. James Rosenquist showed a *Noxzema $100,000 Be-Beautiful Contest* painting which can be partly made out in some photographs. John Rublowsky, *Pop Art*, New York: Basic Books, 1965, p.174. Birillo also mentioned Mel Ramos' participation though the work could not be identified. George Segal had been invited to take part in the exhibition but later decided not to participate. Interviews with Ben Birillo, 5 Oct. 2001 and 14 May 2002.

5 Sheppard, 'The Two Dollar Egg'. Birillo recalls that the lady examining a Campbell's Minestrone Soup can in Henri Dauman's *Life* magazine photograph actually wanted to shop in *The American Supermarket*. Birillo interview.

Billy Apple **Apples, 2 for 25 cents** 1962–64

6   Dorothy Herzka was not able to attend the opening after she broke her leg. Birillo
    interview. For an account by Dorothy Herzka Lichtenstein see 'Remembering the
    American Supermarket', in Constance W. Glenn (ed.), *The Great American Pop Art
    Store: Multiples of the Sixties*, Santa Monica, California: Smart Art Press 1997, p.95.

7   Birillo interview; interview with Sara Seagull and Larry Miller, The Robert Watts
    Studio Archive, New York, 15 May 2002.

8   Birillo also recalls a working stamp machine by Watts which, however, was banished to
    the backroom because of the risqué nature of some of the stamps designed by Watts.

9   Frank J. Charvat, *Supermarketing*, New York: Macmillan Company 1961, p.29.

10 Glueck, 'Gallery Market', p.51.

11 Calvin Tomkins, 'Art or not, it's food for thought', *Life*, 20 Nov. 1964, p.143.

12 By 1958 there were 20,413 supermarkets in the US and a 1956 report stated that 80–
    90% of customers used car for grocery shopping. Charvat, *Supermarketing*, pp.29, 63.

13 Ibid. p.29.

14 'At an early date in its history the super found that mass displays of merchandise
    psychologically tended to make the people buy. Mock-ups, mirrors, and lighting have
    been used to give the illusion of bigness. Modern display fixtures, refrigerators, and
    freezers have been developed. Manufacturers constantly have studied package
    design to make the product more appealing. Studies have been made on the value of
    display space to increase sales. Multiple packaging has been developed to create
    "billboard illusions" in stores, as well as make display space more usable directly on
    floors of supermarkets.' Ibid. pp.60–61.

15 Rublowsky, *Pop Art*, p.7.

16 'The American Supermarket', press release, 24 March 1965, for presentation at
    Galeria Il Segno, Rome.

17 Interview with Birillo.

18 Rublowsky, *Pop Art*, p.7.

The American Supermarket Bianchini Gallery, New York, 1964
(Photograph and © Henry Dauman/Dauman Pictures, NYC, 2002)

The American Supermarket Bianchini Gallery, New York, 1964
(Photograph and © Henry Dauman/Dauman Pictures, NYC, 2002)

Roy Lichtenstein **Turkey** 1961

Andy Warhol **Campbell's Soup Cans (Chicken with Rice, Bean with Bacon)** 1962

Gerhard Richter/Konrad Lueg **Living with Pop – A Demonstration for Capitalist Realism** in the Furniture Shop Berges, Dusseldorf, 1963 (Photograph: Reiner Ruthenbeck)

Konrad Lueg and Gerhard Richter, Living with Pop – A Demonstration on behalf of Capitalist Realism

Martin Hentschel

Invitation for the Opening of the Exhibition **Living with Pop**

The year is 1963. It has long been obvious that art has to redefine its position. Jean Dubuffet may have provided a decisive impetus when, in December 1951, he spoke at the Arts Club of Chicago about 'Anticultural Positions': 'Our culture is a piece of clothing, which does not fit – or at least it is one, which no longer suits us. It is like a dead language, which no longer has anything in common with the language of the street.'[1] Dubuffet's vote for his art, which emanates from daily life, was heard by Claes Oldenburg, whose early environments take as their subject two central aspects of urban life: *The Street* (1960) and *The Store* (1961). Back in 1958 Allan Kaprow evoked the unprecedented 'happenings and events', which 'are found in garbage cans, police actions, hotel corridors, in display windows and seen on the street'.[2] The German opposite number of the happenings founder, Wolf Vostell, coupled his *Cityrama (1)* project in Cologne on 15 September 1961 with, amongst other things, the invitation, 'Go ... into a launderette and ask in which year we are living; then look next without interruption at the window display of a sausage shop.'[3]

The topos is already well established when, on 11 May 1963, Manfred Kuttner, Konrad Lueg, Sigmar Polke and Gerhard Richter rent a former butcher's shop in the Kaiserstraße in Düsseldorf in order to deliver their first demonstration on behalf of 'Capitalist Realism'. Although it is was actually a conventional exhibition, great store was set on its non-commercial, 'demonstrative character', which was advertised using the vocabulary of Pop Art.[4] This is known thanks to the Swiss periodical *art international* (25 January 1963), in which precisely those concepts used by the German Pop artists on their invitation cards were

formulated: 'Nouveau-Réalisme', 'Pop-Art', 'Common Object Painting', 'Know-Nothing-Genre', 'New Vulgarismus'...[5] It is even emphasised that Pop Art is 'not an American invention and not an imported article for us'.

But the essay in question, 'Dada Then and Now' by Barbara Rose, also forms a kind of leitmotiv for *Leben mit Pop – Eine Demonstration für den Kapitalistischen Realismus* (*Living with Pop – A Demonstration on behalf of Capitalist Realism*), a project conceived jointly by Lueg and Richter. It takes place five months later, on 11 October 1963, in Berges furniture store in Dusseldorf. For the advertisement in the daily newspaper *Der Mittag* of 5 October – under the caption 'Autumnal Visions' – the artists use the reproduction of an illustration that also appeared with the text by Rose. It shows works by Baj, Wesselmann, Hains, Baruchello, Oldenburg and Thiebaud from the *New Realists* exhibition, which took place in 1962 at the Sidney Janis Gallery, New York. The subtitle in *Der Mittag* reads, 'The exhibition "Living with Pop" at Berges will be something like this.'[6]

The fact that Rose also discusses the way Pop Art is derived from the ready-mades of Duchamp falls on fruitful ground with Lueg and Richter. As part of their demonstration they declare on the one hand that the whole furniture store 'without alteration' forms part of the exhibition, which equates with a radicalisation of the ready-made concept. On the other hand they set up a separate exhibition room on the upper storey of the furniture store 'as a compression of the demonstration': 'Exhibition of an average functioning living room, i.e. inhabited; decorated with utensils, food, drink, books, household junk of the period *and the two painters*. The only pieces of furniture are placed on pedestals like sculptures, their natural distances from each other are

New Realists Exhibition at the Sidney Janis Gallery, New York, 1962
From left to right, Baj, Wesselmann, Hains, Baruchello, Oldenburg, Thiebaud

enlarged, in order to realise a state of being exhibited.'[7] A foretaste of this is imparted by the 'waiting room', which is designated as such by two notice boards with large letters. It is furnished with plain chairs, on each of which is lying a current edition of the *Frankfurter Allgemeine Zeitung*. The walls are adorned with fourteen roebuck antlers ('shot in Pommerania 1938–42,' as Richter's report notes in a fastidious manner). The reference is clear: the guests are transported as if into a conservative German doctor's waiting room, for 'Healing and Improvement' as it will later be called in a picture by Sigmar Polke,[8] and stand in line – grouped by numbers – as they are called in. The waiting-room atmosphere is barely relieved by two life-size figures made from painted papier mâché. One represents the artistic spirit of the age: Alfred Schmela, avant-garde gallery owner and father figure of the Düsseldorf artists; the other depicts the political spirit of the age: John F. Kennedy, the US President (still living at the time), a Berliner by choice and model for all good Germans. The way the figures are made suggests the presence of Pop Art (they can in that respect be regarded as homage to Claes Oldenburg) as well as that of the Düsseldorf carnival (where such figures are carried in the processions on Shrove Monday). The twin ascriptions provide a pointer to the character of the demonstration: it vacillates between German Pop and a carnivalesque reversal of the traditional way of thinking.

In fact for many visitors the order of things is reversed when, in the next exhibition room, they see not art formed in the usual manner but in its stead an average living room. The diagnosis, which the viewer himself has to provide, can only be the following: You are just as ordinary and narrow-minded as anyone else, just look at your living room! As a living part of the inventory, divided between armchair and sofa, Lueg and Richter radiate the customary boredom of every evening: beer and

spirits are at the ready; the evening news is on but they are not looking at it, for news of the world at large is merely of peripheral interest to the petit bourgeois – the artists appearing as such. Everything supposedly important is reflected within these familiar four walls. Thus, compared with the waiting room, the living room is now comfortably warm, illuminated by the light of the standard lamp, and the scent of pine needles is sprayed off and on in order to perfect the 'idyll'.

In the exhibition room the talk is once again of Duchamp's ready-made paradigms. The pedestal solution makes the art context apparent in order, at the same moment, to dispel it all the more clearly. In addition, the artists vanish from sight while appearing as living stock items, as auctorial subjects. Complementing the proceedings are the few paintings brought by the artists, not into the exhibition room itself but scattered around the showrooms of the furniture store like normal accessories. That is where the subsequent, circular tour of all participants finally leads. In the meantime the artists have stepped down from their pedestals and are leading the guests from room to room. The tour is accompanied by dance music, which is interrupted time and again by 'texts taken from furniture store catalogues'. It should, by this point, have become apparent to the visitors that the demonstration applies to their own behaviour and habits as consumers. For the slow-witted, however, the programme provides a final (unfulfilled) point, namely: 'After the circular tour ... see A. etc.', that is to say, it continues in an endless loop until the eyes drop out – a brainwave that certainly pays homage to Dada.

The participation of Joseph Beuys is notable. Richter later specifically recorded the fact that the Fluxus exhibitions, which took place in Düsseldorf in 1962 and 1963 with substantial involvement on the part

Gerhard Richter/Konrad Lueg **Living with Pop – A Demonstration on behalf of Capitalist Realism** in the Furniture Shop Berges, Dusseldorf, 1963 (Photographs: Reiner Ruthenbeck)

of Beuys, were the trigger for his photographic portrayals.[9] That may be the reason for the contribution by Beuys, who adorns the cloakroom to the exhibition room with hat, yellow shirt, blue trousers, socks, shoes and a carton of margarine and 'palmin'. With his provision of brown crosses for these consumer goods, he carries on – as a shrewd complement to the two principal actors – his own healing process with the conquering of the capitalist ideas of value. For the brown crosses bring to mind the incarnation, in which the profanely material is spiritualised and becomes transubstantiated.[10] Therefore, while Lueg and Richter hold out to the viewer the magnifying mirror of his own behaviour, through the intervention of Beuys the latter is already involved in an act of salvation.

How may one now understand the title of the project? From Richter we learn about the coining of the phrase 'Capitalist Realism': 'It was not really meant seriously. There was already Socialist Realism, with which I was very well acquainted. This, however, was precisely the opposite ..., for 'Capitalist Realism' was another form of provocation ...This expression attacked both sides: it made Socialist Realism appear laughable and likewise the possibility of Capitalist Realism.'[11] We can explain the term demonstration thanks to Bertold Brecht. In his article 'Small Contribution on the Subject of Realism', he quotes the astute censor who criticised the portrayal of the suicide of an unemployed person in the film *Kuhle Wampe* as excessively typified: 'The censor stressed that we should have given the suicidal act an unmitigatedly *demonstrative character.*'[12] A similar thing happens with *Leben mit Pop* in that Lueg and Richter typify the inventory of the room with the pedestals according to all the rules of the style of the period. The consumer-critical impulse of the happenings (as Richter called it from time to time)[13] finds its expression with Lueg and also in the painting

of the same period, while with Richter it yields to that well-known indifference. A parallel can certainly be drawn in the double strategy of the Berges project: a) the whole furniture store being part of the exhibition, and b) the compression in a separate exhibition room and Richter's treatment of everyday photos. For Richter chooses a photo because its colour composition and three-dimensional character are already specified and do not have to be discovered first. 'Because it is, however, difficult to make the photo into a picture simply by declaration, I have to paint it.'[14] It is precisely this type of declaration that is undertaken in Berges furniture store on 11 October 1963.

[1] Quoted in *Dubuffet Retrospective*, exh. cat., Berlin, Vienna and Cologne 1981, p.65. Cf. also Andreas Franzke, 'Jean Dubuffet und die amerikanische Kunst' in *Europe/ America*, exh. cat., Ludwig Museum, Cologne 1986, p.111ff.

[2] Allan Kaprow, 'The Legacy of Jackson Pollock', *Art News*, vol.57, no.6, Oct. 1958, p.56, see also pp.24-6.

[3] Jürgen Becker and Wolf Vostell, *Happenings, Fluxus, Pop Art, Nouveau Réalisme – Eine Dokumentation*, Reinbek: Rowohlt 1965, p.382.

[4] The letter signed by Gerhard Richter to the *Neue Deutsche Wochenschau* dated 29 April 1963 is reprinted in Gerhard Richter, *Text. Schriften und Interviews*, ed. Hans-Ulrich Obrist, Frankfurt am Main: Insel 1993, p.11f.

[5] The invitation card is reprinted in the catalogue 'Ich nenne mich als Maler Konrad Lueg', ed. Thoman Kellein, Kunsthalle, Bielefeld 1999, p.12. The appropriate terms in the introductory lines to the essay by Barbara Rose, 'Dada Then and Now', *art international*, vol.7, no.1, 25 Jan. 1963, pp.22–8.

[6] Cf. Martin Hentschel, *Die Ordnung des Heterogenen: Sigmar Polkes Werk bis 1986*, Phil. Diss., Ruhr-Universität, Bochum 1991, p.60ff., and Susanne Küper, 'Konrad Lueg and Gerhard Richter: *Leben mit Pop – Eine Demonstration für den Kapitalistischen*

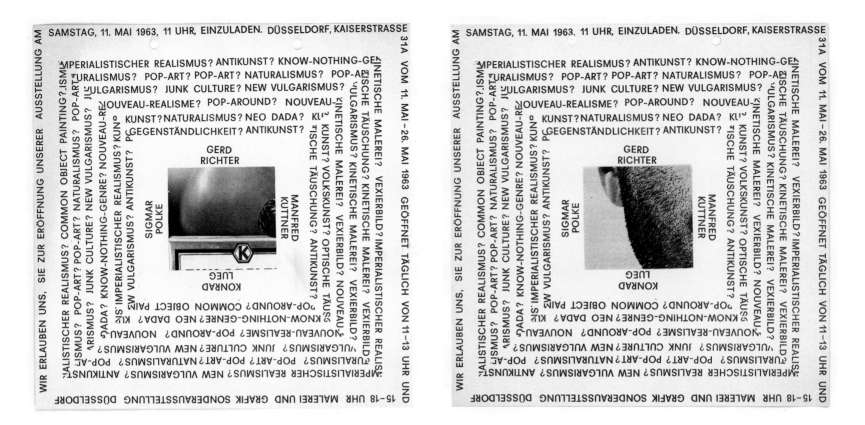

Invitation for the **Demonstrative Exhibition** 1963

Realismus' in Wallraf-Richartz-Jahrbuch, vol.LIII, Cologne 1992, p.289 ff.

7   The programme and concluding report on the project appear in Richter, *Text*,
    pp.14–17 (italics added). Quotations cited, unless stated otherwise, are taken from
    the report.

8   What is meant here is the picture *Die Lebenden stinken und die Toten sind nicht
    anwesend* (1983), in Mary Boone, *Sigmar Polke*, exh. cat., Michael Werner Gallery,
    New York 1985, n.p.

9   Coosje van Bruggen, 'Gerhard Richter: Painting as a Moral Act', *Artforum*, May 1985,
    p.84; cf. Richter, *Text*, p.27.

10 On the use of the brown cross see *Joseph Beuys*, exh. cat., Kunsthaus Zürich 1993,
    p.270f.

11 Quoted in van Bruggen, 'Gerhard Richter', p.84.

12 Bertold Brecht, *Über Realismus*, ed. Werner Hecht, Frankfurt am Main: Suhrkamp
    1971, p.30.

13 Cf. Richter, *Text*, p.57.

14 Ibid. p.27.

<u>Bericht über</u>

<u>"Eine Demonstration für den kapitalistischen Realismus" von Konrad Lueg</u>
<u>und Richter, am Freitag, dem 11.Oktober 1963, in Düsseldorf, Flinger-</u>
<u>straße 11 (Bergeshaus)</u>

(12.September 63): Planung einer Ausstellung in einem Düsseldorfer Möbel-
haus. Zur Verfügung steht ein 32 qm großer Raum im III.Stock des Büroteiles.

Beschlossen nach Verwerfung verschiedener Ausstellungskonzeptionen wird
eine folgende Demonstration:

a) Ausstellen des gesamten Möbelhauses ohne Veränderung.
b) Im separaten Ausstellungsraum als Komprimierung der Demonstration:
   Aufstellung eines durchschnittlichen Wohnzimmers in Funktion, d.h. be-
   wohnt; dekoriert mit den jeweiligen Utensilien, Speisen, Getränken,
   Büchern, Hauskram und den beiden Malern. Die einzelnen Möbel werden in
   der Art von Plastiken auf Sockel gestellt, ihre natürlichen Abstände
   von einander werden vergrößert, um ein Ausgestellt-sein zu verwirk-
   lichen.
c) Programmierter Ablauf der Demonstration für den 11.10.63.

<u>Verzeichnis der am 11.10.63 zu besichtigenden Räume:</u>

I.   Schaufensterpassage (26 große Fenster). Büroeingang. Aufzug zur III.
     Etage.
II. Warteraum (großer Treppenhausflur in der III.Etage). An den Wänden:
     2 Schilder mit der Aufschrift WARTERAUM. 14 Rehbockgeweihe (geschossen
     1938-42 in Pommern). Aufgestellt sind 39 einfache Stühle, auf jedem
     liegt eine "Frankfurter Allgemeine" vom 11.10.63. Auf den Treppenstufen
     liegen verschiedene Illustrierte Zeitschriften, in der Nähe des Auf-
     zuges stehen zwei lebensgroße Figuren (Papier auf Drahtgeflecht ka-
     schiert und bemalt), darstellend den Kunsthändler Alfred Schmela und
     den Präsidenten John F. Kennedy. Der Raum ist von kaltem, etwas schwa-
     chem Neonlicht beleuchtet.
III. Ausstellungsraum. Auf 9 weißen Sockeln stehen: Ein Teewagen mit Blumen
     in einer Vase, im Zwischenfach Churchills Werke und die Zeitschrift
     "Schöner Wohnen". Ein Schrank mit gemischtem Inhalt. Ein weinroter
     Sessel. Ein Gasherd. Ein grüner Sessel, darauf sitzend K.Lueg (dunkler
     Anzug, weißes Hemd, Krawatte). Ein kleiner Versatztisch, darauf ein
     Fernsehgerät (nach der Tagesschau die Ära Adenauer übertragend). Eine
     kleine Stehlampe. Eine Couch, darauf liegend mit einem Kriminalroman
     G.Richter (blauer Anzug, rosa Hemd, Krawatte). Ein Tisch, gedeckt mit
     Kaffeegeschirr für 2 Personen, angeschnittenem Marmor- und Napfkuchen
     und eingeschenktem Kaffee; außerdem 3 Gläser und in einem Plastikbeutel
     3 Flaschen Bier und 1 Flasche Korn. Die Wände sind weiß gestrichen.
     Bilder oder Wandschmuck sind nicht angebracht. Neben der Eingangstür
     befindet sich eine Garderobe. Sie ist mit dem offiziellen Anzug von
     Prof. J. Beuys bestückt (Hut, gelbes Hemd, blaue Hose, Socken, Schuhe.
     Darauf angebracht sind 9 kleine Zettel mit braunen Kreuzen. Darunter
     steht ein Karton mit Palmin und Margarine). Der Raum ist von sehr
     hellem, warmen Neonlicht und einer Stehlampe beleuchtet und durch
     wiederholtes Einsprühen mit Fichtennadelozon mit anhaltendem Geruch
     erfüllt.
IV. Umfangreiche Möbelausstellung aller gängigen Stile in 4 Etagen.
     (81 Wohnzimmer, 72 Schlafzimmer, Küchen, Einzelstücke. Lagerräume.
     Eng gereihte Nischen, Kojen, Zimmer, mit Möbeln vollgestellte Treppen
     und Gänge, Teppiche, Wandschmuck, Geräte, Utensilien). -
     In verschiedenen Einrichtungen der Schlaf- und Wohnzimmerabteilungen
     sind Bilder von Lueg und Richter aufgestellt.
     Von K.Lueg: Vier Finger; Betende Hände; Bockwürste auf Pappteller;

- 2 -

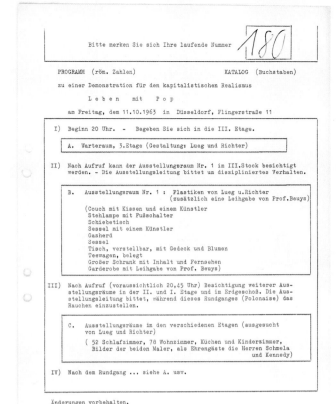

- 2 -

Bügel.
Von G.Richter: Mund; Papst; Hirsch; Schloß Neu-Schwanstein.
Die Räume sind normal beleuchtet.

<u>Bericht über den Verlauf der Demonstration vom 11.10.63:</u>

(20 Uhr. Zwei Angestellte des Hauses stehen am Eingang und verteilen Programme, die mit einer laufenden Nummer versehen sind. (gezählt wurden
122 Gäste), davon verließ ein geringer Teil vorzeitig die Veranstaltung.

Die Besucher fahren mit dem Aufzug zur III.Etage und befinden sich im
WARTERAUM. Lautsprecher übertragen im ganzen Haus Tanzmusik und die Durch-
sagen eines Sprechers, der die Gäste begrüßt und in Abständen von 3 - 5
Minuten nach laufender Nummer Gruppen von 6 - 10 Besuchern auffordert, den
Ausstellungsraum zu besichtigen. Die zuerst aufgerufenen Gäste betreten
nur zögernd den Raum. Bald darauf füllt sich der Raum. Gegen 20,30 Uhr
richtet sich keiner mehr nach den Aufrufen, sondern jeder drängt sich hin-
ein. Die ausgestellten Speisen und Getränke werden sämtlich von den Besuchern verzehrt, der Schrankinhalt wird zum Teil geplündert.

20,35 Uhr verlassen die ausgestellten Künstler ihre Sockel und rufen, eben-
so wie die Lautsprecher, zum großen Rundgang auf.
Richter führt eine erste Gruppe von Gästen in die im II. Stock gelegene
Schlafzimmerabteilung. Lueg folgt mit den weiteren Besuchern.
Die Lautsprecher übertragen fortwährend Tanzmusik, unterbrochen von ausge-
suchten Texten aus Möbelkatalogen. Der Rundgang verläuft vom II.Stock ab-
wärts in die Wohnzimmerabteilung, von da durch das Lager in die im Keller
gelegene Küchenabteilung.
Die meisten Besucher halten die vorgeschriebene Route nicht ein, zerstreu
en oder verlaufen sich in den einzelnen Abteilungen.
Um 21 Uhr sind alle Gäste in der Küchenabteilung. Sie nehmen in den 41
Kücheneinrichtungen Platz und trinken das bereitgestellte Bier. Ein Besucher (Kunststudent) zieht sich aus Protest gegen diese Demonstration
bis auf die Badehose aus. Er wird mit seinen Kleidern unter dem Arm aus
dem Haus gewiesen.
Um 21,30 Uhr hat der letzte Gast das Haus verlassen.

Gerhard Richter, Report on **A Demonstration on behalf of Capitalistic Realism** 1963

Gerhard Richter / Konrad Lueg **Living with Pop – A Demonstration on behalf of Capitalist Realism** in the Furniture Shop Berges, Dusseldorf, 1963 (Photographs: Reiner Ruthenbeck)

Konrad Lueg **Hanger** 1963

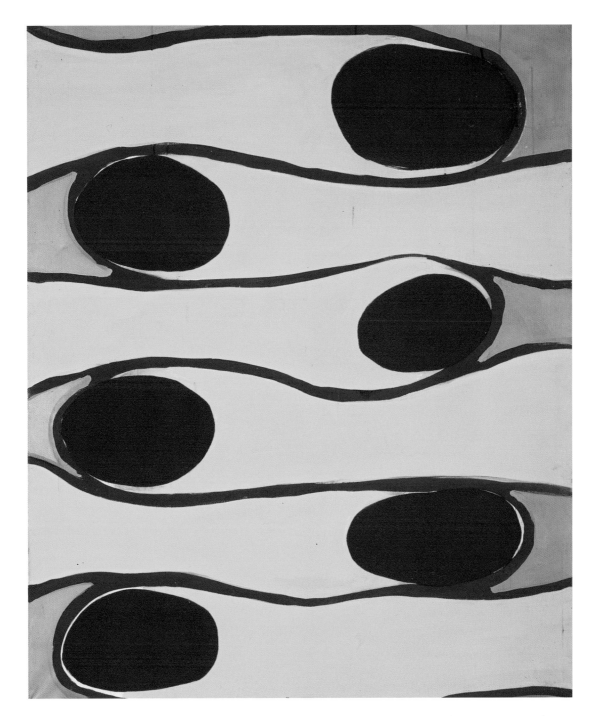

Konrad Lueg **Praying Hands** 1963

Willem de Ridder **European Mail-Order Warehouse/Fluxshop** 1964–65 (Reconstruction 1985)   188

Poster for **Festum Fluxorum** 1963

Fluxus Consumption:
A Strange Form of
Happiness

Thomas Kellein

The only achievement of dialectics is

that eternal development

is eternal dissatisfaction.

Nam June Paik[1]

A special party, a big celebration, an important birthday; to do the occasion proud there is a Grapefruit Flux Banquet with grapefruit hors d'œuvre, marinated grapefruit, grapefruit-seed soup, grapefruit dumplings, grapefruit mashed potatoes, grapefruit pancakes, grapefruit cocktail and grapefruit wine, pressed in 1970 by George Maciunas for his presentation of work by John Lennon with Yoko Ono.[2] Earlier, on New Year's Eve in 1969, at a political turning point for Western countries as the 1970s dawned, Fluxus artists in Wooster Street in New York celebrated with strange dishes like 'shit cookies' or 'clouds' consisting of 'mashed potatoes in ten flavours'.

It was Maciunas who conceived of Fluxus food and drink as 'mono meals'.[3] Grapefruit could be replaced by fish: besides fish cakes and other solid foods made from fish, there would also be pale drinks made from fish meal, fish tea, fish ice cream for dessert, fish jam or fish pudding. And in the same vein there were also ideas for food that was wholly white, black or transparent. Salt replaced sugar in tea, or – following compositional advice from John Cage – eggs could be boiled for between one and ten minutes, producing ten 'different' egg dishes. Anything could be served except the usual dishes that found favour in bourgeois circles, although Maciunas asked that new ideas should be

registered for the sake of maintaining some order. Traditional diversity and richly varied foods were supplanted by his grotesque, anti-hedonist principle of reduction. Fluxus artists were to eat, drink and even build only mono meals, as in real-life socialism. As far as Maciunas was concerned, whenever a new Fluxus product appeared, whether as a substitute for art or food, there was no need for a noble original, good manners or an aura. Even when it came to his own dwelling, Maciunas wanted a plain concrete prefabricated structure.[4] Something simple was sufficient, and as a rule an idea worked for him if the new work promised to rattle capitalist culture.

While the world of consumer goods and consumption frequently featured in paintings from Manet to Warhol and in works by photographers from the Bauhaus to the Becher School – be it as an object of admiration, inquisitive curiosity, imitation or ridicule – in 1963, following in the footsteps of Karl Marx and Friedrich Engels, Fluxus turned its attention to the way in which revolutionary forces within the production process could alter the conditions of production. In the eyes of Chairman Maciunas, the *flâneur* and the gourmet were to be replaced by the comrade, who was not only to strip the consumer world of its magic but, ideally, of the very basis of its existence.

For a time Fluxus consumption meant – in a wry, almost Jesuit sense – preparation, practice and *exerzitium*. Traditionally enjoyable art gave way to simple exercises like *Exit* or *Drip Music* by George Brecht. In performances of the former, people would exit under a sign that read 'Exit', and for the latter there might be a stage with water dripping from a ladder into a bowl. Thus the spirit of Fluxus was disseminated, consisting – according to Maciunas – of a chain of monomorphic works that could be summed up by the term 'concretism': form and content

Fluxus Collective **cc VTRE No5** March 1965

in art were to come closer to each other and to converge in a rudimentary, non-illusionistic manner. It was not only things bourgeois that were rejected, above all the Baroque was prohibited.[5] There was anti-art promoting the cause of a culture that shunned existing galleries and museums, but this was not long to the liking of many artists who would gladly have continued to develop their work with Maciunas. It was not only culinary pleasures that were replaced by macabre recipes. In a purifying drive, multiple means, colours and tastes were no longer wanted where singularity could satisfy hunger and give happiness, artistically speaking. Why seek variety, especially when one and the same product would help to lower the cost of this new cultural project?

In Maciunas' home, he and his guests would eat whatever was especially cheap at the time. On his table there would generally be whatever had to be 'used up' before it went off. Sometimes he would eat only apples or oranges, for days on end, if and for as long as they cost next to nothing. And so precious dollars would be saved for Fluxus. Picasso's *Repas frugal* – summing up the fate of so many artists – with its Bohemian portrayal of the Christian suffering of an artist and his lover in a Parisian bistro shortly after 1900, was now replaced by Maciunas with an everyday rationalism, which did not so much anticipate the success of individual artists as the derailing of established high culture. The money saved and the carefully re-used materials were intended for a production system that everyone could make use of, everyone in his or her own surroundings. As Chairman, Maciunas entrusted other artists with the world itself as Fluxus West, North, South and East, although the Kafkaesque vision of a democratic art that would ultimately lead to an America or Europe populated by artists and free of millionaires and art markets did not come to pass, even with compliant commanders. Like the *Fluxshop & Mail Order Warehouse* that

opened in New York in 1964, the small production business that Maciunas alone stayed with throughout his life had insufficient takings and lacked investors.

Barbara Moore reported that the Chairman developed a system for his own personal nutrition that not only involved leftovers and special offers, but also eating in advance. Every two or three days he would have lunch in a Scandinavian smoregasbord restaurant because the 'All You Can Eat' offer supposedly boosted his food intake for the next few days.[6]

He reproached colleagues for their extravagant eating habits and recommended that they should adopt his own 'Spartan diet'. In his view, more than a dollar a day for food and drink was too much for a Fluxus artist, alcohol and cigarettes were taboo and instead of marijuana – that popular, innocuous drug of the 1960s – he preferred 'grass tea', brewed from real grass and boiling water, which was itself a work that appeared after 1969 under 'Tea Variations' in his lists of serial products.[7] He was constantly making these lists and creating products in small amounts, despite the fact that over the years there was virtually no demand for them, even amongst colleagues and friends.

At the earliest Fluxus festivals in Wiesbaden, Copenhagen, Paris and Düsseldorf between September 1962 and February 1963, it was only the consumption of high culture that was questioned. Instead of a concerto with string players, on the concert programme there was La Monte Young's *Composition 1960 # 7*, consisting solely of an interval of a fifth. It was to be played on the violin for a protracted period of time, if possible for an hour or more. Instead of a piano piece, four or five Fluxus artists performed Philip Corner's *Piano Activities*, which involved

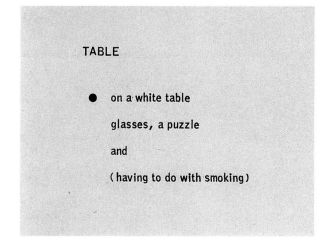

TABLE

● on a white table

glasses, a puzzle

and

(having to do with smoking)

George Brecht **Water Yam** 1964

loosening the screws of the sounding board of a grand piano, sawing up the lid or the body of the instrument and weighing down the strings or cutting through them with tools of some kind.

'Fluxus was a catalyst. It was a signal for us, and we became cynical and brazen and told each other that art is rubbish and Cézanne was stupid', to quote Gerhard Richter looking back at a visit to the *Festum Fluxorum Fluxus* in Düsseldorf. Like his colleague Konrad Lueg, he understood that traditional thematic painting and the expressive gestures of the painters of the 1950s had now become obsolete and even comical in the light of the brightly coloured, increasingly mechanised world of consumer goods. Later that year, in October 1963, the two Düsseldorf artists occupied a furniture store with paintings after photographs and consumer motifs, sitting and lying in a stylised living room – with a television set constantly on – in the cause of 'Capitalist Realism'.[8]

Joseph Beuys, who had opened the doors of the Düsseldorf Art Academy to Maciunas in February 1963 and put on a performance with two mechanical toy monkeys with bells, was also moved to fundamental change in his own work by the impoverished, amorphous materials of the Fluxus artists. His own second exhibition in 1963, put on by the van der Grinten brothers, was called *Fluxus*, and in the accompanying catalogue he accordingly renamed a large proportion of the three-dimensional works he had made since 1947.[9] When the toy monkeys stopped ringing their bells after twenty seconds the piece was over and a melancholy silence set in, as was so often the case in Fluxus pieces. Although the most faithful Fluxus artists recognised an aesthetic starting point for their own ideas in Duchamp's notion of ready-mades, Joseph Cornell's nostalgia filled boxes and John Cage's aleatoric music, was

derivative. The twenty or so artists involved – Eric Andersen, Ay-O, George Brecht, Robert Filliou, Henry Flynt, Geoffrey Hendricks, Dick Higgins, Joe Jones, Milan Knizak, Alison Knowles, Artur Köpcke, Takehisa Kosugi, Shigeko Kubota, Yoko Ono, Nam June Paik, Tomas Schmit, Mieko Shiomi, Ben Vautier, Robert Watts and Emmett Williams – were specifically interested in introducing to the booming world of the economic miracle, on a long-term basis, the philosophy of doing nothing, and the emptiness of never-ending accumulations: a challenge that the consumer society has not accepted to this day.

In 1962, for instance, as a homage to the calculating machine, Maciunas wrote a piece named *In Memoriam to Adriano Olivetti* for four or five players, which could be performed at almost any festival. Each player held a paper roll with a list of numbers or a long till receipt, making a mental note of one number in particular. Keeping to a beat, each silently read all the numbers on the list for a fixed length of time, marking the appearance of the chosen number by raising a hat, opening an umbrella or making a noise. Whether this was ridiculing Taylorism or forms of military discipline, the alternating stoic immobility and mechanical bobbing up and down was not only divertingly amusing but also seemed disturbing and disobedient. For it was never clear how to handle art of this kind. It was neither theatre, nor music, nor visual art, and it was not up for sale.

According to Maciunas' early promises, Fluxus was – by means of a monopoly of distribution – to develop an alternative culture for the works of avant-garde artists. Books, sheet music, newsletters, a journal, boxes, the institutions of the *Fluxshop & Mail Order Warehouse* in New York and Amsterdam, *Flux Food*, *Flux Furniture*, the *Flux Housing Cooperative* and even a Fluxus circumnavigation of the world were

Fluxus Collective **Fluxboxes** 1970

Ben Vautier **Mystery Box** New York, 1964

specifically designed to constantly propagate the notion of distribution. In fact the name itself already existed when Maciunas fled to Wiesbaden in 1961 to escape his creditors in New York.

Fluxus was also a matter of moving an unsecured cheque from one place to another. In everything he did Maciunas looked for what was practical and pursued a path characterised by tireless work and small savings. In the eyes of the artists, and of many promoters and publishers too, none of what he did seemed to work. While it is true that the first concerts did promise a new forum to a loose group of visual artists, authors, musicians and composers, at the same time there were problems when it came to sharing out the takings, publishing the works near to the time of the performance, and with professional publicity for the events. From the outset finances were in short supply, then conviction also began to run low. When the major Fluxus concerts were over in Europe in spring 1963, Maciunas did nothing to tackle the problems in his organisation, but insisted instead on doing away with traditional modes of art consumption, on physically interrupting the urban traffic that went with it, and on claiming recognition for his doctrinaire aesthetic monotheism which some Fluxus pieces, including those by his colleagues, visibly evoked. While his 'movement' was disintegrating, he tightened up its laws – like Breton and Tzara in their day – with a kind of cadre training for the faithful and excommunication for any rebels. Shockingly ordinary forms of artistic activity now occupied a prominent position in his programme.

In keeping with Maciunas' precepts, the standard edition of Ben Vautier's *Mystery Box* was to be filled with dust. A larger, luxury edition, measuring 5 x 20 x 20 cm, was to have a filling of egg shells. And the cuboid version, measuring 25 x 25 x 25 cm, was to be filled with garbage:

'chipped plaster, used mimeograph stencils, dried up tea bags (used), orange skins, etc.', as he wrote from New York in February 1964 when he was seeking Vautier's approval for his suggestions. With macabre pragmatism he then added, 'This will be very practical since we can dispose of garbage by this method and even get money for it.'[10]

Manifestations of Fluxus appeared on the stage, in publications, even in the streets: in its day La Monte Young's *Composition 1961*, consisting of the sentence 'Draw a straight line and follow it', became a Fluxus paradigm and, in the author's view, a piece suitable for performance in front of important museums or on overcrowded sidewalks. It was listed in 1963 in the *Fluxus News-Policy Letter No. 6* under revolutionary propaganda measures, with which the world of higher art was to be sabotaged and destroyed.[11] Karlheinz Stockhausen's performance of *Originale* in New York in August 1964 was picketed by Maciunas and Henry Flynt because it did not meet the new norms.

In 1966 the Japanese group Hi-Red-Center put on their *Street Cleaning Event*, an action at the Grand Armory Plaza in New York in which the four artists, wearing white doctor's coats and wielding toothbrushes, thoroughly cleaned a good square-metre of pavement, using water and Ajax scouring powder.[12] In this performance – as in the *Flux Films* with the smiling face of Mieko Shiomi, which scarcely ever altered, or in the *Flux Wallpaper* repeating the same photograph of Yoko Ono's backside – the work was about a stoic form of new beginning, one that moreover spurned the extended production of art that had evolved in the meantime. While the New York art scene was going from Pop Art to Minimal Art and Conceptual Art, and after 1968 widened its circle of collectors, galleries and museums to include Land Art, Body Art and new forms of processual art, Maciunas remained faithful to the princi-

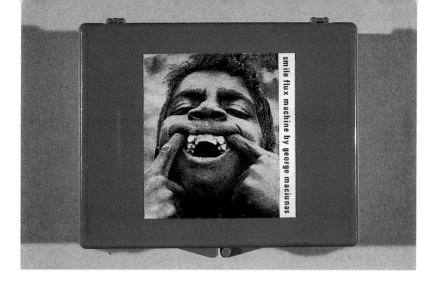

George Maciunas **Smile Flux Box** 1970

ples set up in 1963. By the early 1970s he stood almost entirely alone in the circles of his old acquaintances, although now certain younger artists, including Per Kirkeby for one, came to him filled with curiosity. Mail Art and the culture of artists' books also owe much to Fluxus art, with its distinct lack of commercial success.

As late as 1977 Maciunas was still working out an alternative postal system with stamps bearing faces taken from a reference work on abnormal dental patterns. In 1963 Robert Watts, one of his most faithful followers who stayed until the end, had 'revamped' a stamp dispenser in order to distribute just such artists' stamps. In the same year Willem de Ridder had set up his *European Mail-Order Warehouse/Fluxshop* in Amsterdam, intending it as a bastion of the commercial distribution of Fluxus products. This was meant to create a market for the individual boxes, the *Fluxkits*, the Fluxus journal *VTRE* and the *Yearboxes*. It was de Ridder's task to collate the contents of the products, in some cases to assemble them, and at the same time to delay distribution until such time as the parts Maciunas was delivering were either all there or any possible complaints had been warded off. The small white cards for George Brecht's *Water Yam*, for instance – one of the most important anthologies of so-called 'word events' – came from New York.[13]

Despite de Ridder's enthusiasm for his shop in Amsterdam, he was able to sell only very little, like Maciunas in New York. The products were priced between $2 and $100; yet even if they had sold, the costs for materials, postage, rent and labour would scarcely have been covered. And the shop in the Amstel 47 Gallery had to be temporarily left unattended when the owner was away elsewhere. One of the most important records of the planned but unfulfilled Fluxus business is a photograph showing de Ridder's then girlfriend in a display window, in amongst *Water Yams*, *Fluxkits*, issues of VTRE, La Monte Young's *Compositions 1961* and various luxury editions. All the displays and labels were designed and produced by Maciunas personally.[14]

'While Rome burns', wrote Dick Higgins, a Fluxus participant in the early years, 'I work with butter and eggs for a while, George Brecht calls for "at least one egg" and Alison Knowles makes an egg salad and La Monte Young plays B–F sharp on a fiddle hour after hour.'[15] Two years before his death from cancer in 1978, Maciunas invited his colleagues to take a walk around the farm he had bought with a mortgage in Massachusetts. By that time, due to a lack of demand and for want of an effective organisation, the global cultural revolution of Fluxus had evidently been postponed. But towards the end, looking at the upshot of his work, Maciunas told the much younger Larry Miller that what he and his colleagues had been doing was making jokes. Over the course of a quarter of a century that was all they had achieved with Fluxus: 'We came out to be like a bunch of jokers.'[16]

1   From a manuscript by Nam June Paik on his exhibition *Exposition of Music* 1963 in the Galerie Parnass in Wuppertal, as cited in Jon Hendricks, *Fluxus etc./Addenda II: The Gilbert and Lila Silverman Collection*, exh. cat., Baxter Art Gallery, California Institute of Technology, Pasadena 1983, p.296. On p.297 Paik varied this statement: with the help of Akutagawa, he attributed the 'only achievement' to the German philosopher Georg Wilhelm Friedrich Hegel.

2   Maciunas had published Yoko Ono's artistic work as early as 1963. According to the

Robert Watts **Affixations by Implosions, Inc.** 1962–67

title the banquet was a homage to grapefruit; a copy of the grapefruit menu is included in Jon Hendricks, *Fluxus Codex: The Gilbert and Lila Silverman Fluxus Collection*, Detroit, New York: Abrams 1988, pp.68f.

3 Ibid. pp.67, 340f.

4 See 'Appendix 1: Soviet Prefabricated Building System', in Henry Flynt and George Maciunas, *Communists Must Give Revolutionary Leadership in Culture*, New York 1966; repr. in Jon Hendricks, *Fluxus etc./Addenda I: The Gilbert and Lila Silverman Collection*, New York: Ink & 1983, pp. 40–2.

5 The verbal basis of the Fluxus Aesthetic was formulated by Maciunas in a text leaflet published for his programme – lasting several weeks – for *Musica Antiqva et Nova* in 1961 in the New York AG Gallery. For more on this, see Thomas Kellein, *Fluxus*, London: Thames & Hudson 1995, pp.18–21, 52.

6 Barbara Moore, 'George Maciunas: A Finger in Fluxus', *Artforum*, vol.21, no.2, Oct. 1982, p.39.

7 Hendricks, *Fluxus Codex*, p.355.

8 Coosje van Bruggen, 'Gerhard Richter. Painting as a Moral Act', *Artforum International*, vol.23, no.9, May 1985, p.84. Thomas Kellein, *Ich nenne mich als Maler Konrad Lueg*, exh. cat., P.S. I Center for Contemporary Art, New York, Kunsthalle Bielefeld, S.M.A.K. Gent 1999/2000, pp.15–21.

9 Thomas Kellein, 'Zum Fluxus-Begriff von Joseph Beuys', in Volker Harlan, Dieter Koepplin and Rudolf Velhagen (eds.), *Joseph Beuys Tagung: Basel 1.-4. Mai 1991*, Basel 1991, pp. 137–42.

10 Letter in the Gilbert and Lila Silverman Fluxus Collection, New York (Inv. 01037).

11 Facsimile reprint in Hendricks, *Fluxus etc./Addenda I*, p.156.

12 Illustrations in Kellein, *Fluxus*, pp.63–5.

13 He wrote to the recipient, 'Now you have complete set and can put one of each in box & sell, sell, sell!!!', as cited in Hendricks, *Fluxus Codex*, p.231.

14 Illustrations and text documents, ibid. pp.231–7. For more on Fluxus products in general, see Ina Conzen, *Art Games: Die Schachteln der Fluxus-Künstler: Sohm Dossier 1*, Staatsgalerie Stuttgart, Cologne: Oktagon 1997.

15 Dick Higgins, *Postface/Jefferson's Birthday*, New York: Something else 1964, p.5.

16 Hendricks, *Fluxus etc./Addenda* I, p.27.

Ben Vautier **The Bizarre Bazaar** 2002

Ben Vautier **The Bizarre Bazaar** 2002

Joseph Beuys **Wirtschaftswerte (Economic Values)** 1980 (detail)

Joseph Beuys, Wirtschaftswerte, 1980

Rolf Quaghebeur

The crucial element pervading all of Beuys' output is what he himself termed 'Sozialplastik' ('social sculpture'). At a time when it was still possible to have great ideals and believe in social utopias, he was aiming at the total liberation of man through an amalgamation of art and life. *Wirtschaftswerte* ('economic values') is undoubtedly one of the most monumental, grand and representative pieces in Beuys' oeuvre. It was produced in 1980 during the *Art in Europe after '68* exhibition in what was then the Museum of Contemporary Art in Gent.

Intuitively and spontaneously Beuys stacked packets containing all kinds of primary food stuffs, mostly from what used to be the German Democratic Republic, onto six metal racks positioned diagonally in the room. The installation is surrounded by late nineteenth-century paintings and in front of the racks there is a damaged block of chalk of which the bottom has been smeared with butter. Other 'fatty' materials, such as oil, honey and margarine, are also used in abundance. To Beuys, these elements worked as sources of energy, emitting a healing power. Their symbolic value derives from Beuys' Second World War experiences, when his reconnaissance plane was shot down over the Crimea. Nomads saved his life by smearing his body with wax and butter and wrapping him up in felt. The block of plaster had been in his studio for a long time and had suffered wear and tear. The palette knife and the dish of butter that he used to correct the 'scars' on the block were integrated into the installation later on. The fat is slowly absorbed by the chalk, which symbolises culture – the product of Western person's urge to order – as opposed to nature, symbolised by the fluid, uncontrollable butter, melting and hardening at different

temperatures and through manipulation. Nature is ever changing, without fixed form. In his drawings Beuys would often use browns and russet colours to indicate this – the colour of soil, but also of blood. In installations butter and other fats are often used in this way. He believed in the healing power of nature, which for him consisted entirely of energy.

However, culture – the geometric, mathematical hardness of the chalk – cannot survive without the energy of nature. The energy that is produced here by the contrast between hard and soft, culture and nature, is symbolically fed to all the economic values on the rack through a radio cable that has been connected up to the block of chalk. With this installation, Beuys wished to bring synthesis to the world, a world dominated by capitalist values – some of the East German foodstuffs turn out to be hard to distinguish from West German ones. At the same time he expressed his conviction that our tie with nature and its healing powers never can and never should be broken. He is proposing a new world order in which everything is harmoniously arranged in cycles of rise and decline.

None the less, it would be nonsensical to restrict ourselves to the so-called magical side of Beuys. This is a highly critical and political piece. Selecting the products – the 'Wirtschaftswerte' – from what was then the Communist East Germany constituted a questioning of the separation of the two Germanies, something he did on another occasion by ironically suggesting that the Berlin Wall should be heightened by five centimetres 'to improve the proportions of the wall'. Since its inception in 1980, the installation has been shown in various countries as part of different exhibitions, at the Musée d'Orsay in Paris, the Stedelijk Museum in Amsterdam, the Prado in Madrid and the

Joseph Beuys **Wirtschaftswerte (Economic Values)** 1980 (details)

Nationalgalerie in Berlin. During the exhibition *von hier aus* in Dussel-dorf (1984), Beuys personally altered the work by completely enclosing it in chicken wire. This not only prevented theft of the packets of food, but was viewed by Beuys as an addition to the piece. Later, at the request of the artist, it was restored to its original state. The differing installations have one thing in common; they are always surrounded by paintings dating from the period of Karl Marx and taken from the collection of the host museum itself. For Beuys, this was not only a way to join the present to the past and so nullify the separation of new art from old, but also to show the link between Marxist communism and the products on the racks.

Obviously, the political and social context has changed considerably since 1980, with the fall of communism in Europe and the many social and economic changes that followed as a result. Nevertheless, this piece has not lost any of its relevance. On the contrary, change and evolution are an integral part of the works of Beuys and are strongly represented in this installation. Although the artist initially selected items with a fairly long shelf life, such as wax, dry biscuits and pre-serves, over the past twenty years the packaging has degraded, the butter has become rancid and quite a number of articles have deterio-rated. The changing shape, odour and colour of the piece march along-side evolutions in society, and continue to give the contents, as well as the material aspects of the installations, their topical relevance.

With this piece, Beuys brought daily life into the museum and expressed his strong social involvement as an artist. Politics, art, science, econ-omy and religion were all as one to him. The artist functions as a kind of shaman, a healer who should attempt to bring about a catharsis. This is why he had the following inscription made on the chalk: 'Der Eurasier lässt schön grüssen' ('Greetings from the Eurasian'). Through the radio cable connected up to this message, the written commu-nication is broadcast. As Beuys once said about himself, 'Ich bin ein Sender, Ich strahle aus' ('I am a transmitter, I send out waves'). Beuys believed there was creativity in everyone and that humans should arrive at a new society through art and creativity. This philosophy not only set in motion the social and political movement that led to the founding of the ecology party in Germany, but also broadened the tra-ditional understanding of art. He took banal objects and put them in a museum, elevating them to art by putting them on metal racks, when normally one would come across objects on racks only in storage depots. He turns the museum inside out by expressing the function of 'collecting' in the galleries in a literal way. By signing all the packets on the racks and giving them the title *1 Wirtschaftswerte*, Beuys empha-sised the direct link between daily, trivial life and the 'transcendental' world of the arts. At one stage, some packets were even taken off the racks by Beuys and sold separately.

Wirtschaftswerte is a complex piece. It shows the division of Europe, the similarities and differences between the known and the unknown; the subtle contrasts between angular and straight, hard and soft, point us towards the continuing existential crisis of our society. The tensions Beuys managed to generate by the continual combination of artistic, scientific, ecological and political ideas were pioneering and influen-tial on an entire generation of artists. Any viewer who is confronted with the piece, the enormous austerity of the packagings, the stale smell and the faded colour, cannot fail but be moved by the grandeur and the monumentality of the installation.

Joseph Beuys **Wirtschaftswerte (Economic Values)** 1980 (details)

Bibliography

↘ Adriani, Götz. Winfried Konnertz and Karin Thomas, *Joseph Beuys: Life and Works*, Woodbury, New York: Barron's Educational Series, 1979.

↘ Hoet, Jan, Norbert De Dauw and Veerle Van Durme, 'Joseph Beuys', in *Catalogus van de Verzameling van het Museum voor Hedendaagse Kunst, Gent*, Brussels 1982.

↘ Hoet, Jan, et al., *Kunst in Europa na '68*, exh. cat., Gent: Museum van Hedendaagse Kunst, 1980.

↘ Hoet, Jan and Frederika Huys, 'Vervangbare authenticiteit', in *KM. Tijdschrift van de stichting Kunstenaarsmateriaal*. Amsterdam 2000.

↘ Horsfield, K., 'On Art and Artists: Joseph Beuys', in *Profile*, vol.1, 1981.

↘ Stachelhaus, Heiner, *Joseph Beuys*. Trans. David Britt, New York: Abbeville Press, 1991.

↘ Staeck, Klaus and Gerhard Steidl (eds.), *Joseph Beuys: Das Wirtschaftswertprinzip*, Heidelberg: Edition Staeck, 1990.

↘ Szeemann, Harald, *Joseph Beuys*, Kunsthaus Zürich, 1993.

↘ Zweite, Armin (ed.), *Joseph Beuys – Natur, Materie, Form*. Exh. cat., Munich, Paris and London: Schirmer/Mosel, 1991.

Joseph Beuys **Wirtschaftswerte (Economic Values)** 1980

The Glamour of Things

Max Hollein

The world of consumer goods, its aesthetics and strategies are a vital, integral part of our urbane surroundings. Branded products, everyday objects, mass-produced consumer goods are primary hallmarks of a consumer-orientated society based upon a free-market economy. At the same time the rituals and characteristics of shopping are often not far removed in their effect from those of the art world. Changing the context, appropriation, subversive infiltration or analyses are deliberate artistic strategies. Reflecting and utilising the elements, objects and methods of the commercial environment are important integral parts of a specific artistic statement and creativity. Presentation, order, routine, alignment, superabundance: a strongly aestheticised form of representation holds sway. Artists such as Jeff Koons, Haim Steinbach, Katharina Fritsch, Damien Hirst, Guillaume Bijl and Andreas Gursky – so varied in their background and their work – are all great artistic directors amid the consumer world.

The aesthetics of consumer goods, the glamour of things, creates a synthetic environment of permanent desire and of wanting to be desired. Goods thereby acquire a new identity, significance and soul; and with no one more so than with Jeff Koons. It is not only with his *The New* series – in which in various formations and arrangements, with the aid of plexi covers and neon light, he helps mass-produced Hoover vacuum cleaners achieve eternal life, perpetual freshness and completely altered significance – that he displays in a subtle manner the longings and desires of the bourgeoisie, the striving for security and attainment of social status. The objects with which he works wish to be desired. Attraction, elegance, wrapping and presentation are the messengers and agents of this expectation. The form of the presentation is a privilege, a status symbol for a new class of importance within the scale of values. Koons, the master of presentation, uses it to create the ideal picture for an altar of the present. 'I don't seek to make consumer icons but to decode why and how consumer objects are glorified.'[1] In this Koons rejects a purely aesthetic view of his work:

On the contrary I understand my work as being wholly conceptional from top to bottom. It is true I use certain aesthetic means as a tool, but regard them, however, as psychological means. My work is concerned with my own psychology of the public. For me 'aesthetics' means a discriminating stage between humans, something which intimidates people, so that they believe art is too far above them. Of course there are aesthetic ground rules, which I use as a means of communication.[2]

These objects attract our attention, they wish to communicate but in doing so, however, they are also provocative, bold and superior. In spite of their supposed coldness, perfection and restraint, Koons' works are stamped with emotion and longing. While he, like no other person, understands the aura of consumer goods in our everyday culture and the dreams, desires and expectations that we project upon this world of consumer goods, Koons creates the perfect, most desirable objects in all their artificiality. What is presented is 'The New': the new thing, the latest novelty – a designation after which our consumer world always strives, just like the art world. Unlike the radical and provocative works of Marcel Duchamp, with Koons objects have the task of conscious seduction – with considerable success. In this Koons himself is a great seducer, just like his objects. He knows his public and its voyeuritic tendencies. He knows about the power of attraction, of the superficial, of visual manipulation. He accelerates

Jeff Koons **The New** 1980– 81

our fascination with the artificial-synthetic, the perfectly new, the easily consumable but supposedly noble. And thus arises the double seduction, the glossy, spotless object from the consumer world in its aseptic packaging, which already carries the seductive character as an inherent quality within itself, hand in hand with the seductive power of an aureate work of art. 'As far as art is concerned, I am totally disillusioned – totally. Art lacks any kind of effect upon others. I try to attain that effect through the material; I also try to manipulate the public and to control the surroundings and the emotions. The public is my "ready-made".'[3] The elevation of consumer goods, the fine appearance of product display and the enticement of new, unused things that we recognise from the displays in the shopping malls, acquire a new reputation and eminence through the transformation of these products into art objects. The presentation in all its perfection and focus drains the objects of their actual economic value, but establishes them as materialised manifestations of longing, aims and existences. They suggest that which the consumer world pretends to offer: the absolutely beautiful, the eternally new, the consumable perfection. The cocoon in which they find themselves, is on the one hand a display window and on the other a shield, an enveloping aura, which should protect out-dated models from ageing quickly, giving them eternal newness, security and relevance – although the next generation of vacuum cleaning devices is already waiting at the door. Even the method of sale is inherent in *The New*.

I believe that salesmen stand at the forefront of our culture. Society changes very rapidly and nowadays quite different things are sold compared with previously. There was a time when representatives went from door to door. In America the knock on the door meant that the Hoover man was there. These reps were one of the triggers for my vacuum cleaner series.[4]

Haim Steinbach also finds the objects for his work and the basis for what he installs in the everyday world of consumer goods. His whole output revolves around the idea of an object and its presentation, the illuminating, manipulative, existential power of the display and grouping. The interest relates to our experience of the aesthetics of things, no matter whether they are now objects of art or mass-produced consumer goods. The smoothness and perfection of the arrangement, the symmetrical, ordered, sparkling clean set-up is an integral part of his work.[5] An essential aspect of this is the surface area as a determining element in our world of transitory visual impressions. It has the potential suddenly to create new identity and appreciation just as the fashionable consumer seeks to acquire a new image for herself/himself through clothes of a certain brand. 'I do not think as a sculptor but as a painter. To me all the surfaces are cultural surfaces, the most interesting is the overdetermination of the object identity. The way the object presents itself, how it is dressed.'[6] Steinbach's works are emblems of our consumer culture and the fetish with consumer goods, whilst within their artistic arrangements they speak of levels of use and significance, origins, old and new, original or derivative, relationships and influences. 'The focus in my work is not the new; the work also extends to old objects, and to objects that have been damaged – they may be aging, aged, disintegrating, or disintegrated, but they are objects nonetheless – they may have or have had an ideal reality at one point.'[7] Steinbach investigates, makes connections plain and then manipulates them again. In the centre stands the question as to the meaning and relationship of everyday objects and their representative power. He explains the feelings, associations and perceptions towards and between objects while the latter are usually presented in systematic and composed ranks on the top of triangular stands. The interplay of the method of presentation, colour aesthetics and arrangement of an object results in a fresh

Katharina Fritsch **Display Stand with Madonnas** 1987–89

statement about its origins, history, content and quality, as well as its reception. In so doing the artist simultaneously adopts a variety of roles: as *flâneur* and consumer he searches for appropriate, already-produced, actual objects; as curator he assembles the latter into suitable arrangements; as collector he creates from the enormous fund of things he has gathered together. With Steinbach the artist mutates from traditional artistic creator to the *flâneur* in the world of things. Observed from this standpoint, he does not create, but selects and places. With the aid of techniques from the worlds of shopping and art – the stand surface as pedestal – Steinbach isolates objects from their natural context and undermines their original, simple, peripheral identity by arrangement in rows and repetition. The objects are rescued from their insignificant existence and redeemed from our disdain and lack of attention – transmutation through presentation.

The might of seriality, of the aesthetic surface, of the staging of every-day life is also familiar to Andreas Gursky. In works such as *Prada I* (1996), *Prada II* (1997), *Prada III* (1998), *Untitled V* (1996) or *99 Cent* (1999), he radicalises and exaggerates the forms of expression of consumerism. One sees the attraction and power of the presentation of consumer goods, the fetishisation in the elegant shop windows, the visual power of the layout accentuated, improved and exaggerated by the large for-mat and technically enhanced photo works. The motifs thus become ideal forms of the fetish with consumer goods, perfected, fabricated, radicalised ensembles of our consumer-fixated leisure society. Gursky's works have considerable analytical power in this respect. As with Koons or Steinbach, the motifs are taken from everyday commercial life, how-ever Gursky does not use the objects themselves, he does not lift an actual vacuum cleaner onto the artistically prepared pedestal, but cap-tures this ensemble of consumer goods in an artistic medium – pho-tography. As Andreas Gursky puts it, 'They are presented everywhere and in the final analysis we have to deal with an exaggerated form of consumer goods' fetishism. That is all. This social aspect interested me ... As I have already said, there is this type of consumer goods' pres-entation, but not in the radical form as expressed by me.'[8] As an observer of this work, one is influenced by both the presentation surface of photomurals and the commercial presentation surfaces illustrated. The interest in the aesthetics of the display window and stand, in the sculp-tural quality of the shop window, becomes apparent particularly if one sees *Prada II* as a further development of *Prada I*: The presentation of consumer goods as a motif does not actually need the consumer goods themselves – the stands are empty.

With Katharina Fritsch the motif of the serial, the never-ending, the superabundance of pure, beautiful objects takes place once again in three-dimensional space. Fritsch's stands of consumer goods, based on geometrical forms (double cones, cylinders, pyramids), with arrange-ments of vases, Madonnas or brains, play with the suggestive power of the supposed thing on offer. The monotony and multiplication of the art products develops the theme on various levels. The individual works of art in themselves, taking into account their multiplicity, are already a commentary on the art world. Conversely, the method of production, reproducibility, simplification and presentation of the art multiples makes prototype consumer goods out of these objects – vase, Madonnas or brains. This is all the more astonishing since basically one is con-cerned with very intimate objects, things connected with highly personal experiences: a statue of the Madonna, a vase for knick-knacks, a casting of a brain. Though logically a display, they do not lead to a supply. Repetition and stylisation of these uncanny arrangements result in an introspective, enigmatic aura. Fritsch's racks do not say 'buy me'.

Damien Hirst **Pharmacy** 1992 (detail)

Clinical cleanliness, ascetic coolness, purity and orderly layout, opening out into the ornamental, a longing for order and perfection in the arrangement: these are also characteristic traits of the works of Damien Hirst, especially in his key work *Pharmacy* (1992). He knows about the calming power of the aesthetic design: 'With clear forms and perfect edges then people can feel secure. It's a confidence.'[9] The pharmacy itself as an institution (which, however, would more honestly be described as a shop) as well as the packaging and the ambience must instil the necessary sense of confidence in the sick, the customers, the purchasers. Hirst comments on the seductive power and the aestheticising of the moment of sale in pharmacies:

They weren't looking at it logically. They were looking at shiny colours and bright shapes and nice white coats and cleanliness and they were going right – this is going to be my saviour ... In the supermarkets there's a massive battle going on between brands – Coca Cola fighting KP Crisps – a big battle for attention and it's very messy, it's very ugly. Whereas in the chemist, they all harmonise with each other in a much more beautiful way, which is kind of what goes on in artwork, so all the drug companies – they're not fighting each other, there's a kind of unwritten law.[10]

The Calming Moment of the pure, the beautiful, the perfectly produced design object or the aesthetically staged everyday consumer goods: visual seduction is everywhere – on the streets, in the department stores, in the galleries and museums. *Pharmacy* evolved as an installation through the conflict between gallery, exhibition room and sales' place:

I realised that an art gallery is like a shop. I said before once 'the difference between an art gallery and a car showroom and art and

cars – an art dealer and a car salesman' – you realise that all these rooms are just rooms and they're all the same – they have a similar function ... One is the confidence that it had, the simple confidence of it and the other was the confidence of the medicine cabinets in their own right.[11]

Guillaume Bijl brought the reality of our artificial consumer society into the unreality of the art gallery with his transformations. Bijl's three-dimensional 'still lifes', devoid of human beings – like the *New Supermarket* constitute a very analytical and also subversive way of treating the representation of our everyday staged reality, overlaid by a manipulated artificiality. The familiar places of trust, which surround us permanently, the form, composition and demands of which we accept with confidence as natural, logical and rational, undergo a completely unexpected detachment of observation and unmasking reflection. Suddenly we are standing before eerie places – platforms of our collective as well as of our individual desires, dreams and longings.

In 1979 the British punk band The Clash sang the refrain, '*I'm all lost in the supermarket – I can no longer shop happily*' – perhaps a final, impotent revolt against the superabundance of consumer goods and their suggestive power over the formation of our personality. The public did not detect such a critical attitude in 1987 towards the Pet Shop Boys, and although their song 'Shopping' in itself was also of a subversive nature only the refrain stuck: '*We're S-H-O-P-P-I-N-G, we're shopping*'. Exactly the same would happen to the visual arts of that period and anyone primarily looking for socially critical content in these works will be disillusioned, misjudging their whole content and power. Naturally they have their subversive elements, they open the eyes in their exaggeration and incisiveness, but it is much more –

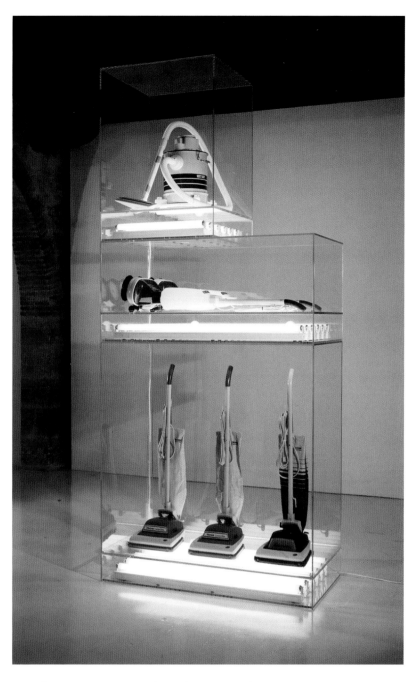

Jeff Koons **New Hoover Deluxe Shampoo Polishers, New Hoover, Quick-Broom, New Shelton Wet/Dry Triple Decker** 1987

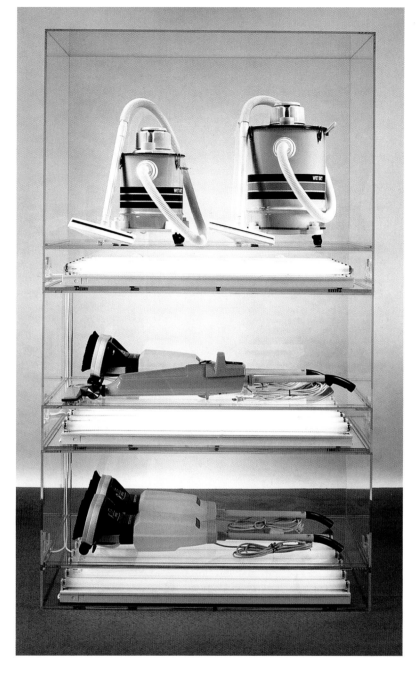

Jeff Koons **New Hoover Convertibles Green, Green, Red, New Hoover Deluxe Shampoo Polishers, New Shelton Wet, Dry 5 Gallon Displaced Tripledecker** 1981–87

by means of playful analyses and affected reaction to our everyday life – a question of creating ideal works of art for our age, perfect arrangements, altars and ensembles in the midst of our affluent society, marked by its goods-orientated lifestyle.

1 Jeff Koons in an interview with Allan McCollum and Daniela Slavioni, 'McCollum and Koons', *Flash Art*, vol.131, 1986/7.

2 Jeff Koons in an interview with David Sylvester in *Easyfun – Ethereal*, Solomon R. Guggenheim Museum, New York 2000, p.39.

3 Jeff Koons in an interview with Anthony Haden-Guest in Angelika Muthesius (ed.), *Jeff Koons*, Cologne: Taschen 1992, p.72.

4 Jeff Koons in an interview with David Sylvester in *Easyfun – Ethereal*, p.43.

5 Cf. Max Hollein, *Zeitgenössische Kunst und der Kunstmarktboom*, Vienna: Böhlan 1999, p.70.

6 Haim Steinbach in a letter to Ettore Spalletti, 15 July 1992, in Ettore Spalletti, *Haim Steinbach, Osmosis*, Solomon R. Guggenheim Museum, New York 1993, p.9ff.

7 Ibid. p.60.

8 Andreas Gursky in a conversation with Heinz-Norbert Jocks in 'Das Eigene steckt in den visuellen Erfahrungen', *Kunstforum*, vol.145, May–June 1999, p.248ff.

9 Damien Hirst in conversation with Gordon Burn, www.tate.org.uk/pharmacy part 4.

10 Ibid. part 1.

11 Ibid. part 5.

Haim Steinbach **supremely black** 1985

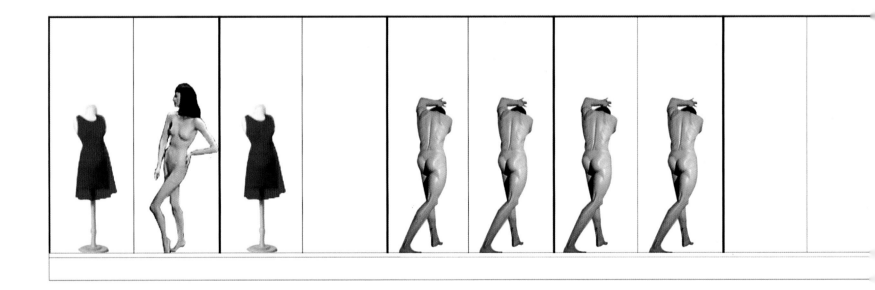

Haim Steinbach **Untitled (Art Déco bust, display mounts, necklaces)** 1989

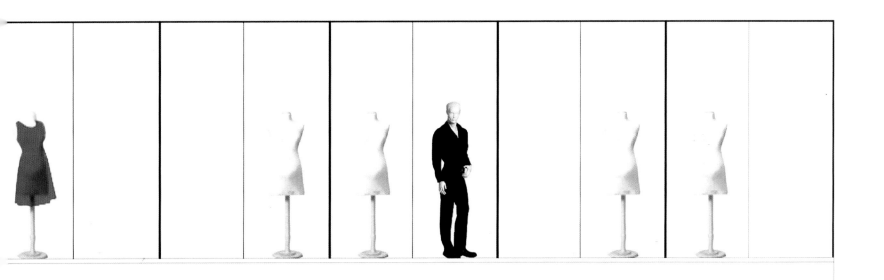

Haim Steinbach **Display #60 (41 figures)** 2002

Andreas Gursky **Prada I** 1996

Andreas Gursky **Prada II** 1997

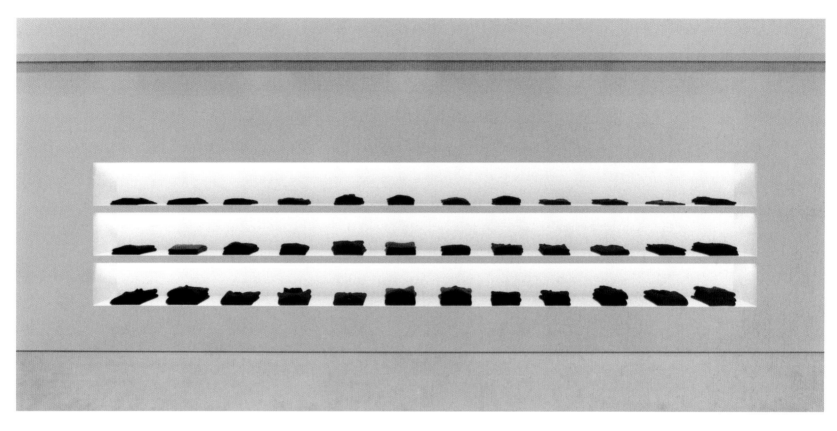

Andreas Gursky **Prada III** 1998

214

Andreas Gursky **99 Cent II** 2001 (diptych)

overleaf: Damien Hirst **Pharmacy** 1992

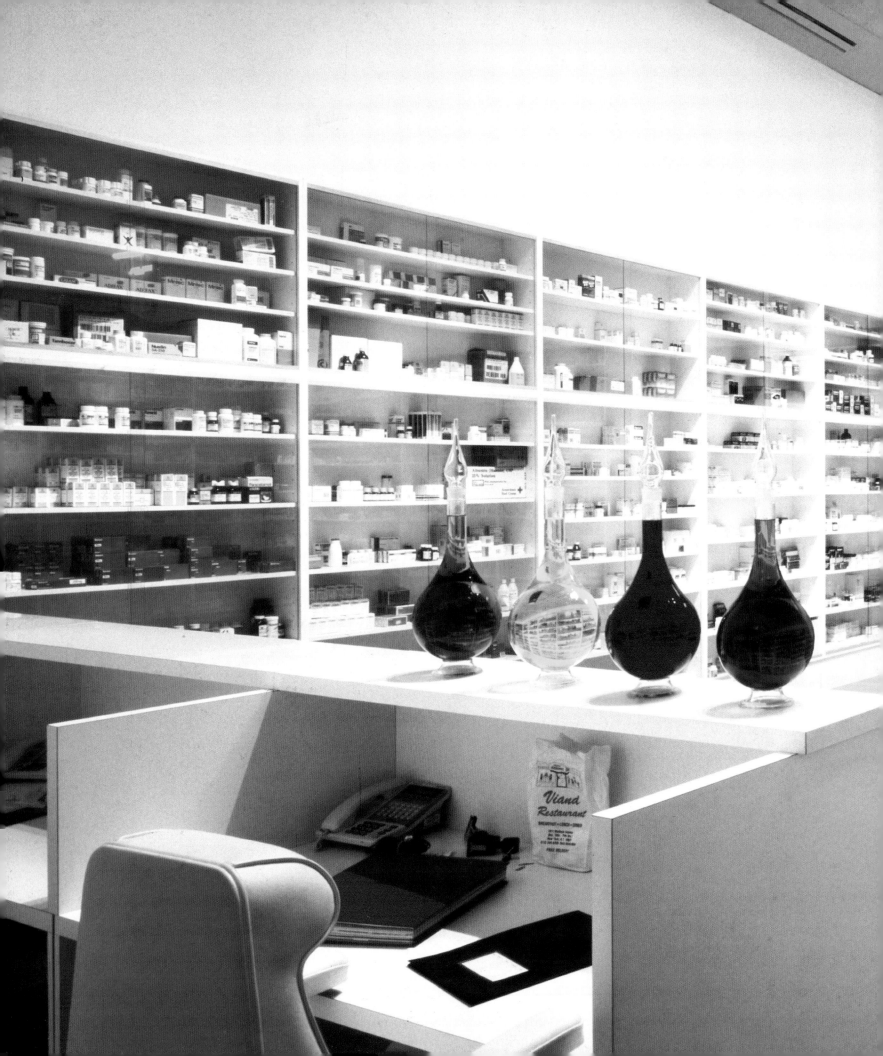

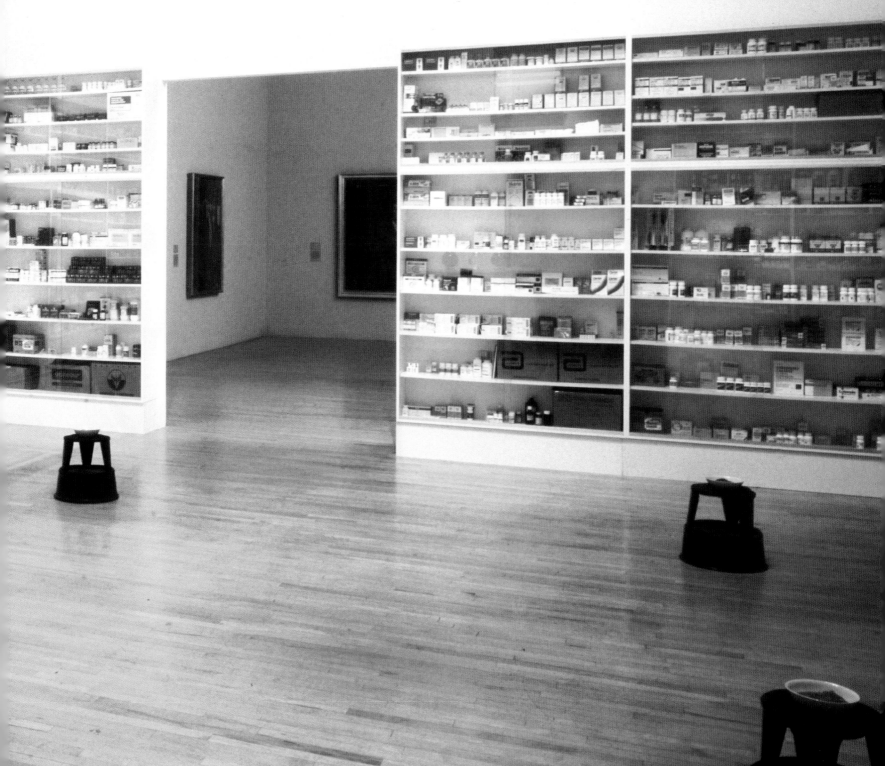

Guillaume Bijl, Installation **New Supermarket** Galerie Littmann Basel, 1990

Guillaume Bijl, Installation **New Supermarket** Galerie Littmann Basel, 1990

Guillaume Bijl, Installation **New Supermarket** Galerie Littmann Basel, 1990

Barbara Kruger **Untitled (Shopping)** 2002

Shop Until You Stop

Julian Stallabrass

Art and fashion have always gone hand in hand. Sometimes radical and shocking, sometimes traditional and conservative, both are judged according to subjective standards of taste. Each represents in its own way the moods and spirit of the times. They stimulate the senses and create objects of desire as fetishes of an affluent society and legacies of culture.[1]

If contemporary art tends to handle the issue of consumer culture with both fascination and nervousness, there is good reason for both reactions. Fascination because consumerism appears to become ever more cultural, less the realm of selling things than of selling or merely displaying images, sounds and words. Nervousness because the engines of this production are so vast and lavishly funded, their output so ubiquitous and strident. If commodities tend towards being cultural, what space is left for art?

It is an old concern, found in modernism as well as in postmodernism, though taking different forms in each. Fernand Léger stood before the machine exhibits of the Paris Fair, marvelling at how such immaculate productions outshone the poor, self-conscious efforts of artists.[2] The argument that art is no longer possible because the world of products is saturated with aesthetics is the postmodern variant of that anxiety, and also on the surface of it a modernist dream realised, though in a false sublation, less in synthesis than surrender.[3]

While the issue of art's separation from or mergence in commodity culture has a long history, during the 1990s, there was an intensifica-

tion of the forces, many of them old features of capitalism, that contributed to the dominance of triumphant consumer culture over art, and indeed over all other cultural production. Commodities appeared to become even less like functional objects and more like evanescent cultural moves within a sophisticated, self-referential game played out over a wide range of identifications. The greatest profits continued to be made not in industry but in services, data processing and finance, and the success of those sectors was most associated with the neoliberal economies, particularly with the United States.[4] In the West, this change was felt as early as the mid 1970s but the 1990s saw the collapse of alternative models, not only in Eastern Europe where formerly Communist nations adopted neoliberal policies, often with catastrophic results, but also in the great industrial economies, Germany and Japan, which both suffered stagnation and decline, while continental Europe moved to embrace the neoliberal model, sugar-coated though it was with nominally social-democratic governance. Like commodification itself, the neoliberal model – encompassing privatisation, high unemployment, low wages for workers, the weakening of the unions and neglect of public services – widened its ambit and deepened its hold.

In some of these territories (including Scandinavia) which recession had newly opened to unrestrained and corrosive market forces, art served as an unwitting agent of neoliberalism, trampling over the comforting if suffocating amenities of social democracy, while giving expression to the liberated concerns of identity politics, consumerism, vulgarity, and pleasure in the degraded.[5] Such works opened up previously suppressed perspectives, yet at the same time served as useful, if minor, allies of privatisation and the colonising force of commodification. The parallels between the orthodoxies of postmodernism and the free market ethos have often been drawn out:

Michael Landy **Closing Down Sale** 1992 (detail)

The ideology of the world market has always been the anti-foundational and anti-essentialist discourse par excellence. Circulation, mobility, diversity and mixture are its very conditions of possibility. Trade brings differences together and the more the merrier! Differences (of commodities, populations, cultures, and so forth) seem to multiply infinitely in the world market, which attacks nothing more violently than fixed boundaries; it overwhelms any binary division with its infinite multiplicities.[6]

Corporate culture has thoroughly assimilated the discourse of a tamed postmodernism, which in the first place it had a strong hand in bringing to hegemony. As in mass culture, art's very lack of convention has become entirely conventional. Ubiquitous and insistent voices urge consumers to express themself, be creative, be different, break the rules, stand out from the crowd, even rebel, but these are no longer the words of radical agitators but of business. The writers of the US magazine of cultural analysis, *The Baffler*, vividly describe the extent and standardisation of these injunctions. Their wonderfully condensed example of this imperative is William Burroughs' appearance in an advert for Nike.[7] Much in the art world since 1990 has offered a tame exemplification of those virtues purloined by corporate culture.

Postmodern theory itself, as it moved from being an account of a potential utopia or dystopia to being a flat description of an existing reality, lost its critical and ethical force. In its reduced state, consumerism and the supposed empowerment of the shopper were central to postmodernism's disquisitions. While in the 1990s postmodern theory was buffeted by attacks on its internal absurdities, and its browbeating of readers with meaningless scientific jargon, in much of the art world, at least, it was less replaced than lost sight of by its acceptance.[8]

The spectral character of the contemporary commodity goes hand-in-hand with the rise of neoliberalism. This militant form of capitalism was aided by far-reaching technological changes that made the exchange of information cheap, quick and simple. Vast programmes of computer networking were driven by profiteering on the privatisation of publicly owned telecommunications industries.[9] The digitisation of data could turn previously free information (for instance, in libraries) into commodities, in an enclosure of data commons.[10]

In another development that tended to make the commodity less material, branding achieved greater importance throughout the 1990s as corporations spent money saved on outsourcing production on their own images. As Naomi Klein has argued in her justly renowned book, *No Logo*, as production was exported to low-wage economies, so the link between the consumers of a product and its makers was sundered.[11] The brand was elevated in compensation, floating free of mere products, to become an allegorical character, a reliable embodiment of particular combinations of virtues or admirable vices. Sometimes, as with Ronald McDonald, it solidifies into an animated figure.

While commodification generally expanded, so that, for example, sequences of genetic code are patented and companies advertise in schools, limits were still drawn. John Frow lists some areas, such as religion, aspects of personal life, politics and art that, while not free of the effects of commodification, are not subject to the strict demands of profit maximisation.[12] If, in reading the list, the words 'politics' and 'art' are stumbled over, perhaps it is because democracy has become more plainly plutocracy, while art and business have drawn nearer to each other.

Peter Zimmermann **Exchange Rates** 1993

Claude Closky **Untitled (Supermarket)** 1996–99

Again, the 1990s saw an intensification of trends that had been initiated earlier. Business sponsorship of the visual arts and partnerships between large corporations and art institutions increased and as a matter of course tended to suppress the display of dissenting art works, while importing business practice into galleries and museums.[13] Art has increasingly tended to be used as an instrumental device to stimulate shopping (and perhaps this is part of the role of a show called 'Shopping').

Branding in the art world has also flourished. Galleries and museums burnish their new logos, striving to impress the character of their brand upon the public. The branding of 'Tate' (marketers conduct systematic warfare against definite and indefinite articles) produces an entity that exceeds its various physical branches, and achieves cross-branding symbiosis through deals to endorse, for example, a range of household paints sold at D-I-Y giant B&Q. Many artists similarly strive to achieve brand recognition, and a few succeed: Tracey Emin has become a brand out of which her art is made. Such artists as brands are again allegorical figures that, like robots, deliver particular and predictable behaviour along with other outputs. At a meeting on arts sponsorship held at the Royal Society for the Arts, a representative of Selfridges put the matter with candour: the recent display of Sam Taylor-Wood pictures across the façade of the shop was a bringing together of two brands, to the benefit of both.[14]

On going to the links page of Claude Closky's site, the viewer is presented with an alphabetical list of .com sites composed of familiar names: it begins adams, akerman, alys, amer, andre, araki. All the links are in fact to company sites, so clicking on www.billingham.com, for example, takes you to a site selling camera bags.[15] Expectations are frustrated,

and the range of products and services brought together that share artists' names is a curious little database, yet the work encourages the user to think about artists' names as brands, and about the dotcom character of their work.

As commodities have become more cultural, art has become more commodified. Even in the early days of postmodernism, Adorno recognised the parallel between art and consumer goods, especially in an age of over-production

> ...where the material use-value of commodities declines in importance, where consumption becomes vicarious enjoyment of prestige ... and where, finally, the commodity character of consumables seems to disappear altogether—a parody of aesthetic illusion.[16]

The result is an attitude to art which is similar to people's attitude before commodities. Yet this is no irreversible or inevitable historical development, borne out of the essence of art and commodity, but one that is tied to the rising and falling rhythm of the economic cycle, and enjoyed only by those wealthy enough to conspicuously consume.

A number of artistic practices in the 1990s responded to the trajectory of these changes, feeding off them and pushing them further. Sylvie Fleury took the results of her shopping trips to high-class boutiques and laid them on the gallery floor; or she (literally) placed desirable, fashionable items on pedestals. Guillaume Bijl simply opened shops (amongst other institutions) within the museum. For Wolfgang Tillmans the same photographic material may serve in gallery installations or as publicity pictures in 'lifestyle' (that is, shopping) magazines, and his approach is sanctioned by the rise of increasingly arty

Jean Pigozzi **Lots of Silver Pans, Man on Phone** 1996

Allan Sekula **Fish Story** 1990–95

fashion magazines and increasingly fashionable art magazines, along with some genuine hybrids.

For Marx, the commodity is a strange and complex thing, being at once a material object valued by its buyer in part because it has a use and, because of the action of the market, a bearer of monetary exchange value. While uses are diverse and incommensurable, exchange values are all set on a single scale. For Benjamin Buchloh, in his pessimistic accounts of contemporary art, use value is increasingly surrendered, and art (like money) has become a commodity of nearly pure exchange value.[17] (As long as they remain material objects, neither money nor art can shed all use value; books can be printed on money, and a Rembrandt used as an ironing board.)[18] In a further stage, even the pretence to achieving use value is dropped, as artists simply reflect and examine the new scene in which there is no distinction between art and commodity culture, and they do so without critique, irony or the desire for change. This is, for instance, the view generally taken by critics about the work of Sylvie Fleury.[19]

Thus art approaches the condition of that most abstract of commodities, money, and it is actually used like that by the rich, as a quasi-liquid form of speculative capital, with the consequence that great numbers of the objects in which that value inheres are locked away unseen in secure, purpose-built depositories.

Yet there are disturbances to this simple scheme in which art and other commodities grow closer in character, as do galleries and shops: to begin with the materiality of the art object persists, even of media art which has been accepted as art only by paying the price of becoming partly material. The art market is still dependent upon the buying and

selling of rare or unique objects which are far removed from the mass-produced commodities found in ordinary shops. In many markets, a few dominant companies control production, but there are few in which consumption is regulated. The commercial art world tries to hold both reins tight, for the buyers of these objects are very few, and are known to the sellers, production is artificially limited, and patronage often has a personal dimension. To look at the contemporary art world is to take a glimpse into an older, pre-industrial market system.[20] A suggestion of this difference is found in Andreas Gursky's various photographs of top-flight shops and famous galleries. The shops seem to reproduce the forms of minimalist sculpture with such pristine perfection that matter becomes uncannily spectral, while in the galleries the muddy craft character of the objects displayed is evident, for instance, in the ragged shadows they cast on white walls.

Furthermore, and here one limit of profit maximisation is drawn, in many nations the state plays a large role in hoarding and displaying art objects, influencing the determination of taste and the course of art writing. If art works were truly commodities like any other, states should be happy to leave their purchase, conservation and disposal to market forces. While commodities are thought to divide as well as define identity, appealing to competing impulses within the individual, there is an ideological presumption that the art work within the museum forges social cohesion even as it celebrates difference, and collective memory even as it recycles and recombines a diversity of references.

Above all, while ordinary commodities live or die by millions of individual decisions to buy or not to buy, the feedback mechanisms which determine the track of contemporary art are regulated and exclusive, and the ordinary viewer of art is permitted no part in them. Komar and

Seamus Nicolson **Bobbyann** 2000   Seamus Nicolson **Wajid** 2000

Melamid highlighted this issue by applying the standard methods of the consumer questionnaire to painting, producing results guided by catering to the average taste of different national populations.[21] This separation from the full rigours of the market confers advantages and disadvantages. From the art enclave, flirtations can be engaged with the world of shopping, with an assurance that one will not be subsumed into the other. Indeed, those works that appear to threaten such subsumption (such as those of Bijl) serve to reinforce the boundary by making it visible. Isolation turns the gaze inwards, as within a mirrored box, so that reflections assume an unwarranted significance, and artists' moves tend to be seen in relation to those of other artists, rarely within the context of the outer world. Increasingly recursive games are played with predecessors' work, as well as with material drawn from mass culture. Thus Mike Bidlo appropriates Warhol's appropriation of Brillo pads, transforming the appropriation of a consumer item into the appropriation of art, while suggesting that Warhol's images have themselves become reduced to consumer items.

This specialist internal discourse only provides the illusion of escape from the commodity form. Marx has the fetishised commodity speak of its own condition, and it says the following:

> ...our use value may interest men, but it does not belong to us as objects. What does belong to us as objects, however, is our value. Our own intercourse as commodities proves it. We relate to each other merely as exchange values.[22]

While art seeks to protect itself with specialist, internal discourse, in works and words, it only emulates the play of free-floating exchange values in a time of glut.

From the moment that it was established, the safety of the enclave has, of course, been challenged by artists. Yet while those challenges were tied to time and context, the objects in which they were incarnated were not, and as they persisted through history, their tinge of radicalism added to their aesthetic lustre and market value as they became increasingly conventional art commodities.

From the mid 1990s, with rise of web browser, the dematerialisation of the art work, and especially its weightless distribution over digital networks, has threatened the protected system of the arts. What is the market to make of a work that is reproducible with perfect accuracy, which can simultaneously exist on thousands of servers and millions of computers, and which can be cannibalised or modified by users? How can one buy, sell or own such a portion of data? This is a situation, central to Marxist theory, in which modernisation of the means of production comes into conflict with the relations of production. In digital art, the use of the most up-to-date technological means to make and distribute work comes into conflict with the craft-based practice, patronage and elitism of the art world.

Artists have inhabited online space alongside corporations that made concerted efforts to force the change from forum to mall. That commercial colonisation has been a rich subject for net artists who have produced many sharp and sophisticated pieces designed to draw the shopper up short. One of the most notorious was etoy's *Digital Hijack* which diverted surfers who had typed in keywords such as 'Madonna', 'Porsche' and 'Penthouse' into a search engine, and clicked on etoys' top-rated site, being greeted with the response: 'Don't fucking move. This is a digital hijack', followed by the loading of an audio file about the plight of imprisoned hacker Kevin Mitnick, and the hijacking of the

Michael Landy **Breakdown** 2001

Internet by Netscape.[23] Others, including Rachel Baker with her examination of customer surveys, data mining and loyalty cards, have come into dispute with corporations using the copyright laws to suppress freedom of speech. Baker made a site promising Web users who registered for a Tesco's loyalty card points as they surf, provided they filled in a registration form that asked questions such as 'Do you often give your personal data to marketers?' and 'How much is your personal data worth to marketing agents?' She soon received a letter from Tesco threatening an injunction and damage claims.[24]

This form of art is indicative of a wider, extraordinary development: that out of a renewed and virulent species of capitalism, at the point of its apparent triumph, there condensed from fragmented single-issue politics, a coherent movement of opposition.[25] Michael Hardt and Antonio Negri argue that this is no accident, for cooperative values emerge from the very change of the primary economies towards data processing:

> Today productivity, wealth, and the creation of social surpluses take the form of cooperative interactivity through linguistic, communicational, and affective networks. In the expression of its own creative energies, immaterial labour thus seems to provide the potential for a kind of spontaneous and elementary communism.[26]

The Open Source or free software movement provides an example of such collective and unremunerated work in action.[27]

The combination of productive and reproductive technologies in the digital world handed astonished artists a route back to social and political engagement, sidestepping art institutions (which, as we have seen,

were thoroughly imbued with the corporate ethos), and promptly raising once more the spectre of the avant-garde.

Marx argued that production and consumption were bound up with one another to the point of identity. Not only does one depend upon and complete the other, but in production is found consumption (for instance, of raw materials), and in consumption production (for instance, eating produces the body).[28] The exclusive focus on consumption in much of the art world is an ideological matter, one that flows from the prominence of advertising and other corporate propaganda, for which the less that is thought about production (who labours and for what pay, in what circumstances and at what risk, under what form of coercion, with what environmental consequences?), the better. This blindness is reinforced in the art world by its own archaic production practices. There are huge numbers of art works that have dealt, for instance, with the uncanny character of toys in the realm of consumption; few touch on the equal charge of the contrast between their intended use and the circumstances in which the majority of them are made – in China, say, by the harshly disciplined sweated labour of young women living between unsafe factory and crowded dormitory.

There are exceptions to this ideological blindness: Allan Sekula with *Fish Story*, his extraordinary series of photographs and texts about maritime trade, makes visible those who labour in distribution, and in a very different register Sebastião Salgado with his vast, elegiac book of photographs about workers attempted to revive the humanistic engagement of the documentary tradition.[29]

Finally, there are artists who in diverse ways bring the fields of production and consumption into connection and contention. Gursky's

www.toywar.com

www.etoy.com

photographs, of shops and galleries as well as factories examine the cultural, rather than the economic, identification between consumption and production. His depictions of, say, a Grundig factory, the Pompidou Centre and a 99c thrift store all show muted human figures dominated by large-scale grids. These could be textbook illustrations to Adorno's arguments about the secret affinity and interdependence of work and leisure, in which leisure, only apparently partitioned from work, adopts work's structure and forms.[30]

In his installation and performance piece, *Breakdown*, set in a disused shop on London's Oxford Street, Michael Landy brought the two spheres into manifest contact by cataloguing and destroying every possession he owned.[31] The labour of many people, working on a production line, was used to disassemble into component parts and finally pulverise commodities. Labour was used, in destruction, to bring attention to the labour expended in production, which the seamless, slick surface of many commodities seeks to render invisible. The constitution of the self through the ownership of commodities was also brought to the fore, leading viewers to ask of themselves, without all these things, what would be left of me?

For Buchloh, a key example of art that had a use value was Soviet Constructivism, made following revolution for particular, well-defined purposes.[32] Particularly online, where the boundaries between production and reproduction are faint, artists have been rediscovering use value. With activist works, allied to the new political movements, such as Floodnet designed by Brett Stalbaum, they have even engaged in the direct disruption of shopping, notably with a campaign against the giant online corporation, Etoys, which had used legal action to close down art site, etoy.[33] They did so with such effectiveness that their action (along

with the recession) destroyed the company. Perhaps the most radical and productive works of the last years were not those that dwelt within the power of consumerism but those that explored its limits, and what lies beyond.

1 Sponsor's statement by Hugo Boss in Renate Wiehager, (ed.), *Sylvie Fleury*, Osfildern-Ruit: Cantz, 1999, p. 8.

2 'The Machine Aesthetic: The Manufactured Object, the Artisan, and the Artist' (1924), in Fernand Léger, *Functions of Painting*, ed. Edward F. Fry, London: Thames and Hudson, 1973.

3 On that saturation, see Jean Baudrillard, 'Symbolic Exchange and Death', in *Selected Writings*, ed. Mark Poster, Cambridge: Polity Press, 1988, pp. 146-7.

4 See Manuel Castells, *The Information Age: Economy, Society and Culture*. Volume I. *The Rise of the Network Society*, Oxford: Blackwells, 1996, ch. 2.

5 This was apparent in the survey show of Scandinavian art in the 1990s, *Organising Freedom: Nordic Art of the '90s*, Stockholm: Moderna Musset, 2000.

6 Michael Hardt / Antonio Negri, *Empire*, Cambridge, Mass.: Harvard University Press, 2000, p.150.

7 For a selection of articles, see Thomas Frank/ Matt Weiland, (eds.), *Commodify Your Dissent: Salvos from The Baffler*, New York: Norton & Company, 1997.

8 On absurdities, see Terry Eagleton, *The Illusions of Postmodernism*, Oxford: Blackwell 1996 and Christopher Norris, *What's Wrong with Postmodernism: Critical Theory and the Ends of Philosophy*, Hemel Hempstead: Harvester Wheatsheaf, 1990; on jargon, see Alan Sokal / Jean Bricmont, *Intellectual Impostures: Postmodern Philosophers' Abuse of Science*, London: Profile Books, 1998. For the controversy caused by Sokal, see Editors of *Lingua Franca*, (ed.), *The Sokal Hoax: The Sham that Shook the Academy*,

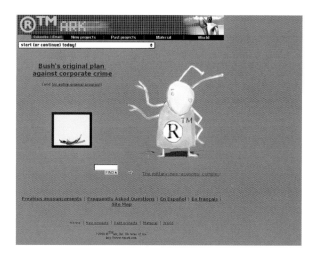

www.RTMark.com

Lincoln: University of Nebraska Press, 2000.

9 Dan Schiller, *Digital Capitalism: Networking the Global Market System*, Cambridge, Mass.: The MIT Press 1999, ch. 2.

10 Herbert I. Schiller, *Culture Inc.: The Corporate Takeover of Public Expression*, Oxford: Oxford University Press,1989, ch. 4.

11 Naomi Klein, *No Logo*, London: Flamingo, 2000.

12 See John Frow, *Time and Commodity Culture: Essays in Cultural Theory and Postmodernity*, Oxford: Clarendon Press, 1997, p. 131.

13 For a striking account of the way sponsorship altered the art world, see Chin-tao Wu, *Privatising Culture: Corporate Art Intervention Since the 1980s*, London: Verso, 2001.

14 Royal Society of Arts debate, May 2001.

15 www.sittes.net/links

16 Theodor W. Adorno, *Negative Dialectics*, trans. E.B. Ashton, London: Routledge, 1973, pp. 24-5.

17 See Benjamin H.D. Buchloh, 'Moments of History in the Work of Dan Graham' and 'Parody and Appropriation in Picabia, Pop, and Polke', in *Neo-Avantgarde and Culture Industry: Essays on European and American Art from 1955 to 1975*, Cambridge, Mass.: October, 2000.

18 According to Mayakovsky, following the Revolution books were sometimes printed on money which had gone out of use. 'Broadening the Verbal Basis', *Lef*, no. 10, 1927; reprinted in Anna Lawton (ed.), *Russian Futurism Through its Manifestoes, 1912-*

1928, Ithaca: Cornell University Press, 1988, p. 260. The use for the Rembrandt was Duchamp's provocation. Marcel Duchamp, 'Apropos of "Ready-mades"', talk delivered at the Museum of Modern Art, New York, 19 October 1961, in Michel Sanouillet/ Elmer Peterson, (eds.), *The Essential Writings of Marcel Duchamp*, London: Thames and Hudson, 1975, p. 142.

19 To take one example, see Renate Wiehager's essay, 'Freddy Mercury Feels Good', in Wiehager (ed.), *Fleury*.

20 See Eric Hobsbawm, *Behind the Times: The Decline and Fall of the Twentieth-Century Avant-Gardes*, London: Thames and Hudson, 1998.

21 See Joann Wypijewski, *Painting by Numbers: Komar and Melamid's Scientific Guide to Art*, Farrar, New York: Straus and Giroux, 1997.

22 Karl Marx, *Capital: A Critique of Political Economy, Volume I*, trans. Ben Fowkes, Harmondsworth, Middlesex: Penguin 1976, pp. 176-7.

23 *Digital Hijack* no longer runs but a simulation can be seen at http://146.228.204.72:8080/. Mitnick became a cause celebre for the hacking community, and for those wishing to ensure freedom of expression on the Net generally. For a site devoted to his support, see www.kevinmitnick.com

24 For the letter, see http://www.irational.org/tm/archived/tesco/; for the work, see http://www.irational.org/tm/archived/tesco/front2.html

25 For a guide to this new politics, see Emma Birchams / John Charlton (eds.), *Anti-Capitalism: A Guide to the Movement*, London: Bookmarks Publications, 2001.

Robert Gober **Untitled** 1993–94

26 Michael Hardt / Antonio Negri, *Empire*, Cambridge, Mass.: Harvard University Press, 2000, p.294.

27 The interpetation of Open Source is controversial. For a business-friendly view, see Eric S. Raymond, *The Cathedral and the Bazaar: Musings on Linux and Open Source by an Accidental Revolutionary*, Sebastapol, CA: O'Reilly, 1999; for a more radical analysis, see Richard M. Stallman, 'Why Software Should Not Have Owners'; http://www.gnu.org/philosophy/why-free.html

28 Karl Marx, *Grundrisse. Foundations of the Critique of Political Economy (Rough Draft)*, trans. Martin Nicolaus, Harmondsworth, Middlesex: Penguin 1973, pp. 90-4.

29 Allan Sekula, *Fish Story*, Düsseldorf: Richter Verlag 1995; Sebastião Salgado, *Workers: An Archaeology of the Industrial Age*, London: Phaidon Press, 1993.

30 See 'Free Time' in Theodor W. Adorno, *The Culture Industry: Selected Essays on Mass Culture*, (ed.) J.M. Bernstein, London: Routledge, 1991, pp. 162-70.

31 See *Michael Landy / Breakdown*, London: Artangel 2001.

32 Buchloh, *Neo-Avantgarde and Culture Industry*, p. 198.

33 For Stalbaum's account of Floodnet, see http://www.nyu.edu/projects/wray/ ZapTactFlood.html For information about the eToys dispute, see http://www.toywar.com/ See also http://www.RTMark.com

Roy Arden **Wal-Mart Store (Royale) Burnaby B.C.** 1996

Roy Arden **Wal-Mart Store (Royale) Burnaby B.C.** 1996

Roy Arden **Wal-Mart Store (Apple Jacks) Burnaby B.C.** 1996

Roy Arden **Wal-Mart Store (Plastic Stools) Burnaby B.C.** 1996

Zwelethu Mthethwa **Untitled** 1998/99

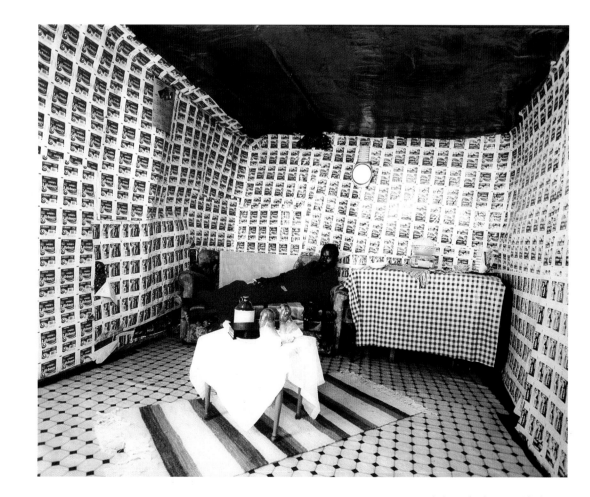

Zwelethu Mthethwa **Untitled** 1999

Lisa Ruyter **Givenchy 1 (The Green Pastures)** 2001

Tom Sachs **Prada Valuemeal** 1998

Tom Sachs **Crispy Chicken Deluxe (Hermès)** 1999

Tom Sachs **Tiffany Gift Meal** 1999

Tom Sachs **Chanel Special Meal** 1999

Surasi Kusolwong **La-la-la Minimal Market (Welcome 1 Euro)** 2002

Surasi Kusolwong **1,000 Lira Market (La vita continua)** 2001

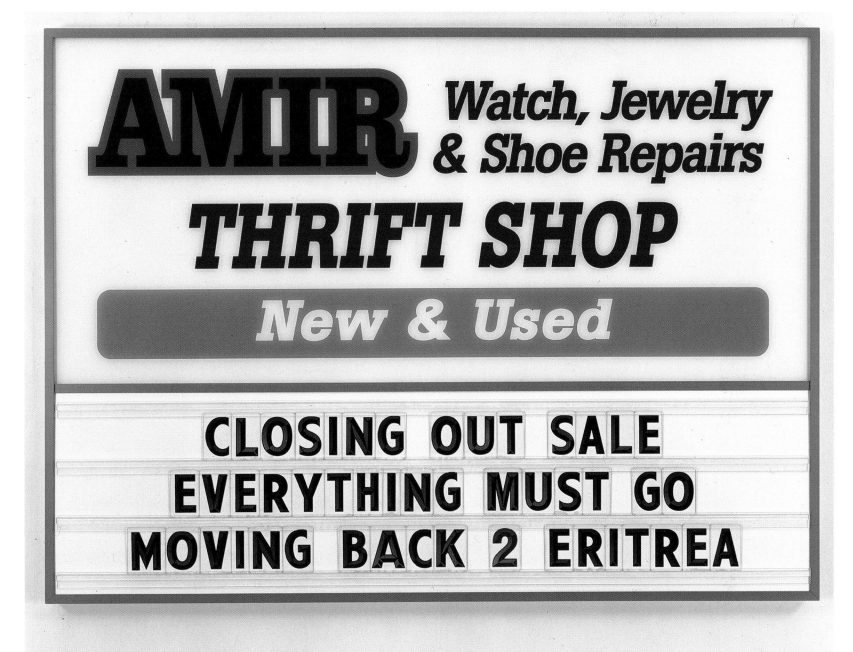

Ken Lum **Amir, Watch, Jewelry & Shoe Repairs, Thrift Shop, New & Used** 2000

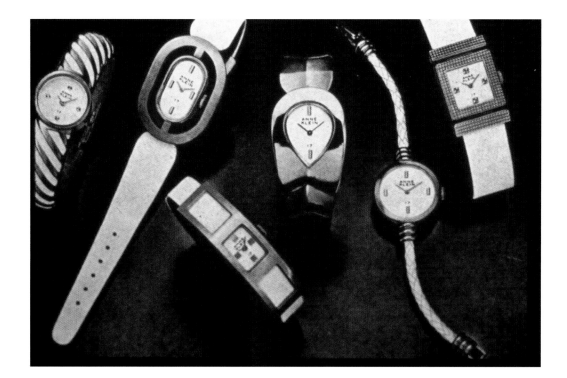

Richard Prince **Untitled (Watches)** 1977–78

Martha Rosler **Kassel Barefoot #3** 1981

Martha Rosler **Vienna** 1987

Martha Rosler **Madison Avenue, New York** 1986

Martha Rosler **Subway Station, Frankfurt** 1983

Paul McCarthy **Fear of Mannequins, Wig-heads, Hollywood Boulevard,** 1971/2002

Paul McCarthy **Fear of Reflections** 1971/2002

Tracey Emin and Sarah Lucas **The Last Night of the Shop 3.7.1993** 1993

Seamus Nicolson **Jason** 2000

Wolfgang Tillmans **Supermarkt** 2000

Martin McGinn **Mini Market** 2001

Michael Landy **Costermonger's Stall** 1992–97

Jenny Holzer **Xenon for Liverpool** 2002

Common Culture **Colour Menu Installation 4** 2002

villa spies
on the island torö (s)
by staffan berglund (1969)

she wears suede dress with phyton insert by trussardi, shoes by callaghan, small handbag from freitag. she wears t-shirt by bless, satin pencil skirt from future ozbek, 'air max' metallic trainers by nike

'606 universal' shelving system in beech-veneered mdf by dieter rams. book: jeff noon, vurt, ringbull press (1993); if / then (0.1/ 1999); mike davis, city of quartz, verso (1990). 'g3 powerbook' by apple

Gunilla Klingberg **Spar Loop** 2000

List of Works

Berenice Abbott
↘ *Newsstand, 32nd Street and Third Avenue*, 1935
Silver gelatin print, 20.3 x 25.4 cm
Miriam and Ira D. Wallach Division of Art, Prints and
Photographs, The New York Public Library, Astor, Lenox
and Tilden Foundations ↘ **96**

Berenice Abbott
↘ *Blossom Restaurant*, 1935
Silver gelatin print, 20.3 x 25.4 cm
Miriam and Ira D. Wallach Division of Art, Prints and
Photographs, The New York Public Library, Astor, Lenox
and Tilden Foundations ↘ **95**

Berenice Abbott
↘ *Whelan's Drug Store,* 1936
Silver gelatin print, 20.3 x 25.4 cm
Miriam and Ira D. Wallach Division of Art, Prints and
Photographs, The New York Public Library, Astor, Lenox
and Tilden Foundations ↘ **104**

Berenice Abbott
↘ *A & P (Great Atlantic & Pacific Tea Co.)*, 1936
Silver gelatin print, 20.3 x 25.4 cm
Miriam and Ira D. Wallach Division of Art, Prints and
Photographs, The New York Public Library, Astor, Lenox
and Tilden Foundations ↘ **105**

Berenice Abbott
↘ *Rope Store*, 1936
Silver gelatin print, 19.1 x 22.9 cm
Miriam and Ira D. Wallach Division of Art, Prints and
Photographs, The New York Public Library, Astor, Lenox
and Tilden Foundations ↘ **104**

Berenice Abbott
↘ *Chicken Market*, 1937
Silver gelatin print, 41.9 x 35.3 cm
Miriam and Ira D. Wallach Division of Art, Prints and
Photographs, The New York Public Library, Astor, Lenox
and Tilden Foundations ↘ **96**

Berenice Abbott
↘ *Bread Store, 259 Bleecker Street, New York*, 1937
Silver gelatin print, 25.4 x 20.3 cm
Miriam and Ira D. Wallach Division of Art, Prints and
Photographs, The New York Public Library, Astor, Lenox
and Tilden Foundations ↘ **95**

Berenice Abbott
↘ *Hardware Store*, 1938
Silver gelatin print, 35.6 x 40.6 cm
Miriam and Ira D. Wallach Division of Art, Prints and
Photographs, The New York Public Library, Astor, Lenox
and Tilden Foundations ↘ **105**

Josef Albers
↘ *Stille Geste* (Silent Gesture), c. 1929
Photograph, 22.9 x 15.4 cm
The Josef and Anni Albers Foundation, Bethany,
Connecticut ↘ **138**

Josef Albers
↘ *Neue Nike* (New Nike), c. 1929
Photograph on board, 23.5 x 17.2 cm
The Josef and Anni Albers Foundation, Bethany,
Connecticut ↘ **138**

Josef Albers
↘ *Untitled (Mannequins)*, c. 1930
Photo-collage on board (2 photographs), 29.7 x 41.7 cm
The Josef and Anni Albers Foundation, Bethany,
Connecticut ↘ **139**

Josef Albers
↘ *Erdmannsdorfer Puppen* (Erdmannsdorf Dolls), *30*, 1930
Photo-collage on board (3 photographs), 41.7 x 29.7 cm
The Josef and Anni Albers Foundation, Bethany,
Connecticut

American Supermarket
↘ *The American Supermarket* (Announcement),
Bianchini Gallery, New York, 1964
Silkscreen on paper, 43.1 x 55.8 cm
Estate of Robert Watts. Courtesy of Larry Miller
and Sara Seagull, Robert Watts Studio Archive,
New York ↘ **170**, ↘ **171**

Billy Apple
↘ *Apples, 2 for 25 Cents*, 1962–64
Off-set lithograph on canvas, extruded aluminium strip
with printed plastic, 127 x 101 cm
Museum of New Zealand, Te Papa Tongarewa, Wellington
Collection of Te Papa Tongarewa (I.002864) ↘ **174**

Billy Apple
↘ *A for Apple*, 1962/2002
Screenprint on canvas with neon, 76.2 x 63.5 cm
Courtesy of the artist, Auckland, New Zealand

Roy Arden
↘ *Wal-Mart Store (Apple Jacks) Burnaby B.C.*, 1996
Giclée print, 51 x 61 cm
Courtesy of Gilles Peyroulet & Cie., Paris ↘ **231**

Roy Arden
↘ *Wal-Mart Store (Plastic Stools), Burnaby B.C.*, 1996
Giclée print, 51 x 61 cm
Courtesy of Gilles Peyroulet & Cie., Paris ↘ **231**

Roy Arden
↘ *Wal-Mart (Royale) Burnaby B.C.*, 1996
Giclée print, 51 x 61 cm
Courtesy of Gilles Peyroulet & Cie., Paris ↘ **231**

Roy Arden
↘ *Wal-Mart (Tide) Burnaby B.C.*, 1996
Giclée print, 51 x 61 cm
Courtesy of Gilles Peyroulet & Cie., Paris ↘ **231**

Eugène Atget
↘ *Au Soleil d'Or, Place de l'Ecoles*, 1902
Albumen print, 21.6 x 18 cm
International Museum of Photography at George Eastman
House, Rochester, New York ↘ **92**

Eugène Atget
↘ *Au Port Salut*, 1903
Albumen print, 21.9 x 17.9 cm
International Museum of Photography at George Eastman
House, Rochester, New York ↘ **93**

Eugène Atget
↘ *Rue de Petit Thouars*, 1910–11
Albumen print, 23.7 x 17.6 cm
International Museum of Photography at George Eastman
House, Rochester, New York ↘ **99**

Eugène Atget
↘ *Boulevard de Strasbourg*, 1912
Albumen print, 22.5 x 17.8 cm
International Museum of Photography at George Eastman
House, Rochester, New York ↘ **100**

Eugène Atget
↘ *Avenue des Gobelins*, 1925
Silver gelatin print, 17.8 x 22.8 cm
International Museum of Photography at George Eastman
House, Rochester, New York ↘ **84**

Eugène Atget
↘ *Rue Mouffetard*, 1925
Silver gelatin print, 22.4 x 17.8 cm
International Museum of Photography at George Eastman
House, Rochester, New York ↘ **94**

Eugène Atget
↘ *Boulevard de Strasbourg*, 1926
Silver gelatin print, 22 x 18 cm
International Museum of Photography at George Eastman
House, Rochester, New York ↘ **101**

Eugène Atget
↘ *Avenue de l'Obervatoire*, 1926
Silver gelatin print, 18 x 22.4 cm
International Museum of Photography at George Eastman
House, Rochester, New York ↘ **103**

Eugène Atget
↘ *Avenue des Gobelins*, 1926
Silver gelatin print, 23 x 17.8 cm
International Museum of Photography at George Eastman
House, Rochester, New York ↘ **94**

Eugène Atget
↘ *Bon Marché*, 1926–27
Silver gelatin print, 17.8 x 22.9 cm
International Museum of Photography at George Eastman
House, Rochester, New York ↘ **102**

Stewart Bale
↘ *F. W. Woolworth & Co. Ltd, London Road, Liverpool*, 1931 **
Silver gelatin print (reprint), 50.8 x 61 cm
Stewart Bale Archive, Courtesy of the Board of Trustees of
the National Museums & Galleries on Merseyside
(Merseyside Maritime Museum) ↘ **110**

Stewart Bale
↘ *F. W. Woolworth & Co. Ltd, London Road, Liverpool*, 1931 **
Silver gelatin print (reprint), 50.8 x 61 cm
Stewart Bale Archive, Courtesy of the Board of Trustees of
the National Museums & Galleries on Merseyside
(Merseyside Maritime Museum) ↘ **110**

Stewart Bale
↘ *Lewis's Ltd, Ranelagh Street, Liverpool*, 1949 **
Black and white photograph (reprint), 50.8 x 61 cm
Stewart Bale Archive, Courtesy of the Board of Trustees of
the National Museums & Galleries on Merseyside
(Merseyside Maritime Museum) ↘ **110**

Stewart Bale
↘ *Blacklers Stores Ltd, Great Charlotte Street, Liverpool*,
1954 **
Black and white photograph (reprint), 50.8 x 61 cm
Stewart Bale Archive, Courtesy of the Board of Trustees of
the National Museums & Galleries on Merseyside
(Merseyside Maritime Museum) ↘ **110**

Stewart Bale
↘ *Blacklers Stores Ltd, Great Charlotte Street, Liverpool*,
1954 **
Black and white photograph (reprint), 50.8 x 61 cm
Stewart Bale Archive, Courtesy of the Board of Trustees of
the National Museums & Galleries on Merseyside
(Merseyside Maritime Museum)

Stewart Bale
↘ *Marks & Spencer Ltd, Church Street, Liverpool*, 1954 **
Black and white photograph, 50.8 x 61 cm
Stewart Bale Archive, Courtesy of the Board of Trustees
of the National Museums & Galleries on Merseyside
(Merseyside Maritime Museum) ↘ **111**

Stewart Bale
↘ *Liverpool Co-operative Society, Interior of Kirkby
Premises*, 1959 **
Black and white photograph, 50.8 x 61 cm
Stewart Bale Archive, Courtesy of the Board of Trustees
of the National Museums & Galleries on Merseyside
(Merseyside Maritime Museum)

Stewart Bale
↘ *Arcofoods, Ranelagh Street, Liverpool*, 1962 **
Black and white photograph, 50.8 x 61 cm
Stewart Bale Archive, Courtesy of the Board of Trustees
of the National Museums & Galleries on Merseyside
(Merseyside Maritime Museum)

Thomas Bayrle
↘ *Glücksklee*, 1969
4,200 milkcans, 180 x 170 cm
Private Collection, Frankfurt ↘ **167**

Denise Bellon
↘ *Rue de la glacière, Mannequin by Marcel Jean*, 1938
Black and white photograph (reprint), 30 x 24 cm
Les films de l'équinoxe – Fonds photographique Denise
Bellon ↘ **132**

Denise Bellon
↘ *Mannequin by Oscar Dominguez*, 1938
Black and white photograph (reprint), 30 x 24 cm
Les films de l'équinoxe – Fonds photographique Denise
Bellon ↘ **137**

Denise Bellon
↘ *Maurice Henry and his Mannequin*, 1938
Black and white photograph (reprint), 30 x 24 cm
Les films de l'équinoxe – Fonds photographique Denise
Bellon ↘ **133**

Denise Bellon
↘ *Mannequin by Sonia Mossé*, 1938
Black and white photograph (reprint), 30 x 24 cm
Les films de l'équinoxe – Fonds photographique
Denise Bellon ↘ **137**

Denise Bellon
↘ *Mannequin by Paul Eluard*, 1938
Black and white photograph (reprint), 30 x 24 cm
Les films de l'équinoxe – Fonds photographique
Denise Bellon ↘ **133**

Denise Bellon
↘ *Salvador Dalí and his Mannequin*, 1938
Black and white photograph (reprint), 30 x 24 cm
Les films de l'équinoxe – Fonds photographique Denise
Bellon ↘ **136**

Joseph Beuys
↘ *Wirtschaftswerte* (Economic Values), 1980
Six metal shelves, food packages from the German
Democratic Republic, block of plaster, pencil, grease,
290 x 400 x 265 cm
Stedelijk Museum voor Actuele Kunst (S.M.A.K.), Gent
 ↘ **198–201**
 Installation includes six paintings from the exhibiting
 institution, painted during the time of Karl Marx.

Mike Bidlo
↘ *Not Warhol (Brillo Boxes, 1969)*, 1991
Acrylic on wood, 51 x 51 x 43 cm each
Galerie Bruno Bischofberger, Zurich ↘ **210**

Guillaume Bijl
↘ Installation *New Supermarket*, 2002
Mixed media, dimensions variable
Courtesy of the artist ↘ **218**, ↘ **219**

Peter Blake
↘ *Toy Shop*, 1962
Mixed media, glass and painted wood, 156.8 x 194 x 34 cm
Tate. Purchase 1970 ↘ **161**

KP Brehmer
↘ *Schachtel 'Für Beuys'* (Box 'For Beuys'), 1965
Laminated print on board, 14 x 5.5 x 5.5 cm
KP Brehmer Estate, Berlin

KP Brehmer
↘ *Aufsteller 12* (Display 12), 1965
Laminated print on board, 57.2 x 63 x 25.7 cm
KP Brehmer Estate, Berlin

KP Brehmer
↘ *Aufsteller 15* (Display 15), 1965
Laminated print on board with fabric, 40 x 30 x 25 cm
Block Collection, Berlin ↘ **160**

KP Brehmer
↘ *Aufsteller 'Reklame für Fräulein F'* (Display 'Advertisement for Miss F'), 1965
Laminated print on board with fabric, 26 x 21 cm
Block Collection, Berlin ↘ **160**

KP Brehmer
↘ *Schachtel 3* (Box 3), 1966
Laminated print on board fabric and wood, 25 x 14 x 3 cm
KP Brehmer Estate, Berlin ↘ **160**

KP Brehmer
↘ *Aufsteller 21 'Eye-Cream-2'* (Display 21 'Eye-Cream-2'), 1967
Laminated print on board, 65 x 80 x 10 cm
KP Brehmer Estate, Berlin

KP Brehmer
↘ *Schachtel 17, Hinzurück* (Box 17, Back and Forth), 1968
Laminated print on board, 57 x 37 x 3 cm
KP Brehmer Estate, Berlin

Maurizio Cattelan
↘ *Less than Ten Items*, 1997
Galvanized metal, plastic and rubber,
107 x 211.5 x 57.2 cm
Olbricht Collection ↘ **89**

Christo
↘ *Pousette (wrapped supermarket cart)*, 1963
Mixed media, 105 x 78 x 42 cm
Onnasch Collection, Berlin ↘ **162**

Christo
↘ *Four Store Fronts Corner*, 1964–65
Galvanized metal, clear and coloured Plexiglass,
Masonite, canvas and electric light, 248 x 569 x 61 cm
Collection Christo and Jeanne-Claude ↘ **163**

Claude Closky
↘ *Sans titre (supermarché)* (Untitled (Supermarket)), 1996–99
Wallpaper, silkscreen print, dimensions variable
Courtesy of the artist and Galerie Chouakri Brahms, Berlin ↘ **38**, ↘ **224**

Common Culture
↘ *Colour Menu Installation 4*, 2002 **
Light boxes, dimensions variable
Courtesy of the artists ↘ **251**

Marcel Duchamp
↘ Window display for Breton's *Le Surréalisme et la Peinture*, New York, November 1945
Photograph by Maya Deren? (reprint), 23.9 x 17.8 cm
Friederike and Thomas Girst Collection, Munich/New York
↘ **142**

Marcel Duchamp
↘ Window display for André Breton's *Arcane 17*, 1946
Photograph by Maya Deren? (reprint), 23.9 x 17.8 cm
Philadelphia Museum of Art ↘ **146**, ↘ **147**

Don Eddy
↘ *Hosiery, Handbags and Shoes*, 1974
Acrylic on canvas, 91.5 x 145 cm
Ludwig Forum für Internationale Kunst, Aachen – Ludwig Collection ↘ **165**

Michael Elmgreen & Ingar Dragset
↘ *Powerless Structures, Fig. 342*, 2002 *
Plastic lettering, paper
Courtesy of the artists ↘ **68**

Tracey Emin & Sarah Lucas
↘ *The Last Night of the Shop 3.7.93*, 1993
Fabric and paper badges, 151.5 x 135 cm
Tate. Presented by the Factual Nonsense Trust and the family of Joshua Compston in memory of Joshua Compston 2000 ↘ **245**

Max Ernst
↘ *Fiat Modes – Pereat Ars*, 1919
Three lithographs (I, II, III),
45.5 x 30 cm each
Galerie Brusberg, Berlin ↘ **134**

Erró
↘ *Foodscape*, 1964
Oil on canvas,
201 x 302.5 cm
Moderna Museet, Stockholm ↘ **159**

Richard Estes
↘ *The Candy Store*, 1969
Oil and synthetic polymer on canvas, 121.3 x 174.6 cm
Whitney Museum of American Art, New York. Purchased with funds from the Friends of the Whitney Museum of American Art ↘ **164**

Walker Evans
↘ *Household Supply Store*, 1935
Photograph (reprint), 18.6 x 23.5 cm
Library of Congress, Washington, D.C., Prints and Photograph Division

Walker Evans
↘ *Seed Store Interior. Vicksburg, Missisippi* , 1936
Photograph (reprint), 23.5 x 18.6 cm
Library of Congress, Washington, D.C., Prints and Photograph Division ↘ **107**

Walker Evans
↘ *General Store Interior. Moundville, Alabama*, 1936
Photograph (reprint), 18.6 x 23.5 cm
Library of Congress, Washington, D.C., Prints and Photograph Division

Walker Evans
↘ *Roadside Fruit. Ponchatoula, Louisiana*, 1936
Photograph (reprint), 18.6 x 23.5 cm
Library of Congress, Washington, D.C., Prints and Photograph Division ↘ **106**

Walker Evans
↘ *Seed Store Interior. Vicksburg, Missisippi*, 1936
Photograph (reprint), 18.6 x 23.5 cm
Library of Congress, Washington, D.C., Prints and Photograph Division

Walker Evans
↘ *Grocery store. Moundville, Alabama*, 1936
Photograph (reprint), 18.6 x 23.5 cm
Library of Congress, Washington, D.C., Prints and Photograph Division

Walker Evans
↘ *Storefront. Greensboro, Alabama*, 1936
Photograph (reprint), 18.6 x 23.5 cm
Library of Congress, Washington, D.C., Prints and Photograph Division

Walker Evans
↘ *Auto Parts Shop. Atlanta, Georgia*, 1936
Photograph (reprint), 18.6 x 23.5 cm
Library of Congress, Washington, D.C., Prints and Photograph Division ↘ **106**

Walker Evans
↘ *Photographer's Window of Penny Portraits. Birmingham, Alabama*, 1936
Photograph (reprint), 18.6 x 23.5 cm
Library of Congress, Washington, D.C., Prints and Photograph Division

Walker Evans
↘ *Storefronts*, 1936
Photograph (reprint), 18.6 x 23.5 cm
Library of Congress, Washington, D.C., Prints and
Photograph Division ↘ **97**
Walker Evans
↘ *The Old Reliable House Mover*, 1936
Photograph (reprint), 18.6 x 23.5 cm
Library of Congress, Washington, D.C., Prints and
Photograph Division ↘ **97**

Hans Finsler
↘ *Pralinensorten* (Praline Selection), 1927–28
Photograph, 24 x 30 cm
Museum für Kunst- und Kulturgeschichte der
Hansestadt Lübeck ↘ **120**
Hans Finsler
↘ *Mosttafeln III* (Most Bars III), 1927–28
Photograph, c. 24 x 18 cm
Staatliche Galerie Moritzburg Halle, Landesmuseum
Sachsen-Anhalt
Hans Finsler
↘ *Most Edelmokka* (Most Superior Mocha), 1927–28
Photograph, c. 24 x 18 cm
Staatliche Galerie Moritzburg Halle, Landesmuseum
Sachsen-Anhalt
Hans Finsler
↘ *Kaffeegeschirr I* (Coffee Service I), 1930
Photograph, c. 24 x 18 cm
Staatliche Galerie Moritzburg Halle, Landesmuseum
Sachsen-Anhalt ↘ **120**
Hans Finsler
↘ *Konfektschalen* (Sweets Dishes), 1930
Photograph, c. 24 x 18 cm
Staatliche Galerie Moritzburg Halle, Landesmuseum
Sachsen-Anhalt
Hans Finsler
↘ *Tafelservice, zwei Anordnungen* (Dinner Service, Two
Arrangements), 1930–31
Photograph, c. 24 x 18 cm
Staatliche Galerie Moritzburg Halle, Landesmuseum
Sachsen-Anhalt ↘ **120**

Sylvie Fleury
↘ *Untitled*, 1992
Carpet, couch, shoe boxes, shoes,
80 x 340 x 240 cm
Andrea Caratsch Collection, Zurich ↘ **12**

Sylvie Fleury
↘ *Pleasures*, 1996
Wall painting, dimensions variable
Monika Sprüth/Philomene Magers,
Cologne/Munich ↘ **12**
Sylvie Fleury
↘ *ELA 75/K, Easy. Breezy. Beautiful.(Nr.6)*, 2000
Supermarket trolley on pedestal, 83 x 55 x 96 cm
Courtesy of the artist and Galerie Hauser & Wirth &
Presenhuber, Zurich ↘ **235**

Katharina Fritsch
↘ *Warengestell mit Vasen* (Display Stand with Vases),
1987–89
Plastic, screenprint, aluminium,
270 x 112.5 x 12.5 cm
Courtesy of the artist, Dusseldorf ↘ **211**

Robert Gober
↘ *Untitled*, 1993/94 **
Photolithography on archival paper,
56.8 x 30.5 cm and 28.3 x 30.5 cm
Gerard Faggionato, London ↘ **230**

Andreas Gursky
↘ *Prada I*, 1996
C-Print, 134 x 226 cm
Courtesy of the artist, Dusseldorf ↘ **212**
Andreas Gursky
↘ *Prada II*, 1997
C-Print, 165 x 316 x 5.4 cm
Kunstmuseum Wolfsburg ↘ **212**
Andreas Gursky
↘ *Prada III*, 1998
C-Print, 177 x 307 x 6 cm
Goetz Collection, Munich ↘ **213**
Andreas Gursky
↘ *99 Cent II*, 2001 (diptych)
C-Print, 206 x 341 x 8 cm each
Courtesy of Galerie Monika Sprüth, Cologne ↘ **214–215**

Nigel Henderson
↘ *Wig Stall, Petticoat Lane, London*, 1952
Photograph, 20.3 x 24.5 cm
Estate of Nigel Henderson ↘ **108**

Nigel Henderson
↘ *Barber's Shop Window, London*, 1949–53
Photograph, 20.3 x 24.5 cm
Estate of Nigel Henderson ↘ **109**
Nigel Henderson
↘ *W & F Riley, Newsagents and Confectioners, London*,
1949–53
Photograph, 20.3 x 24.5 cm
Estate of Nigel Henderson ↘ **108**
Nigel Henderson
↘ *Roman Road Street Market, London*, 1949–53
Photograph, 20.3 x 24.5 cm
Estate of Nigel Henderson ↘ **109**

Damien Hirst
↘ *Pharmacy*, 1992
Mixed media, installation, dimensions variable
Tate. Purchase 1996 ↘ **206**, ↘ **216–217**

Jenny Holzer
↘ *Xenon for Liverpool*, 2002 **
Xenon projection, dimensions variable
Courtesy of the artist ↘ **250**

Frederick Kiesler
↘ *Details of Display Design*, 1927–28
Black and white photograph, 25 x 16 cm
Österreichische Friedrich und Lillian Kiesler-
Privatstiftung
Frederick Kiesler
↘ *Top View of a Display Furniture*, 1927–28
Black and white photograph, 24 x 18.5 cm
Österreichische Friedrich und Lillian Kiesler-
Privatstiftung
Frederick Kiesler
↘ *Window Display*, 1927–28
Black and white photograph, 25.5 x 20 cm
Österreichische Friedrich und Lillian Kiesler-
Privatstiftung ↘ **127**
Frederick Kiesler
↘ *Frederick Kiesler and Display Furniture*, 1927–28
Black and white photograph, 25.3 x 20.2 cm
Österreichische Friedrich und Lillian Kiesler-
Privatstiftung ↘ **128**

Frederick Kiesler
↘ *Window Display for Saks Fifth Avenue*, 1927–28
Black and white photograph, 25.3 x 20.5 cm
Österreichische Friedrich und Lillian Kiesler-
Privatstiftung

Frederick Kiesler
↘ *Window Display for Saks Fifth Avenue*, 1927–28
Black and white photograph, 25.5 x 20.1 cm
Österreichische Friedrich und Lillian Kiesler-
Privatstiftung

Frederick Kiesler
↘ *Detail of Window Display for Saks Fifth Avenue*,
1927–28
Black and white photograph, 21.3 x 16.4 cm
Österreichische Friedrich und Lillian Kiesler-
Privatstiftung

Frederick Kiesler
↘ *Detail of Window Display for Saks Fifth Avenue*,
1927–28
Black and white photograph, 21.4 x 16.4 cm
Österreichische Friedrich und Lillian Kiesler-
Privatstiftung

Frederick Kiesler
↘ *Detail of Window Display for Saks Fifth Avenue*,
1927–28
Black and white photograph, 25.5 x 20.3 cm
Österreichische Friedrich und Lillian Kiesler-
Privatstiftung ↘ **129**

Frederick Kiesler
↘ *Window Display for Saks Fifth Avenue*, 1927–28
Black and white photograph, 25.5 x 20.3 cm
Österreichische Friedrich und Lillian Kiesler-
Privatstiftung ↘ **129**

Frederick Kiesler
↘ *Window Display for Saks Fifth Avenue*, 1927–28
Black and white photograph, 20.1 x 25.4 cm
Österreichische Friedrich und Lillian Kiesler-
Privatstiftung ↘ **129**

Frederick Kiesler
↘ *Window Display for Saks Fifth Avenue*, 1927–28
Black and white photograph, 25.5 x 20.3 cm
Österreichische Friedrich und Lillian Kiesler-
Privatstiftung ↘ **129**

Frederick Kiesler
↘ *Window Display for Saks Fifth Avenue*, 1927–28
Black and white photograph, 20.5 x 25.3 cm
Österreichische Friedrich und Lillian Kiesler-
Privatstiftung ↘ **129**

Frederick Kiesler
↘ *Window Display for Saks Fifth Avenue*, 1927–28
Black and white photograph, 20.2 x 25.7 cm
Österreichische Friedrich und Lillian Kiesler-
Privatstiftung ↘ **129**

Frederick Kiesler
↘ *Detail of a Window Display for Saks Fifth Avenue*, 1927–28
Black and white photograph, 21.4 x 16.4 cm
Österreichische Friedrich und Lillian Kiesler-
Privatstiftung ↘ **129**

Frederick Kiesler
↘ *Detail of a Window Display for Saks Fifth Avenue*, 1927–28
Black and white photograph, 21.4 x 16.4 cm
Österreichische Friedrich und Lillian Kiesler-
Privatstiftung ↘ **129**

Frederick Kiesler
↘ *Detail of a Window Display for Saks Fifth Avenue*, 1927–28
Black and white photograph, 21.4 x 16.4 cm
Österreichische Friedrich und Lillian Kiesler-
Privatstiftung ↘ **129**

Frederick Kiesler
↘ *Study for a Façade Design for a Department Store*, 1927–28
Collage, cardboard, photograph, pencil, ink, 50.7 x 47 cm
Österreichische Friedrich und Lillian Kiesler-
Privatstiftung ↘ **124**

Frederick Kiesler
↘ *The Modern Show Window and Store Front*, 1929
Paper, print, 27.5 x 20.5 cm
Österreichische Friedrich und Lillian Kiesler-
Privatstiftung

Frederick Kiesler
↘ *Contemporary Art Applied to the Store and its
Display*, 1930
Book (four copies), 28 x 21 cm
Österreichische Friedrich und Lillian Kiesler-
Privatstiftung ↘ **64**

Frederick Kiesler
↘ *Some Notes on Show Windows*, 1930
Paper, typescript, 29.5 x 22 cm
Österreichische Friedrich und Lillian Kiesler-
Privatstiftung

Gunilla Klingberg
↘ *Spar Loop*, 2000 **∗∗**
Video animation
Courtesy of the artist ↘ **253**

Jeff Koons
↘ *New Hoover Deluxe Shampoo Polishers, New Hoover
Quick-Broom, New Shelton Wet/Dry Triple Decker*, 1987
Three shampoo polishers, three vacuum cleaners,
Plexiglass, fluorescent lights, 231 x 137.8 x 71 cm
Courtesy of the Dakis Joannou Collection, Athens ↘ **207**

Jeff Koons
↘ *New Hoover Deluxe Shampoo Polishers*, 1980–86
Three shampoo polishers, Plexiglass, fluorescent lights,
142.2 x 91.4 x 38.1 cm
Courtesy of Anthony d'Offay Gallery, London ↘ **202**

Jeff Koons
↘ *New Hoover Convertibles Green, Green/Red, New
Hoover Deluxe Shampoo Polishers, New Shelton Wet/Dry
5 Gallon Displaced Tripledecker*, 1981–87
Five vacuum cleaners, two shampoo polishers, Plexiglass,
fluorescent lights, 312 x 137 x 71 cm
Fonds Régional d'Art Contemporain-Collection
Aquitaine ↘ **207**

Barbara Kruger
↘ *Untitled (I Shop Therefore I Am)*, 1987
Photographic screenprint on vinyl, 284.5 x 287 cm
Private Collection. Courtesy of Thomas Ammann
Fine Art, Zurich ↘ **54**

Barbara Kruger
↘ *Untitled (Shopping)*, 2002 **∗**
Installation, Galeria Kaufhof, Frankfurt,
2300 square metres
Courtesy of the artist ↘ **220**

Germaine Krull
↘ *Sans titre, Passages – Paris* (Untitled, Passages –
Paris), 1928/1980s
Gelatin silver print (reprint), 31 x 26 cm
Ann and Jürgen Wilde Collection, Zülpich ↘ **135**

Germaine Krull
↘ *Sans titre, Paris* (Untitled, Paris), 1927–28/1980s
Gelatin silver print (reprint), 33 x 21 cm
Ann and Jürgen Wilde Collection, Zülpich ↘ **131**

Surasi Kusolwong
↘ *1 Euro Market (Shop till You Fly)*, 2002 **∗**
Installation, Airport Gallery, Terminal 1,
Frankfurt am Main
Courtesy of the artist ↘ **238**

Surasi Kusolwong
↘ *One Pound Market (Just What Is It that Makes Today's Homes so Different, so Appealing?)*, 2002 **
Mixed media, dimensions variable
Courtesy of the artist ↘ **238**
Surasi Kusolwong
↘ *Suitcase Market (Selected Collection)*, 2002 **
Mixed media, dimensions variable
Courtesy of the artist

Michael Landy
↘ *Costermonger's Stall*, 1992–97 **
Wood, gloss-paint, tarpaulin, plastic buckets, electric lights, flowers, 182.8 x 213.3 x 213.3 cm
Collection Anita and Poju Zabludowicz, London ↘ **248**
Michael Landy
↘ *Closing Down Sale*, 1992/2002 **
Mixed media, dimensions variable
Courtesy of the artist ↘ **16**, ↘ **223**

Marko Lehanka
↘ *Ohne Titel (Zigarettenautomat)* (Untitled (Cigarette Vending Machine)), 1990 *
Wood, chipboard, varnish, 85 x 62 x 23.5 cm
Beckers Collection, Darmstadt ↘ **89**

Sze Tsung Leong
↘ *Evolution of Shopping*, 2001
Wall graphic, dimensions variable
Courtesy of Sze Tsung Leong, New York ↘ **80–83**

Roy Lichtenstein
↘ *Turkey*, 1961
Oil on canvas, 66 x 76.2 cm
Private collection ↘ **176**
Roy Lichtenstein
↘ *Turkey Shopping Bag*, 1964
Colour screenprint on smooth white wove paper bag with handles, 49 x 43.4 cm
Printed by Ben Birillo for *The American Supermarket* exhibition, Bianchini Gallery, New York, 1964
Ben Birillo, Great Neck, New York
Roy Lichtenstein
↘ *Button with ribbon*
Mixed media
Produced by Ben Birillo for *The American Supermarket* exhibition, Bianchini Gallery, New York, 1964
Collection Benjamin Birillo II, New York

Konrad Lueg
↘ *Betende Hände* (Praying Hands), 1963
Acrylic on canvas, 120 x 100 cm
Private Collection. Courtesy of Konrad Fischer Galerie, Dusseldorf ↘ **187**
Konrad Lueg
↘ *Bügel* (Hanger), 1963
Acrylic on canvas, 140 x 90 cm
Marzona Collection ↘ **186**

Ken Lum
↘ *Amir, Watch, Jewelry & Shoe Repairs, Thrift Shop, New & Used*, 2000 *
Plexiglass, powder-coated lacquered aluminium, plastic letters, enamel paint,
152.5 x 213.3 x 5 cm
Private collection ↘ **239**
Ken Lum
↘ *Parvi, Fresh Meat and Poultry*, 2000
Plexiglass, powder-coated lacquered aluminium, plastic letters, enamel paint,
152.5 x 213.3 x 5 cm
Courtesy of The Agency, London

Paul McCarthy
↘ *Fear of Reflections*, 1971/2002 **
Installation, dimensions variable
Courtesy of the artist, Altadena, California ↘ **244**
Paul McCarthy
↘ *Fear of Mannequins, Wig-heads, Hollywood Boulevard*, 1971/2002 **
Installation, dimensions variable
Courtesy of the artist, Altadena, California ↘ **244**

Martin McGinn
↘ *Mini Market*, 2001 **
Oil on canvas, 304.8 x 183 cm
Houldsworth, London ↘ **248**

Hannes Meyer
↘ *Gesamtansicht Vitrine Co-op, Gent* (Co-op Vitrine, Gent (First Version)), 1924
Black and white photograph, 22.6 x 17.9 cm
Institut für Geschichte und Theorie der Architektur (gta) ETH Zürich ↘ **117**

Hannes Meyer
↘ *Aufsicht Vitrine Co-op, Basel* (Top View Co-op Vitrine, Basel (Second Version)), 1925
Black and white photograph, 21 x 17 cm
Institut für Geschichte und Theorie der Architektur (gta) ETH Zürich ↘ **117**
Hannes Meyer
↘ *Aufsicht Vitrine Co-op, Basel* (Top View Co-op Vitrine, Basel (Second Version)), 1925
Black and white photograph, 20.5 x 15.5 cm
Institut für Geschichte und Theorie der Architektur (gta) ETH Zürich ↘ **112**
Hannes Meyer
↘ *Horizontalansicht Vitrine Co-op, Basel* (Horizontal View of Co-op Vitrine, Basel (Second Version)), 1925
Black and white photograph, 22 x 18.5 cm
Institut für Geschichte und Theorie der Architektur (gta) ETH Zürich ↘ **113**
Hannes Meyer
↘ *Detailansicht Vitrine Co-op, Basel* (Detail of Co-op Vitrine, Basel (Second Version)), 1925
Black and white photograph, 13 x 11.6 cm
Institut für Geschichte und Theorie der Architektur (gta) ETH Zürich ↘ **113**

Julien Michel
↘ *Les Policiers* (The Police), 2000 *
Oil on canvas, 115 x 160 cm
Private Collection, Krefeld. Courtesy of Galerie Chouakri Brahms, Berlin ↘ **249**

László Moholy-Nagy
↘ *Store Alexander Simpson*, 1936
Black and white photograph (reprint), 13 x 18 cm
Courtesy of Hattula Moholy-Nagy ↘ **121**
László Moholy-Nagy
↘ *Model for Courtaulds*, 1936
Black and white photograph (reprint), 13 x 18 cm
Courtesy of Hattula Moholy-Nagy ↘ **121**

Zwelethu Mthethwa
↘ *Untitled*, 1998–99
Cibachrome, 90 x 120 x 5 cm
Dave Fascher Collection ↘ **233**
Zwelethu Mthethwa
↘ *Untitled*, 1999
Photograph, 120 x 175 x 5 cm
Courtesy of Marco Noire Contemporary Art ↘ **233**

Andy Warhol
↘ *Giant Size $1.57 Each*, 1963
Screenprint on record cover, 31.4 x 31.4 cm
Paul Maenz Collection, Berlin ↘ **166**

Andy Warhol
↘ *Giant Size $1.57 Each*, 1963
Screenprint on record cover, 31.4 x 31.4 cm
Paul Maenz Collection, Berlin

Andy Warhol
↘ *Heinz Tomato*, 1964
Painted wood, 21.6 x 39.4 x 30.5 cm
Tate. Lent by the Froehlich Foundation,
Stuttgart 2000

Andy Warhol
↘ *Del Monte*, 1964
Painted wood, 24 x 39.4 x 30.5 cm
Tate. Lent by the Froehlich Foundation, Stuttgart 2000
↘ **152**

Andy Warhol
↘ *Brillo*, 1964
Painted wood, 44 x 43 x 35.5 cm
Tate. Lent by the Froehlich Foundation,
Stuttgart 2000 ↘ **152**

Andy Warhol
↘ *Campbell's Tomato Juice*, 1964
Painted wood, 25.4 x 45.7 x 24 cm
Tate. Lent by the Froehlich Foundation,
Stuttgart 2000

Andy Warhol
↘ *Campbell's Soup Can Shopping Bag*, 1964
Colour screenprint on smooth white wove paper bag
with handles, 49 x 43.4 cm
Printed by Ben Birillo for *The American Supermarket*
exhibition, Bianchini Gallery, New York 1964
Collection Benjamin Birillo II, New York

Andy Warhol
↘ *Button with ribbon*
Mixed media
Produced by Ben Birillo for *The American Supermarket*
exhibition, Bianchini Gallery, New York, 1964
Collection Benjamin Birillo II, New York

Andy Warhol
↘ *Area Rug Sale*,1976–86
Nine gelatin silver prints stitched with thread,
80 x 103.4 cm
Galerie Bruno Bischofberger, Zurich ↘ **61**

Andy Warhol
↘ *Silverware*, 1983
Gelatin silver print, 20.3 x 24.4 cm
Galerie Bruno Bischofberger Zurich

Andy Warhol
↘ *Building, 'Top Equipment'*, 1983
Gelatin silver print, 20.3 x 25.4 cm
Galerie Bruno Bischofberger, Zurich

Andy Warhol
↘ *Window Display Last Eight Days*, 1984
Gelatin silver print, 25.4 x 20.3 cm
Galerie Bruno Bischofberger, Zurich ↘ **169**

Andy Warhol
↘ *Store Signs*, 1984
Gelatin silver print, 20.3 x 25.4 cm
Galerie Bruno Bischofberger, Zurich ↘ **169**

Andy Warhol
↘ *Window Display*, *Mona Lisa*, c. 1985
Gelatin silver print, 20.4 x 25.4 cm
Galerie Bruno Bischofberger, Zurich ↘ **169**

Andy Warhol
↘ *Drugstore Shelves*, 1985–86
Gelatin silver print, 20.4 x 25.4 cm
Galerie Bruno Bischofberger, Zurich ↘ **168**

Andy Warhol
↘ *Window Display Jewelry*, 1986
Gelatin silver print, 25.4 x 20.3 cm
Galerie Bruno Bischofberger, Zurich ↘ **169**

Andy Warhol
↘ *Window Display, Cookout Supplies*, 1986
Gelatin silver print, 20.3 x 25.4 cm
Galerie Bruno Bischofberger, Zurich ↘ **168**

Andy Warhol
↘ *Skeletons*, 1986
Gelatin silver print, 20.4 x 25.4 cm
Galerie Bruno Bischofberger, Zurich ↘ **168**

Andy Warhol
↘ *Hellmann's Mayonnaise*, 1987
Gelatin silver print, 25.4 x 20.4 cm
Galerie Bruno Bischofberger, Zurich ↘ **168**

Robert Watts
↘ *Stamp Machine, No. 4*, 1961
Metal, paint, mixed media, 40.6 x 19.5 x 14 cm
Staatsgalerie Stuttgart ↘ **195**

Robert Watts
↘ *Affixations by Implosions, Inc.*, 1963/67
Three sheets of 100 stamps, offset printing, perforated on
gummed paper, in cellophane and paper package with
metal grommet, 21.9 x 29.8 cm each
Estate of Robert Watts. Courtesy of Larry Miller and Sara
Seagull, Robert Watts Studio Archive, New York ↘ **194**

Robert Watts
↘ *Case of Eggs (with Rainbow Wax Eggs)*, 1964
Plexiglass, vacuum-formed plastic and wax,
35.5 x 63.5 x 35.5 cm
Estate of Robert Watts. Courtesy of Larry Miller and Sara
Seagull, Robert Watts Studio Archive, New York ↘ **173**

Robert Watts
↘ *Bread (Ten Loaves)*, 1964
Paint and aluminium foil on plaster casts,
9.5 x 14 x 28 cm
Estate of Robert Watts. Courtesy of Larry Miller and Sara
Seagull, Robert Watts Studio Archive, New York

Robert Watts
↘ *Chrome Cabbage*, 1984
Two examples
Chrome plated bronze, 14.3 x 14.9 x 13.3 cm
Estate of Robert Watts. Courtesy of Larry Miller and Sara
Seagull, Robert Watts Studio Archive, New York

Miwa Yanagi
↘ *Elevator Girl, House 1F (a & b)*, 1997
Two colour photographs (diptych) mounted on Plexiglass,
240 x 200 x 2 cm each
Aarhus Kunstmuseum, Denmark ↘ **232**

Peter Zimmermann
↘ *Wechselkurse* (Exchange Rates), 1993
Screenprint on paper boxes, dimensions variable
Landesbank Baden-Württemberg, Stuttgart ↘ **224**

* Schirn Kunsthalle Frankfurt only
** Tate Liverpool only

Bibliography

Adburgham, Alison
↘ *Shops and Shopping 1800–1914: Where and in What Manner the Well-Dressed English Woman Bought Her Clothes.* London: Allen & Unwin, 1964.

Andrews, Margaret R. and Mary M. Talbot
↘ *All the World and Her Husband: Women in Twentieth-Century Consumer Culture.* London: Continuum Int., 1999.

Appadurai, Arjun (ed.)
↘ *The Social Life of Things: Commodities in Cultural Perspective.* Cambridge: Cambridge University Press, 1988.

Artley, Alexandra (ed.)
↘ *The Golden Age of Shop Design: European Shop Interiors 1880–1939.* London: Architectural Press, 1975.

Asendorf, Christoph
↘ *Batteries of Life: On the History of Things and Their Perception in Modernity.* Trans. by Don Reneau. Berkeley, Los Angeles and London: University of California Press, 1993.

Baker, Adrienne (ed.)
↘ *Serious Shopping.* London: Free Association Books, 2001.

Baldessari, Anne and Jean Hubert-Martin
↘ *Art & Publicité, 1890–1990.* Paris: Museé National d'Art Moderne, Centre Georges Pompidou, 1990.

Baren, Maurice
↘ *Victorian Shopping.* London: Michael O'Mara Books, 1999.

Baudrillard, Jean
↘ *Selected Writings.* Ed. by Mark Poster. Stanford: Stanford University Press, 1988.
↘ *Simulacra and Simulation.* Trans. by Sheila Glaser. Ann Arbor: University of Michigan Press, 1994.
↘ *The Consumer Society.* London: Sage, 1998.

Bauman, Zygmunt
↘ *Work, Consumerism and the New Poor.* Buckingham: Open University Press, 1998.

Bayley, Stephen (ed.)
↘ *Commerce and Culture.* London: Design Museum, 1989.

Belk, Russell W.
↘ *Collecting in a Consumer Society.* London and New York: Routledge, 2001.

Benjamin, Walter
↘ *The Arcades Project.* Boston: Harvard University Press, 2002.

Benson, John
↘ *The Rise of Consumer Society in Britain 1880–1890.* London: Longman, 1994.

Benson, Susan Porter
↘ *Counter Culture: Saleswomen, Managers, and Customers in American Department Stores, 1890–1940.* Urbana, IL: University of Illinois Press, 1986.

Birkin, Lawrence
↘ *Consuming Desire: Sexual Science and the Emergence of a Culture of Abundance, 1871–1914.* Ithaca: Cornell University Press, 1988.

Blaszczyk, Regina Lee
↘ *Imaging Consumers: Design and Innovation from Wedgwood to Corning.* Baltimore and London: Johns Hopkins University Press, 2000.

Bocock, Robert
↘ *Consumption.* London and New York: Routledge, 1993.

Bourdieu, Pierre
↘ *Distinction: A Social Critique of the Judgement of Taste.* London and New York: Routledge, 1986.

Bowlby, Rachel
↘ *Just Looking: Consumer Culture in Dreiser, Gissing, and Zola.* London: Methuen, 1985.
↘ *Carried Away: The Invention of Modern Shopping.* London: Faber & Faber, 2000.
↘ *Shopping With Freud.* London and New York: Routledge, 1993.

Boyer, Christine
↘ *The City of Collective Memory.* Cambridge, Massachusetts: MIT Press, 1996.

Braudel, Fernand
↘ *Afterthoughts on Material Civilization and Capitalism.* Trans. by Patricia M. Ranum. Baltimore: John Hopkins University Press, 1977.

Breward, Christopher
↘ *The Hidden Consumer.* Manchester: Manchester University Press, 1999.

Brewer, John and Roy Porter (eds.)
↘ *Consumption and the World of Goods.* London: Taylor & Francis Books, 1993.

Briggs, Asa
↘ *Friends of the People: The Centenary History of Lewis's.* London: B.T. Batsford, 1956.

Bronner, Simon J. (ed.)
↘ *Consuming Visions: Accumulation and Display of Goods in America, 1880–1920.* New York and London: Norton, 1989.

Brooks, John
↘ *Showing Off in America: From Conspicuous Consumption to Parody Display.* Boston: Little, Brown, 1981.

Buchli, Victor (ed.)
↘ *The Material Culture Reader.* Oxford and New York: Berg Publishers 2002.

Buck-Morss, Susan
↘ The *Dialectics of Seeing: Walter Benjamin and the Arcades Project.* Cambridge, Mass.: MIT Press, 1991.

Campbell, Colin
↘ *The Romantic Ethic and the Spirit of Modern Consumerism.* New York: Blackwell, 1987.

Carrier, James G.
↘ *Gifts and Commodities: Exchange and Western Capitalism since 1900.* London and New York: Routledge, 1994.

Certeau, Michel de
↘ *The Practice of Everyday Life.* Berkeley and Los Angeles, California: University of California Press, 1984.

Chaney, David
↘ 'The Department Store as a Cultural Form', *Theory, Culture and Society*, vol. 1, no. 3, 1983.

Chang, Chuihua Judy, Jeffrey Inaba, Rem Koolhaas and Sze Tsung Leong (eds.)
↘ *Harvard Design School Guide to Shopping.* Cologne: Benedikt Taschen Verlag, 2001.

Collins, Jim
↘ *High-Pop: Making Culture into Popular Entertainment.* Oxford: Blackwell Publishers, 2002.

Colze, Leo
↘ *Berliner Warenhäuser.* (1908) Berlin: Fannei & Walz, 1989.

Cook, David (ed.)
↘ *Maleshop: Consumerism and Shopping Culture.* New York: New York University Press, 1995.

Cooke, Lynne and Peter Wollen (eds.)
↘ *Visual Display: Culture Beyond Appearances.* Seattle: Bay Press, 1995.

Corrigan, Peter
↘ *The Sociology of Consumption.* London: Sage, 1997.

Cowan, Tyler
↘ *In Praise of Commercial Culture.* Cambridge, Mass.: Harvard University Press, 1998.

Coward, Rosalind
↘ *Female Desires: How They are Sought, Bought and Packaged.* New York: Grove Press, 1985.

Cross, Gary
↘ *Time and Money: The Making of Consumer Culture.* London: Routledge, 1993.
↘ *An All-Consuming Century: Why Commercialism Won in Modern America.* New York: Columbia University Press, 2000.

Crossick, Geoffrey and Serge Jaumain (eds.)
↘ *Cathedrals of Consumption: The European Department Store, 1850–1939.* Aldershot: Ashgate Publishing, 1999.

Cumming, Neil and Marysia Lewandowska
↘ *The Value of Things.* Basel, Boston, Berlin: Birkhäuser, 2000.

Davis, Dorothy
↘ *A History of Shopping.* London: Routledge and Kegan Paul, 1966.

Debord, Guy
↘ *The Society of the Spectacle.* (Paris 1967) New York: Zone Books, 1994.

De Grazia, Victoria with Ellen Furlough (eds.)
↘ *The Sex of Things: Gender and Consumption in Historical Perspective.* Berkeley, Los Angeles, London: University of California Press, 1996.

Desser, David and Garth Jowett (eds.)
↘ *Hollywood Goes Shopping.* Minneapolis: University of Minnesota Press, 2000.

Douglas, Mary
↘ *Thought Styles: Critical Essays on Good Taste.* London: Sage, 1996.

Douglas, Mary and Baron Isherwood.
↘ *The World of Goods: Towards an Anthropology of Consumption.* New York: Norton, 1979.

Durning, Alan
↘ *How Much Is Enough: The Consumer Society and the Future of the Earth.* New York: Norton, 1992.

Edwards, Tim
↘ *Contradictions of Consumption.* Buckingham: Open University Press, 2000.

Edgell, Stephen, Alan Ward and Kevin Hetherington (eds.)
↘ *Consumption Matters.* Oxford: Blackwell, 1997.

Ewen, Stuart
↘ *All Consuming Images: The Politics of Style in Contemporary Culture.* New York: Basic Books, 1988.
↘ *Captains of Consciousness.* New York: Basic Books, 2001.

Falk, Pasi
↘ *The Consuming Body.* London: Sage, 1994.

Falk, Pasi and Colin Campbell (eds.)
↘ *The Shopping Experience.* London: Sage, 1997.

Featherstone, Mike
↘ *Consumer Culture and Postmodernism.* London: Sage, 1990.

Featherstone, Mike and David Frisby (eds.)
↘ *Simmel on Culture.* London, Thousand Oaks, New Dehli: Sage, 1997.

Fine, Ben and Ellen Leopold (eds.)
↘ *The World of Consumption.* London and New York: Routledge, 1993.

Firat, A. Fuat and Nikhileshi Dholakia
↘ *Consuming People.* London: Routledge, 1998.

Fox, Richard Wightman and T. J. Jackson Lears (eds.)
↘ *The Culture of Consumption: Critical Essays in American History, 1880–1980.* New York: Pantheon Books, 1983.

Frank, Thomas
↘ *The Conquest of Cool: Business Culture, Counterculture, and the Rise of Hip Consumerism.* Chicago and London: University of Chicago Press, 1997.

Frei, Helmut
↘ *Tempel der Kauflust: Eine Geschichte der Warenhauskultur.* Leipzig: Edition Leipzig, 1997.

Friedberg, Anne
↘ *Window Shopping: Cinema and the Postmodern.* Berkeley, California: University of California Press, 1994.

Gabriel, Yannis and Tim Lang
↘ *The Unmanageable Consumer.* London: Sage, 1995.

Gaibraith, John Kenneth
↘ *The Affluent Society.* New York: Houghton Mifflin, 1958.

Gardner, Carl and Julie Sheppard
↘ *Consuming Passion: The Rise of Retail Culture.* London: Unwin Hyman, 1989.

Geist, Johann Friedrich
↘ *Arcades: The History of a Building Type.* Cambridge, Massachusetts: MIT Press, 1983.

Glenn, Constance W. (ed.)
↘ *The Great American Pop Art Store: Multiples of the Sixties.* Santa Monica, California: Smart Art Press, 1997.

Glennie, Paul, Nigel Thrift and Sarah Whatmore (eds.)
↘ *Grasping Modern Consumption.* London: Sage, 2000.

Göhre, Paul
↘ *Das Warenhaus.* Frankfurt am Main: Literarische Anstalt Rütten & Loening 1907.

Gottdiener, Mark
↘ *New Forms of Consumption.* Lanham, Maryland: Rowman & Littlefield Publishers, 2000.

Halter, Marilyn
↘ *Shopping for Identity: The Marketing of Ethnicity.* New York: Schocken, 2000.

Hambleton, Ronald
↘ *The Branding of America: From Levi Strauss to Chrysler.* Camden, Maine: Yankee Books, 1987.

Hannigan, John
↘ *Fantasy City: Pleasure and Profit in the Postmodern Metropolis.* New York: Routledge, 1998.

Harrington, Lee C. and Denise D. Bielby (eds.)
↘ *Popular Culture: Production and Consumption.* Oxford: Blackwell, 2000.

Harris, Daniel
↘ *Cute, Quaint, Hungry and Romantic : The Aesthetics of Consumerism.* New York: Basic Books, 2000.

Haug, Wolfgang Fritz
↘ *Critique of Commodity Aesthetics: Appearance, Sexuality and Advertising.* Minneapolis: University of Minnesota Press, 1986.

Hearn, Jeff and Sasha Roseneil (eds.)
↘ *Consuming Cultures.* New York: Palgrave Macmillan, 1999.

Hebdige, Dick
↘ *Hiding in the Light: On Images and Things.* London: Routledge, 1989.
↘ *Subculture: The Meaning of Style.* New York: Methuen, 1979.

Hendrickson, Robert
↘ *The Grand Emporiums: The Illustrated History of America's Great Department Stores.* New York: Stein and Day, 1979.

Horowitz, Roger and Arwen Mohun (eds.)
↘ *His and Hers: Gender, Consumption, and Technology.* Charlottesville, Virginia: University Press of Virginia, 1998.

Humphry, Kim
↘ *Shelf-life.* Cambridge: Cambridge University Press, 1998.

Jackson, Peter, Michelle Lowe, Daniel Miller and Frank Mort (eds.)
↘ *Commercial Cultures.* Oxford: Berg, 2000.

Jeffrey, J. B.
↘ *Retail Trading in Britain 1850–1950.* Cambridge: Cambridge University Press, 1954.

John, Robin
↘ *The Consumer Revolution.* London: Hodder & Stoughton Educational, 1994.

Keat, Russel, Nicholas Abercrombie and Nigel Whiteley
↘ *The Authority of the Consumer.* London and New York: Routledge, 1993.

Kellner, Douglas
↘ *Baudrillard: A Critical Reader.* Oxford: Blackwell Publishers, 1994.
↘ *Jean Baudrillard. From Marxism to Postmodernism and Beyond.* Cambridge: Polity Press, 1989.

Kiesler, Frederick
↘ *Contemporary Art Applied to the Store and Its Display.* New York: Brentano's, 1930.

Klein, Naomi
↘ *No Logo.* London: Flamingo 2000.

Kowaleski-Wallace, Elizabeth
↘ *Consuming Subjects: Women, Shopping and Business in the Eighteenth Century.* New York: Columbia University Press, 1997.

Kowinski, William Severini
↘ *The Malling of America: An Inside Look at the Great Consumer Paradise.* New York: William Morrow, 1985.
Kraus, Chris and Sylvére Lortinger (eds.)
Hatred of Capitalism: A Semiotext(e) Reader. Semiotext(e). Distributed by MIT Press, 2001.
Lancaster, Bill
↘ *The Department Store: A Social History.* Leicester: Leicester University Press, 1995.
Lash, Scott and John Urry
↘ *Economies of Signs and Space.* London: Sage, 1993.
Leach, William
↘ *Land of Desire: Merchants, Power, and the Rise of a New American Culture.* New York: Vintage Books, 1993.
Lears, Jackson
↘ *Fables of Abundance: A Cultural History of Advertising in America.* New York: Basic Books, 1994.
Lebergott, Stanley
↘ *Pursuing Happiness: American Consumers in the Twentieth Century.* Princeton, New Jersey: Princeton University Press, 1993.
Lee, Martyn J.
↘ *The Consumer Society Reader.* Oxford: Blackwell, 1999.
↘ *Consumer Culture Reborn.* London and New York: Routledge, 1993.
Lee, Nick and Rolland Munro (eds.)
↘ *The Consumption of Mass.* Oxford: Blackwell, 2001.
Linden, Eugene
↘ *Affluence and Discontent: The Anatomy of Consumer Societies.* New York: Viking, 1979.
Loeb, Lori Anne
↘ *Consuming Angels: Advertising and Victorian Women.* New York: Oxford University Press, 1994.
Longinotti-Buitoni, Gian Luigi
↘ *Selling Dreams: How to Make Any Product Irresitable.* New York: Simon and Schuster, 1999.
Lunt, Peter K. and Sonia M. Livingstone
↘ *Mass Consumption and Personal Identity: Everyday Economic Experience.* London and New York: Taylor & Francis, 1992.
Lury, Celia
↘ *Consumer Culture.* Cambridge: Polity Press, 1996
Mackay, Hugh
↘ *Consumption and Everyday Life.* London: Sage, 1997.
MacKeith, Margaret
↘ *The History and Conservation of Shopping Arcades.* London: Continuum International, 1986.

Mamiya, Christin J.
↘ *Pop Art and Consumer Culture: American Supermarket.* Austin, Texas: University of Texas Press, 1992.
Marchand, Roland
↘ *Advertising the American Dream: Making Way for Modernity, 1920–1940.* Berkeley, Los Angeles, London: University of California Press, 1985.
Marcus, Leonard S.
↘ *The American Store Window.* London: Architectural Press, 1978.
Mason, Roger
↘ *Conspicuous Consumption: A Study of Exceptional Consumer Behavior.* New York: St Martin's Press, 1981.
McCracken, Grant
↘ *Culture and Consumption: New Approaches to the Symbolic Character of Consumer Goods and Activities.* Bloomington and Indianapolis: Indiana University Press, 1988.
McKendrick, Neil and John Brewer and J. H. Plumb (eds.)
↘ *The Birth of Consumer Society: The Commercialisation of Eighteenth Century England.* London: Europa, 1982.
Miles, Steve
↘ *Consumerism as a Way of Life.* London: Sage, 1998.
Miles, Steve, A. Anderson and Kathy Meethan (eds.)
↘ *The Changing Consumer: Markets and Meanings.* London: Routledge, 1996.
Miller, Daniel
↘ *Material Culture and Mass Consumption.* Oxford: Blackwell, 1987.
↘ *Material Cultures: Why Some Things Matter.* Chicago: University of Chicago Press, 1998.
↘ *A Theory of Shopping.* New York: Cornell University Press, 1998.
Miller, Daniel (ed.)
↘ *Acknowledging Consumption: A Review of New Studies.* New York: Routledge, 1996.
Miller, Daniel, Peter Jackson, Nigel Thrift, Beverly Holbrook and Mi Rowlands (eds.)
↘ *Shopping, Place and Identity.* London and New York: Routledge, 1998.
Miller, Michael B.
↘ *The Bon Marché. Bourgeois Culture and the Department Store, 1896–1920.* Princeton, New Jersey: Princeton University Press, 1981.
Moore, Suzanna
↘ *Looking for Trouble: On Shopping, Gender and the Cinema.* London: Serpent's Tail, 1992.

Mort, Frank
↘ *Cultures of Consumption: Masculinities and Social Space in Late-Twentieth-Century Britain.* London and New York: Routledge, 1996.
Mukerji, Chandra
↘ *From Graven Images: Patterns of Modern Materialism.* New York: Columbia University Press, 1983.
Müller-Tamm, Pia and Katharina Sykora (eds.)
↘ *Puppen, Körper, Automaten: Phantasmen der Moderne.* Dusseldorf: Oktagon, 1999.
Nava, Mica
↘ *Changing Cultures: Feminism, Youth, and Consumerism.* London: Sage, 1992.
Nava, Mica, Andrew Blake, Iian Mackury and Barry Richards (eds.)
↘ *Buy this Book.* London and New York: Routledge, 1996.
Nead, Lynda
↘ *Victorian Babylon: People, Streets and Images in Nineteenth Century London.* New Haven, Connecticut and London: Yale University Press, 2000.
Nye, David A. and Carl Pedersen (eds.)
↘ *Consumption and American Culture.* Amsterdam: VII, 1991.
Orvell, Miles
↘ *The Real Thing: Imitation and Authenticity in American Culture, 1880–1940.* Chapel, Hill and London: North Carolina, London 1989.
Packard, Vance
↘ *The Hidden Persuaders.* Harmondsworth: Penguin, 1977.
Pasdermajian, H.
↘ *The Department Store: Its Origins, Evolution and Economics.* London: Newman Books, 1954.
Pavitt, Jane (ed.)
↘ *Brand.New.* London: Victoria and Albert Museum, 2000.
Pine, B. Joseph and James H. Gilmore
↘ *The Experience Economy: Work is Theatre.* Boston, Mass.: Harvard Business School Press, 1999.
Princen, Thomas, Michael Maniates, Ken Conca (eds.)
↘ *Confronting Consumption.* Cambridge, Mass.: MIT Press, 2002.
Quimby, Ian M. G. (ed.)
↘ *Material Culture and the Study of American Life.* New York 1978.
Radner, Hilary
↘ *Shopping Around. Feminine Culture and the Pursuit of Pleasure.* New York and London: Routledge, 1995

Rappaport, Erika Diane
↘ *Shopping for Pleasure: Women in the Making of London's West End.* Princeton, New Jersey: Princeton University Press, 1999.

Reekie, Gail
↘ *Temptations: Sex, Selling, and the Department Store.* Sydney: Allen and Unwin, 1993.

Richards, Thomas
↘ *The Commodity Culture of Victorian England: Advertising and Spectacle, 1851–1914.* London and New York: Verso, 1991.

Ritzer, George
↘ *The McDonaldization Thesis.* London: Sage, 2000.

Rosenblatt, Roger (ed.)
↘ *Consuming Desire. Consumption, Culture, and the Pursuit of Happiness.* Washington D.C: Island Press, 1999.

Saisselin, Rémy G.
↘ *The Bourgeois and the Bibelot.* New Brunswick, New Jersey: Rutgers University Press, 1984.

Satterthwaite, Ann
↘ *Going Shopping: Consumer Choices and Community Consequences.* New Haven, Connecticut and London: Yale University Press, 2001.

Schaufenster
Die Kulturgeschichte eines Massenmediums. Stuttgart: Württembergischer Kunstverein, 1974.

Schivelbusch, Wolfgang
↘ *Disenchanted Night. The Industrialisation of Light in the Nineteenth Century.* Oxford, New York, Hamburg: Berg, 1988.

Schneider, Sara K.
↘ *Vital Mummies: Performance Design for the Show-Window Mannequin.* New Haven and London: Yale University Press, 1995

Schor, Juliet B.
↘ *The Overspent American: Upscaling, Downshifting and the New Consumer.* New York: Basic Books, 1998.

Schor, Juliet B. (ed.)
↘ *The Consumer Society Reader.* New York: New Press, 2000.

Seelig, Thomas, Urs Staehl and Martin Jaeggi (eds.)
↘ *Trade: Commodities, Communication, and Consciousness.* Zurich: Scalo, 2001.

Selfridge, H. Gordon
↘ *The Romance of Commerce.* London: John Lane, 1918.

Sennett, Richard
↘ *The Fall of Public Man.* New York: Alfred A. Knopf, 1977.

Severini Kowinski, William
↘ *The Malling of America: An Inside Look at the Great Consumer Paradise.* New York: William Morrow, 1985.

Shields, Rob (ed.)
↘ *Lifestyle Shopping: The Subject of Consumption.* London and New York: Routledge, 1992.

Shopping
Jeffrey Deitch Projects, New York, 1996.

Shorris, Earl
↘ *A Nation of Salesmen: The Tyranny of the Market and the Subversion of Culture.* New York: Norton, 1994.

Silverman, Debora
↘ *Selling Culture: Bloomingdale's, Diana Vreeland, and the New Aristocracy of Taste in Reagan's America.* New York: Pantheon, 1986.

Slater, Don
↘ *Consumer Culture and Modernity.* London: Polity Press, 1997.

Smith, Woodruff
↘ *Consumption and the Making of Respectability, 1600–1800.* London and New York: Routledge, 2002.

Sombart, Werner
↘ *Luxury and Capitalism.* Trans. by W. R. Dittmar, 1913. Ann Arbor: University of Michigan Press, 1967.

Sorkin, Michael (ed.)
↘ *Variations on a Theme Park: The New American City and the End of Public Space.* New York: Hill & Wang, 1992.

Stearns, Peter N.
↘ *Consumerism in World History. The Global Transformation of Desire.* London and New York: Routledge, 2001.

Stewart, Susan
↘ *On Longing: Narratives of the Miniature, the Gigantic, the Souvenir and the Collection.* Durham, North Carolina: Duke University Press, 1993.

Storey, John
↘ *Cultural Consumption and Everyday Life.* London: Arnold, 1999.

Strasser, Susan, Charles McGovern and Matthias Judt (eds.)
↘ *Getting and Spending: European and American Consumer Societies in the Twentieth Century.* Cambridge: Cambridge University Press, 1998.

Sulkunen, Pekka, John Holmwood and Hilary Radner (eds.)
↘ *Constructing the New Consumer Society.* New York: St Martin's Press, 1997.

Sussman, Charlotte
↘ *Consuming Anxieties: Consumer Protest, Gender, and British Slavery.* Palo Alto, California: Stanford University Press, 2000.

Taylor, William R.
↘ *In Pursuit of Gotham: Culture and Commerce in New York.* New York and Oxford. Oxford University Press, 1992.

Thrift, Nigel and Ash Amin (eds.)
↘ *The Blackwell Cultural Economy Reader.* Oxford: Blackwell, 2002.

Tomlinson, Alan (ed.)
↘ *Consumption, Identity and Style.* London and New York: Routledge, 1990.

Twitchell, James B.
↘ *Lead Us Into Temptation: The Triumph of American Materialism.* New York: Columbia University Press, 1999.
↘ *Living It Up: Our Love Affair with Luxury.* New York: Columbia University Press, 2002.

Underhill, Paco
↘ *Why We Buy: The Science of Shopping.* London: Orion Business Books, 1999; New York: Simon & Schuster 2000.

Veblen, Thorstein
↘ *The Theory of the Leisure Class: An Economic Study in the Evolution of Institutions.* New York: Macmillan, 1899.

Wallis, Brian
↘ *Damaged Goods: Desire and the Economy of the Object.* New York: New Museum of Contemporary Art, 1986.

Wernick, Andrew
↘ *Promotional Culture.* London: Sage, 1992.

Westerbeck, Colin and Joel Meyerowitz
↘ *Bystander: A History of Street Photography.* Boston: Bulfinch, 2001.

Wightman Fox, Richard and T. Jackson Lears (eds.)
↘ *The Culture of Consumption: Critical Essays in American History.* New York: Pantheon, 1983.

Williams, Gareth
↘ *Branded?* London: Victoria & Albert Museum, 2000.

Williams, Rosalind H.
↘ *Dream Worlds: Mass Consumption in Late Nineteenth-Century France.* Berkeley, Los Angeles, Oxford: University of California Press, 1982.

Williamson, Judith
↘ *Consuming Passions.* London: Marion Boyars, 1995.

Zdenek, Felix, Beate Hentschel and Dirk Luckow (eds.)
↘ *Art & Economy.* Ostfildern-Ruit: Hatje Cantz, 2002.

Zepp, Ira G.
↘ *The New Religious Image of Urban America: The Shopping Mall as Ceremonial Center.* Boulder: University Press of Colorado, 1997.

Zukin, Sharon and Paul Dimaggio
↘ *Structures of Capital.* Cambridge: Cambridge University Press, 1990.

Index

Lenders

We would like to express our deepest gratitude to all Lenders. Without their generous support, this exhibition would not have been possible:

Aarhus Kunstmuseum, Denmark
The Agency, London
The Josef and Anni Albers Foundation, Bethany, Connecticut
Billy Apple, Auckland, New Zealand
Thomas Ammann Fine Art, Zurich
Beckers Collection, Darmstadt
les films de l'équinoxe – Fonds photographique Denise Bellon, Paris
Benjamin Birillo II, New York
Galerie Bruno Bischofberger, Zurich
Block Collection, Berlin
Boros Collection
KP Brehmer Nachlass, Berlin
Galerie Brusberg, Berlin
Andrea Caratsch Collection, Zurich
Chouakri Brahms Berlin
Christo & Jeanne-Claude
Sylvie Fleury, Geneva
FRAC-Collection Aquitaine, Bordeaux
Common Culture
Elmgreen & Dragset, Berlin
Dave Fascher Collection
Konrad Fischer Galerie, Dusseldorf
Katharina Fritsch, Dusseldorf
Foundation Froehlich, Stuttgart
Collection Friederike and Thomas Girst, Munich/New York
Goetz Collection, Munich
Gorney Bravin + Lee, New York
Andreas Gursky, Dusseldorf
Galerie Hauser & Wirth & Presenhuber, Zurich
Estate of Nigel Henderson
Historisches Museum, Frankfurt am Main
Jenny Holzer
Houldsworth, London
Institut für Geschichte und Theorie der Architektur (gta) ETH, Zürich
International Museum of Photography at George Eastman House, Rochester, New York

The Dakis Joannou Collection, Athens
Galerie Kicken, Berlin
Gunilla Klingberg
Leo Koenig Inc., New York
Barbara Kruger, Los Angeles
Surasi Kusolwong, Bangkok
Collection Laurent Laclos, Paris
Landesbank Baden-Württemberg, Stuttgart
Michael Landy, London
Sze Tsung Leong, New York
Library of Congress, Washington, D.C.
Ludwig Forum für Internationale Kunst, Aachen – Sammlung Ludwig
Ludwig Museum Budapest
Paul Maenz Collection, Berlin
Paul McCarthy, Altadena, California
Marzona Collection
Moderna Museet, Stockholm
Museum Boijmans Van Beuningen, Rotterdam
Museum für Kunst- und Kulturgeschichte der Hansestadt Lübeck
Museum Ludwig Köln
Museum of New Zealand Te Papa Tongarewa, Wellington
Museum Wiesbaden
National Museums & Galleries on Merseyside (Merseyside Maritime Museum)
Österreichische Friedrich und Lillian Kiesler-Privatstiftung
The New York Public Library, New York
Olaf Nicolai, Berlin
Marco Noire Contemporary Art
Anthony d'Offay Gallery, London
Claes Oldenburg and Coosje van Bruggen
Olbricht Collection
Onnasch Collection, Berlin
Gilles Peyroulet & Cie., Paris
Inge Rodenstock Collection, Munich
Thaddaeus Ropac Collection
Reiner Ruthenbeck, Ratingen
The Saatchi Gallery, London
The Gilbert and Lila Silverman FLUXUS Collection, Detroit
Skarstedt Fine Art, New York
S.M.A.K., Gent

Sonnabend Gallery, New York
Sprengel Museum, Hannover
Galerie Monika Sprüth/Philomene Magers, Munich
Staatliche Galerie Moritzburg Halle, Landesmuseum Sachsen-Anhalt
Staatsgalerie Stuttgart
Städtisches Museum Abteiberg, Mönchengladbach
The State Russian Museum, Sankt Petersburg
Haim Steinbach, New York
Tate
Ben Vautier, Nizza
The Andy Warhol Museum, Pittsburgh
Robert Watts Studio Archive, New York
Whitney Museum of American Art, New York
Ann and Jürgen Wilde Collection, Zülpich
Kunstmuseum Wolfsburg
Collection of Anita and Pujo Zabludowicz, London

We also would like to thank all those Lenders who wish to remain anonymous.

A number of individuals, besides those mentioned in the Foreword, have been especially generous with their support, help and ideas. We would like to express our gratitude for their generous co-operation:

Lothar Albrecht, Doris Ammann, Elena Bortolotti, Tobias Berger, Jenni Blyth, Adam Boxer, Sebastian Brehmer, Holger Broeker, Lutz Casper, Dominique Chevinesse, Ina Conzen, Jack Cowart, Wystan Curnow, Chris Dercon, Margit Erb, Rosa Esman, Dorothee Fischer, Mark Francis, Marion Fricke, Anna Gentzshein, Carol Greene, Franziska von Hasselbach, Jon Hendricks, Kerstin Hengevoss-Dürkop, Tim Hunt, Nigel Hurst, Yoshiko Isshiki, Joe Ketner, Margery King, Kasper König, Rem Koolhaas, Josy Kraft, Eva Christina Kraus, Susanne Küper, Jutta Küpper, Mark Niklaus Kuenzler, Marie-Louise Laband, Eric LeRoy, Klaus Littmann, Paul Maenz, Lucy Mitchell-Innes, Hattula Moholy-Nagy, Bob Monk, Tobias Mueller, Pia Müller-Tamm, Ruth Neitemeier, Katalin Neray, Michaela Neumeister, Evgenia Petrova, Marla Prather, Donna de Salvo, Marc Scheps, Nina Schleif, Rainald Schumacher, Monika Sprüth, Anu Vikram, Ian Wedde, Kurt Wettengl.